The Road to Murder

Why Driving is the Occupation of
Choice for Britain's Serial Killers

Adam G T Lynes

Foreword Professor David Wilson

 **WATERSIDE** PRESS

The Road to Murder: Why Driving is the Occupation of Choice for Britain's Serial Killers
Adam G T Lynes

ISBN 978-1-909976-37-5 (Paperback)
ISBN 978-1-910979-22-8 (Epub ebook)
ISBN 978-1-910979-23-5 (Adobe ebook)

Main UK distributor Gardners Books, 1 Whittle Drive, Eastbourne, East Sussex, BN23 6QH. Tel: +44 (0)1323 521777; sales@gardners.com; www.gardners.com

North American distribution Ingram Book Company, One Ingram Blvd, La Vergne, TN 37086, USA. Tel: (+1) 615 793 5000; inquiry@ingramcontent.com

Cataloguing-In-Publication Data A catalogue record for this book can be obtained from the British Library.

Printed by Lightning Source.

e-book *The Road to Murder* is available as an ebook and also to subscribers of Myilibrary, Dawsonera, ebrary, and Ebscohost.

Published 2016 by
Waterside Press
Sherfield Gables
Sherfield-on-Loddon
Hook, Hampshire
United Kingdom RG27 0JG

Telephone +44(0)1256 882250
E-mail enquiries@watersidepress.co.uk
Online catalogue WatersidePress.co.uk

Table of Contents

About the author

Adam Lynes is a Lecturer in Criminology at Birmingham City University and Deputy Head of the Homicide and Violent Crime (HaVoC) research cluster within the Centre for Applied Criminology. His research predominantly focuses on the significance of occupational choice for serial murderers leading to publications such as *Serial Killers and the Phenomenon of Serial Murder* (2016) (with David Wilson and Elizabeth Yardley), Waterside Press; "Driving, Pseudo-Reality and the BTK: A Case Study" (2015), *Journal of Forensic Psychology and Offender Profiling* (with David Wilson) and "Zola and the Serial Killer: Robert Black and *La Bête Humaine*" (2012), with others, *International Journal of Criminology and Sociology*. He has also written about other forms of violence in "A Taxonomy of Male British Family Annihilators, 1980–2012" (2014), Elizabeth Yardley and others, *Howard Journal*.

The author of the Foreword

Professor David Wilson is one of the UK's leading criminologists, a National Teaching Fellow and presenter of a number of crime-related TV programmes. Based at Birmingham City University where he is Founding Director of the Centre for Applied Criminology, his books for Waterside Press include *Serial Killers: Hunting Britons and Their Victims 1960–2006* (2007) and *Mary Ann Cotton: Britain's First Female Serial Killer* (2013).

Acknowledgements

First and foremost I want to thank Professor David Wilson both for writing the Foreword to this work and his help with the manuscript generally.

My special thanks also go to Professor Michael Brookes and Professor Craig Jackson, in particular for the latter's suggestions for implementing Holland's RIASEC model (*Chapter Four*) which paved the way for what I believe to be some of the book's most interesting findings.

Last but not least, I would like to thank my family for all their love, support, and encouragement, especially my parents who taught me the value of critical understanding and supported me in all my pursuits, and my grandmother, Brenda, whose love and support made this undertaking a reality.

Adam Lynes
April 2017

Foreword

From my own background working with serial killers and researching and writing about the phenomenon of serial murder, it soon became evident that much of the academic literature tended to be fixated on the 'mind of the killer'. So, based on applied research undertaken in the United States in the 1970s and 1980s, there remains an extensive secondary literature on the biological and psychological makeup of serial killers, most of which attempted to uncover why these individuals repeatedly killed.

Whilst this research — often referred to as the 'medical-psychological' tradition — has perhaps helped to improve what are often loosely described as 'profiling techniques', used when attempting to identify an unknown and still-at-large serial murderer, it was often based on dubious research methods and was largely accepted uncritically. In turn, this has helped to create some ongoing problems and fostered some enduring myths.

For example this particular approach is overly deterministic and tends to overlook other factors that exist outside of an individual serial killer's psyche. Specific focus on how an individual serial killer's biological or psychological makeup, for example, differs from other non-criminals has inevitably lead to an 'otherizing' process. Whilst understandable — after all, they have committed horrific crimes — we tended to forget that many of the most notorious serial murderers that have existed went to school, had friends, got married and were employed. Indeed, Britain's most prolific serial killer was a much respected GP. As such, at the most basic level, this suggested that we needed to think of new ways to theorise about serial killers and the phenomenon of serial murder.

In my own attempts to do so, for example, it became apparent that HOW individuals committed acts of serial murder was just as, if not more important than, WHY they killed. And, more generally, by taking a more sociological, or 'structural approach' to serial murder, my own research showed that there are particular, marginalised groups in society that provide serial killers with a seemingly limitless pool of victims.

However, whilst these groups may indeed be vulnerable to attack by serial killers, and the contribution of the 'structural approach' notwithstanding, the question remained as to whether the social and economic position of the killers themselves might also be a factor that was worthy of greater academic research.

In 2012 I tasked Adam Lynes, my PhD student at the time, to answer this question. In providing an answer into how the socio-economic position of serial killers influenced their offending behaviour, Adam drew attention to how their occupations, or lack thereof, appeared to be a significant factor in their 'success' of committing multiple murder over a long period of time. In particular, his research, based on a multi-faceted case study, provided fresh theoretical insights into how specific occupational choice — namely those that are transient in nature — can significantly influence these offenders' behaviour and HOW they committed their crimes. This is an important and not just a novel contribution.

On a personal note, in welcoming this monograph, it is always a pleasure to be able to endorse the work of one of my former students. However, more than this, it is also wonderful to observe how thinking about the phenomenon of serial murder has progressed from rather simplistic hypotheses based on 'entering the mind of the killer' and inferring their motivation to kill, to more complex and persuasive ideas that might just help us to reduce the incidence of serial murder in our society — surely something that we would all want to see?

Professor David Wilson
Founding Director of the Centre for Applied Criminology, Birmingham City University
April 2017

The Lorry Driver Hidden in Plain Sight

*Oh, it's a wonderful invention you can't deny it ... People travel
fast and know more ... But wild beasts are still wild beasts,
and however much they go on inventing still better machines,
there will be wild beasts underneath just the same.*

Emile Zola, *Le Bête Humaine* (1890; Penguin Classics Edition, 1977)

On 30 October 1975 a woman from the Chapeltown district of Leeds, Wilma McCann, was found murdered. It was determined by police that McCann, who was known to offer sexual services for money (Newton, 2006), was hit twice with a hammer prior to being stabbed 15 times in the abdomen, chest and neck (Bilton, 2003). Traces of semen were also found on her underwear (Keppel and Birnes, 2003), which suggested a sexual motive. Despite a widespread inquiry, which involved over 150 police officers and consisted of 11,000 interviews, no culprit was identified.

This murder would, unfortunately, not be an isolated incident and the following year 42-year-old Emily Jackson was found murdered in that city. Like Wilma, Emily was exchanging sexual services for money due to financial difficulties (Bilton, 2003), and was found with 51 puncture wounds. Yet again a potential suspect was not identified, with the killer free to strike again the following year.

With the police seemingly unable to identify the individual responsible for these murders, the ever-elusive perpetrator appeared to be gaining more confidence, and in 1977 would go on to murder four women. Twenty-eight-year-old Irene Richardson, 32-year-old Patricia Atkinson, 16-year-old Jayne MacDonald, and 20-year-old Jean Jordan all of whom were murdered within the same year. Each shared similar lacerations and signs of blunt force trauma to the head. Of these victims, three were known sex workers, but with 16-year-old Jayne having just left school and working as a shop assistant. The murder of Jayne lead to heightened public anxiety surrounding the investigation, with the fear that any woman, not just sex workers, were now potential targets for this killer who was no closer to being apprehended.

The following year 21-year-old Yvonne Pearson, a sex worker, was found three months after being murdered due to the killer hiding her body under a discarded sofa (Wier, 2011). Two more women were murdered in 1978, 18-year-old Helen Rytka and 40-year-old Vera Millward. Both were sex workers and both were bludgeoned and stabbed to death (Bilton, 2003). It was almost a year before the killer claimed his next victim, 19-year-old Josephine Whitaker, a bank clerk who was attacked whilst she was on her way home (Wilson, 2007). The perpetrator's next murder, that of 20-year-old university student Barbara Leach, would mark his third murder of a woman who did not work as a sex worker and, as a consequence, public outcry in relation to the failures of the investigation reached fever pitch. Despite the public uproar, though, it would take the authorities another year before finally apprehending the person responsible, who always appeared to be a step ahead of the authorities.

Nineteen-eighty-one would prove to be the year that the evasive killer was identified but not before he claimed the lives of two more women. 47-year-old Marguerite Walls and 20-year-old Jacqueline Hill, both from respectable backgrounds, with Marguerite working as a civil servant and Jacqueline studying English at university (Bilton, 2003) who were found murdered and yet again displayed similar lacerations, puncture wounds, and blunt force trauma to their heads. The killer may have continued to kill others if it hadn't had been for one eventful winter's night.

On 2 January 1981, in Sheffield, the police pulled over 34-year-old Peter Sutcliffe, who happened to have 24-year-old sex worker Olivia Reivers in the passenger seat. The police, upon further inspection, discovered that the car was fitted with false number plates—as a result Sutcliffe was arrested. The next day police returned to the scene of the arrest and discovered a knife, hammer and rope he had discarded when he temporarily left their presence upon telling them he needed the toilet. Sutcliffe was questioned for two days before finally admitting that he was the "Yorkshire Ripper"—a label the press had given to the then unidentified perpetrator. At long last the killer who had evaded the police for five long years had been caught. Following from this, Sutcliffe was convicted of the murder of 13 women, along with attacks on seven others in the years between 1975–1980 (Wilson, 2007, p. 77). During this time it also became apparent that he in fact committed all of his crimes with the aid of transport.

As it turned out, Sutcliffe not only drove a variety of cars in order to carry out his crimes, but he also appeared to engage in a series of professions that would result in him being surrounded by mechanics and vehicles (Bilton, 2003). Sutcliffe, who worked at a Water Board (Ibid, p. 730), and as a lorry driver (p. 710) not only appeared to consciously chose jobs that required someone who was practical, conforming, and who would be working with objects, but for whom the work would also be a legitimate way of being alone and away from outside interference. When this ability to be alone with his thoughts and fantasies was interrupted, Sutcliffe stated during his police interviews that he was "deeply upset" (p. 730). During one of these interviews, he explained how he couldn't "concentrate at work" due to working with an assistant who "didn't fully understand the mechanics of the job". As a result Sutcliffe was demoted and "got a steady number at the waterworks base at Gilstead". What is interesting here is that he did not appear to be emotionally upset by the fact that he was demoted and ultimately lost responsibility over other individuals. It could be argued that due to the pressures of working with others, especially those with less experience than him, Sutcliffe was losing the freedom that originally attracted him to the job. Sutcliffe being demoted and his choice of the word "steady" to describe his new position implies a sense of renewed freedom and a job he feels comfortable in doing. As a consequence of these two factors, Sutcliffe was again able to return to his private world and his fantasies. During his time at the

Water Board as a mechanic, and later a lorry driver, both of these jobs required Sutcliffe to constantly be around vehicles, with a shift between working on them as a mechanic to being inside them as a driver. This gives a psychological insight into the significance of vehicles for Sutcliffe, further reinforced by his comments in the formal statement about talking to one of his victims prior to killing her: "I asked if she had considered learning to drive I think she said she rode a horse and that it was a satisfactory form of transport" (p. 715). Comments such as these, though seemingly irrelevant, depict just how much driving meant to Sutcliffe and its role in shaping his occupational choice.

While the psychological motivations as to why he chose these types of professions have become clearer, it was not until he began attacking women that he realised the instrumental advantages of having the type of profession that he had. The most prominent advantage for Sutcliffe was that it offered him a legitimate reason for being in the location in which the ripper was picking up his victims (p. 743). Sutcliffe also later became aware of the advantage of using a different vehicle for work and a different vehicle while off-work, stating in his formal statement that:

> "One day I had to make a delivery in Huddersfield in the afternoon. I noticed a few girls plying for trade near the market area. Two or three nights later I decided to pay them a visit" (p. 710).

For Sutcliffe, his occupation not only gave him a valid reason to be in the location, but also camouflage while he scouted the area, looking for potential victims. With access to both his work vehicle and own car, he was capable of confusing both witnesses and police with visits to the red light district masked behind different vehicles. The implementation of a work lorry would also devalue his status as a potential suspect due to the supposed nature of his visit into the area.

Through this brief overview of Sutcliffe's crimes, it is clear that his occupation played a significant role in the commission of his crimes at both an instrumental and psychological level, but what of other British serial murderers? Are there others that held similar forms of occupation? If so, did they use their job as a means to commit their murders in the same vein as Sutcliffe? Are there also other forms of employment that such offenders also held? And did these other occupations hold the same significance to these individuals in relation to their offending as it did for Sutcliffe? These are just some of the questions this book seeks to answer.

CHAPTER ONE

Introduction

Serial killers, like society in general, have become geographically more mobile. Unlike their counterparts in earlier years, some serial murderers now travel around the country, leaving a trail of human carnage.

Jack Levin and James Alan Fox, *Serial Killers, Like Society in General* (1985, Capo Press)

What is the significance of occupational choice or, more specifically, driving as an occupation, for serial murderers? This book is designed to explore, with reference to pre-existing scholarly work on serial murder and relevant criminological theory, this question, and provide some answers. Specifically, it seeks to uncover how these serial murderers use these occupations to assist them in committing their offences. Through a fusion of a criminological and psychological theoretical framework, the book attempts to ascertain if and how these offenders' thoughts and fantasies of committing murder may have influenced their career choices or, alternatively, if it was the "nature" of their occupations that ignited and then fuelled their need to offend. The answers to these questions will introduce other issues regarding the significance of occupational choice, not only for serial murderers but for other types of offenders. At a more instrumental level, the book seeks to illuminate how the police have attempted to tackle these particular transient offenders with regard to their identification and apprehension.

Both criminologists and psychologists have been noticeably silent about the topic of driving, and more specifically occupational choices which involve driving, with regard to its potential impact on serial murder. Such a lack of scholarly work within this field of study is unusual, as the phenomenon of serial murder has been heavily researched (Gibson, 2006). Serial murder has been a topic of discussion and debate for a variety of academic fields and organizations. At present, the focus appears to be on issues such as the offender's motivations and, more recently, the possible influence of society with regard to creating the suitable conditions that serial murderers are more likely to operate in (Wilson, 2009). These two opposing theoretical approaches have become known as the "medical-psychological" tradition and the "structural tradition". Both of these models are discussed in *Chapter Two*.

Separating Myth from Reality

These diverse and often conflicting approaches to the phenomenon of serial murder have resulted in an interest in the topic that far exceeds its scale and has generated many academic articles, "True Crime" books, and movies (Seltzer, 1998). Through this exposure by both academia and the media, serial murderers have, in many ways, become immortalised and, as a result, dehumanised to the point in which we no longer recognise them. They have become "travellers from another time and space" (Doris, 2010, p. 9). This fascination with and ultimate detachment from these individuals has, as a result, meant that potential factors which may result in a better and more holistic understanding of serial murder, such as their occupational choice and the role of driving, have been greatly overlooked in favour of more seemingly attractive ideas—such as, for example, what motivates them to commit murder. This absence of research surrounding the occupational choice of serial murderers becomes even more irregular when one considers that this broad-based public fascination began as far back as the late-1880s, after a series of unsolved murders occurring in the Whitechapel area of London. These murders were committed by an unknown individual who was nicknamed "Jack the Ripper" (Evans and Gainey, 1998). Both academic groups and the general public have ever since sought to explain, explore and understand why and how people have been driven to commit such an "extreme form of violence" (Young, 2010, p. 148).

It is important to note that much of the general public's awareness and understanding of serial murder comes from fictional accounts and "true crime". Storylines are produced to heighten the interest of audiences, rather than to correctly depict serial murder (Simpson, 2000). By focusing on the violence inflicted on victims by "disturbed" and "unhinged" individuals, the public seems to have become captivated by these unique criminals and their offences. This only leads to more confusion about the true nature of serial murder. Law enforcement agencies are also susceptible to the same questionable information from a different basis: the use of subjective and independent opinion and judgment. Professionals involved in serial murder cases — detectives, prosecutors, and forensic psychologists — may actually have limited experience of cases of serial murder. The relative infrequency of serial murder (Jenkins, 1988) combined with inaccurate, subjective information and fictitious representations of serial murderers have resulted in the creation of a number of myths and misconceptions (see Branson, 2014). Such myths include the notion that a serial murderer is incredibly clever, resulting in them being one step ahead of the authorities, and that it takes the skill of a brilliant criminal profiler to apprehend them (Egger, 1998). For nearly as long as this interest in serial murder has existed within the United Kingdom, and North America, so has the interest in just how these offenders could repeatedly kill without raising suspicion, with the common question being: 'How can serial murders be understood and [their crimes] solved when most of the cases are committed by one person?' (Keppel and Birnes, 2003, p. p. 14).

As already noted, the answer to this question has been attempted from a variety of theoretical standpoints, though none have recognised the significance of the occupational backgrounds of these offenders. Existing literature that examines, for example, "geographically transient" serial murderers has, so far, focused primarily on the use of transport and neglected the importance of occupational choice. It is important to note here that "geographic profiling", created by Stuart Kind in 1980, focuses on the use of a vehicle and the psychological "journey" of the individual whilst they offend. Geographic profiling attempts to use either an actuarial approach, which is a form of profiling that places an emphasis on the investigator's personal knowledge of geographic profiling (Snook et al, 2004), or a statistical approach (Rossmo, 2000). This latter form of geographic profiling uses statistical profiles generated through comparing unsolved crimes with solved crimes that are stored in a "refined database" (Rossmo, 2000:70). Regardless of which approach is implemented, it is evident that the offender's occupational background is not taken into consideration. Thus this book not only intends to try and improve upon the existing knowledge of known instrumental advantages of using a vehicle when committing murder, but also to offer a new perspective on the motivations and occupational choices of such offenders.

The Media and the Transient Murderer

In this attempt to separate myth from reality, it is important to consider how the transient murderer and, more specifically, serial murderer, have been portrayed in the media—arguably the most powerful actor in the shaping on the public's understanding of such offenders. Various films and even songs, spanning several decades, have arguably had detrimental effects on our understanding of the transient killer. Here we will be expanding our analysis to include North America, the primary reason being that the influence of North America's media on other countries has been momentous with '*Hollywood's international* success' (Wasko, 2003, p. 182) being a significant contributor.

The first misconception portrayed by the media is that it is not the driver who is the one to be feared, but the lone hitchhiker. Jim Morrison's song "The Hitchhiker" created a terrifying image with lyrics such as:

> "This guy gave me a ride, and ah ... 'If you give this man a ride' started giving me a lot of trouble 'Sweet family will die' and I just couldn't take it, ya know 'Killer on the road' And I wasted him" (Morrison, 1978: track 16).

It is not only songs, though, that reinforces this notion that the pedestrian was the one to be feared when on the road. Films such as the original *The Hitch-hiker* (1953), focused upon two fishermen who, upon their journey to Mexico, are taken hostage by an escaped criminal who informs the two friends that he plans to kill them once they reach their destination. Two remakes were both called *The Hitcher* (1986 and 2007), with the former focusing upon a lone young man tormented and chased by a seemingly, at first, ordinary drifter who quickly begins to psychologically and physically torment the young driver once he has been picked up. The sequel, while changing the protagonists to a young couple, kept to a similar premise, reinforcing the concept that it is not who is behind the wheel who is to be feared, but the pedestrians who are walking alongside the road. These films, it could be argued, had a detrimental impact on how the public, not only in North America, but Britain too, perceived the hitchhiker. Such was the fear of hitchhikers in North America, the Federal Bureau of Investigation installed signs along roads warning drivers not to pick up pedestrians (Strand, 2012). We are not disputing the potential risks of picking up a hitchhiker, but instead suggesting that such films were perhaps harmful in not identifying other possibly more dangerous hazards faced on the road.

Despite the medium of film focusing heavily upon the pedestrian as opposed to the driver, there have been attempts at shedding light upon the notion of the transient murderer. The most notable, and arguably iconic example is Steven Spielberg's debut film *Duel* (1971). *Duel* tells the story of a middle-aged Los Angeles electronics salesman driving whilst on a business trip who, on a two-lane highway in the California desert, encounters a grimy and rusty tanker truck, travelling slower than the speed limit and expelling thick plumes of sooty diesel exhaust. Throughout the course of the narrative, the tanker truck, whose driver is never seen, stalks the salesman, which leads to a fatal confrontation at the film's climax. While the film draws attention to the fact that it is not only pedestrians that pose a risk on the road, but also drivers, the film's dramatic technique of never revealing the driver of the tanker truck to the audience removes the humanity from the character and simply adds to the mystique and misinterpretation of these offenders on screen.

The 1973 film *Badlands* is loosely based upon the real-life crimes of Charles Starkweather who, during a two-month road trip with his 14-year-old girlfriend, Caril Ann Fugate, went on a two-month killing spree in 1958 crossing several states (Strand, 2012). While the film does not state that it is based upon real life events, its aim for the audience to sympathise with the murderers through a series of events shown through their perspectives results in an ambiguous moral standpoint. What the film does achieve, however, is that driving was a fundamental element of their offences. For example, the couple use the sheer geographical space provided to them as a result of North America's vast interstate road network to evade police detection. *Badlands* (1973) provides an interesting instrumental facet in regards to driving and committing murder, in that if someone kills a person in two separate locations with different police jurisdictions, the ability to link the offences to the same offender becomes much more difficult.

A more contemporary example of a film that depicts a transient murderer is *Death Proof* (2007). This particular film shares similarities with Spielberg's *Duel* (1971), in that the antagonist literally uses their vehicle as means to commit their offences. The killer, due to his previous occupation as a stunt-driver, owns a car, which is rigged with a safety cage inside, but only on the driver's side. The killer's modus operandi consists of driving at an incredibly high speed before causing the car to crash. Due to the safety measures installed in the driver's side, the killer emerged with relatively minor injuries whereas his passengers, who were always young women, would be killed. This particular film, when compared to the other films previously discussed, poses interesting questions in regards to the significance of occupational choice. Did the killer initially have fantasies of committing murder and consciously choose a profession that could facilitate these ambitions? Or did his time working as a stuntman and around cars ignite or act as a catalyst for some latent fantasy? Of course, due to the medium that this material was presented in, such questions were not explored or answered, but this does not mean that such questions are invalid.

Most recently, the hit HBO crime show *True Detective* (2014) perhaps provides the most realistic depiction of how a transient oriented profession can aid in the commission of murder. In the show's first season, our protagonists, two detectives portrayed by Matthew Mcconaughey and Woody Harrelson are on a 17-year hunt for the "Yellow King"—a serial murderer who targets young women. During the course of the investigation, a series of suspects, each one more bizarre and strange than the last, come into the detectives' cross hairs. As it turned out, the serial murderer was in fact a rather unsuspecting odd-job labourer who used his vehicle as a means to take on jobs at schools and other locations where his preferred victim type would be. He was in fact interviewed by Rustin "Rust" Cohle, Mcconaughey's character, and, after answering a few questions, is not given a second thought until the series' dramatic finale. Upon the realisation of who the killer is, it's only in retrospect that the instrumental advantages of the "Yellow King's" job as a travelling handyman come into view—with the ability to drive between various locations he was able to gain both proximity and access to his victims, while all along his presence was not being called into question.

It is apparent that the medium of film has both hindered and, at times, helped in the public's understanding of the transient murderer. Films such as *The Hitcher* (1986 and 2007) have arguably influenced the public and various law enforcements that the real danger is in the form of lone pedestrians as opposed to the driver. When films have attempted to portray the transient killer, the humanity and consequently the reality behind such offenders is lost in favour of dramatic tension as seen is *Duel* (1971). On the other hand, the medium of film and, more recently, TV, has also alerted viewers to important considerations regarding the motivations behind the offender, and how their occupation ties into how and why they commit their offences. It is now time to bring these considerations into reality, while being continually mindful that, despite some films declaring that they are based on real life events, "the majority of their 'facts' are nothing more than fabrications" (Best, 2008, p. 61).

Defining Serial Murder

The term "serial murder" is a social construction (Hickey, 2006). However it is only the labelling of particular offences that is considered to be a social construction, while the actual act of murder that these offenders engage in is very much a physical reality (Ferguson et al, 2003). Due to numerous types of murder—including single, double, triple, mass and spree murder—the term serial murder was initially created as a means to separate this distinctive form of murder from, most notably mass murder (Hickey, 2006). Many different, and often competing (Lundrigan and Canter, 2008), definitions have been produced in an attempt to be the first to create a universal classification that could be applied all over the world. These differences often centre on either the number of victims that are required, the amount of time that has to have passed before an individual can be labelled a serial murderer, or both. However, while there are disagreements, the range of the number of required victims is typically between two to three (Hickey, 1997). On the other hand, the issue of an approximate amount of time needed in order to be classified as a serial murderer has proven to be much harder to agree upon. This facet of serial murder has ranged between simply being an unspecified "cooling off period" (Newton, 2006), most commonly associated with the Federal Bureau of Investigation in the USA, to a much more specific "period which is greater than thirty days" (Newton, 2006) between the first offence and the subsequent offences.

Such conflicting issues in attempting to define serial murder have resulted in many prominent names and, to a lesser degree, various organizational bodies within this particular field of study to produce their own definitions. Bodies such as the Federal Bureau of Investigation (FBI), the National Institute of Justice (NIJ) and well known authors on serial murder including Geberth, Turvey, Brooks, Hickey, Egger, Giannangelo, and Holmes and Holmes have all generated their own interpretation on how exactly serial murder should be classified.

Selecting a Definition of Serial Murder

Defining serial murder, as previously discussed, is a problematic process. It is evident from early definitions that many organizational bodies and researchers have attempted to generate a definition that is a development from earlier definitions. This has consequently resulted in particular offending traits—such as crimes driven by sexual motivation—being more strongly associated with serial murder, than other motivations. Nicole and Proulx (2007) develop this issue further, arguing that:

"The difficulties are glaring: basing a definition of serial killer on both number of victims and the sexual nature of the crime not only eliminates any possibility of distinguishing between serial sexual murderers and non-serial, nonsexual murderers, but also suggests that repetitive murder can only be motivated by sexual drive" (Nicole and Proulx, 2007, p. 100).

Nicole and Proulx's statement is important for it is advantageous for a number of reasons to implement a definition that does not require there to be a sexual motivation behind the offences. This will obviously result in a higher number of offenders that can be applied within this particular analysis of serial murder.

While the issue of motivation behind each offender's offences has been resolved, there is still the concern of the number of victims required and the time required between each offence. To reiterate, there is no universal definition of serial murder to date (Schlesinger and Miller, 2003), despite, as previously discussed, the term being used for decades (Harbort and Mokros, 2001). Before a definition with a particular number of victims can be selected, it is imperative to clarify whether or not the potential candidates for this investigation were found guilty in a court of law of murdering the required number of victims. Wilson (2009), whose research was conducted in the United Kingdom, addresses this matter and concludes that, "I have included in the text only those serial killers who were tried and convicted at court for murdering three or more victims" (Wilson, 2009, p. 4–6). With this in mind, any potential candidates will need to have been charged with, and found guilty of, the murder of at least three victims in a court of law. Through analysing previous definitions, and reviewing current literature, which often reiterates that "most researchers agree that to be classified as a serial murderer, there should be a minimum of three victims" (Jones, 2007, p. 1), the number of victims necessary in order to qualify for treatment here will be at least three.

The final factor to consider when selecting a definition of serial murder is the amount of time required between each offence. With regards to past definitions, this period of time has been described as, to begin with, an unspecified "cooling off period" (FBI definition cited in Newton, 2006), to a more comprehensive, yet broad "days, weeks, months, or years" (Hickey, 1997), to a very precise period of "30-days" (Holmes and Holmes, 1994).

In conclusion, selecting a working definition of serial murder has involved synthesising, classifying, and combining aspects of multiple definitions. The definition that has been used to select appropriate candidates for this book defines a serial murderer as:

> "An individual who has been found guilty in a court of law of the murder of at least three victims (or posthumously determined to be guilty), irrespective of motive, in a period of greater than thirty days, typically killing at least one person per killing episode, with a 'cooling off' period in between."

The above "fusion" of definitions is a combination of the FBI's classification in terms of the number of victims; the Holmes and Holmes (1994) definition provided the precise amount of time required in-between offences; and, Wilson's (2009) consideration regarding the importance of the need to be convicted of the necessary quantity of victims also contributed to its creation.

Approach to the Book and How the Data was Gathered

Any investigation into serial murder comes with inherent limitations with regard to the collation of data. Firstly, despite this investigation predominantly concentrating on British serial murderers, there are a number of concerns that have prevented the opportunity to interview such offenders. The principal area of concern is that of the validity of data given from convicted serial murderers. Hepburn and Hinch (1997) note that not only is it extremely difficult and time consuming to gain access to imprisoned serial murderers, but that any information that they may share with the interviewer is questionable in its reliability. An example of such issues can be witnessed in the case of British serial murderer Fred West. West, upon arrest, took part in interviews that amounted to 145 tape recordings (Wilson, 2009) that have since been dismissed as "worthless except to confirm that nothing that he said could be relied upon as anything near the truth" (Bennet and Gardner, 2005). The issue of validity with regards to what these offenders say is not the only concern if they were to be interviewed. Wilson (2009), who identified and labelled cases, including West as those whose "opinions and emotions they expressed were socially constructed to suit the nature and circumstances of their arrest" (p. 16), noted that there were also serial murderers that were the exact opposite. These, Wilson (2009) states, choose not to discuss their offences once they have been apprehended and instead choose to "keep their secrets well-guarded" (p. 18). These two groups have since been categorised as either the "lay outs" or the "cover ups" (p. 18). These factors contributed to the decision to not interview convicted serial murderers. With these limitations in mind, the collation of secondary sources was the primary method of data collection. The reason for this methodological technique was due to the lack of previous scholarly work with regard to this aspect of serial murder. The collated data came in a variety of forms, including newspaper reports, true crime accounts and court transcripts. With regard to the selection of this data set, newspaper articles were compiled from a predefined search field, whilst true crime books and court transcripts were selected on the basis that they centred on one or more serial murderers related to this research. With regards to newspaper reports, this study used the search engine Nexis. Nexis houses all major UK newspapers, "including both national and regional titles" (Yardley et al, 2014, p.120). The search engine LexisNexis was used when compiling court transcripts. LexisNexis, similar to Nexis, houses legal documents at both a national and international level.

Similar to how Wilson (2007; 2009) shifted attention to the victims of serial murderers in order to provide a more structural account and explanation of serial killing within Britain, this book attempts to provide, through a fresh theoretical lens, further insights into this highly popularised yet vastly misunderstood phenomenon.

CHAPTER TWO

How to Get Away With (Serial) Murder: Modern Developments

Every ounce of information we can extract from a killer about his minds and methods gives us more information to track the next one.

Robert Ressler and Tom Shachtman, *Whoever Fights Monsters* (1992, St. Martin's Paperbacks)

Serial Murder: Theoretical Foundations

Before proceeding, it is important to discuss the differing general theoretical approaches to serial murder. Whilst much has been written on the subject (Egger, 1990; Hickey, 1997; Holmes and DeBurger, 1988; Jenkins 1994 to name just a few), the actual theoretical underpinnings, especially from a criminological perspective, have been less discussed and are now only beginning to grow out from its infancy (Castle and Hensley, 2002). Despite this relatively small amount of explicit works, it is possible to construct two theoretically opposing theories of serial murder from a survey of wider literature, which have come to dominate the topic. These are often described as the "medical-psychological" tradition and the "structural tradition" (Grover and Soothill, 1997). The primary emphasis for those who work with the medical-psychological tradition is upon understanding and rationalising the actions of the individual offender within the context of his or her psyche. The fundamental hypothesis is, in essence, that each individual offender is motivated to engage in extreme behaviour because of a single or, in some instances, an amalgamation of several psychological "abnormalities" (Canter and Youngs, 2009). This particular facet of the debate appears to also be the most "popular" among researchers with, as will be explained, a variety of different scholars each offering their own unique interpretation on just how, and in what form, these "abnormalities" appear and function. The structural tradition, however, suggests that the psychological explanations of serial murder are, by themselves, unable to explain the phenomenon of multiple killing. As Castle and Hensley (2002, p. 453) point out, "the study of serial murder continues to be an exploratory rather than explanatory research topic". In essence, this particular perspective seeks to "divert" attention away from the serial murderers themselves, and instead towards the society in which they inhabit (Wilson, 2009). In short, here we have two very different theoretical perspectives: one that argues that the answers lie within the offenders themselves; and the other proposing that it is the society in which these individuals inhabit that holds the key to understanding why certain individuals can repeatedly kill.

The "Structural Tradition"

One of the earliest and most cited examples of the application of the structural tradition in practice is Canadian anthropologist Leyton's *Hunting Humans: The Rise of the Modern Multiple Murderer* (1986), and his concept of "homicidal protest". Whilst Leyton's focus is upon multiple murderers rather than just serial murderers, the core of his proposal — that psychological explanations alone are unable to account for the occurrence of multiple murder — has caused significant deviations in the study of serial killing. Leyton challenges the arguments held by the medical-psychological tradition by suggesting that the majority of those who commit multiple murder are not suffering from any mental abnormalities or diseases. Instead, Leyton contends that those who want to understand multiple murder need to look past the individual who committed the crime, and instead towards society. Leyton elaborated on this concept, adding that attention should be given to the social structures in which the offender lives and offends. In developing his theory he classified three broad historical epochs, and argues that in these multiple killers and their victims are socially specific. The table below encapsulates these historical structures, and shows the broad socio-economic context of the serial murderers and their victims:

Historical Epochs of Serial Murderers and their Victims

Three Historical Epochs, Serial murderers, and their Victims	Pre-Industrial (Pre-late 19th Century)	Industrial (late 19th Century)	Modern (Post World war II)
Killer	Aristocratic	Middle Classes (e.g. doctors, teachers)	Upper working/ lower middle-class (e.g. security guards, computer operators)
Victim	Peasantry	"lower orders" (e.g. prostitutes, housemaids)	Middle classes (e.g. university students)

Adapted from Leyton, E. (1986) *Hunting Humans: The Rise of the Modern Multiple Murderer,* Toronto: McClelland and Stewart, pp. 269–295

The historical periods are the pre-industrial age (i.e. pre-late 19th century); the industrial period (i.e. late 19th century); and the modern period (i.e. post World War II). In essence, the various socio-economic conditions that dominated throughout the three historical epochs produced serial murderers who reacted in what Leyton called "homicidal protest." Leyton, cited in Grover and Soothill, explains this as follows:

"In each of the historical periodisations, the configuration of the social structure is such that some persons when faced with challenges to their position in the social hierarchy react to those challenges through the 'protest' of killing members of the threatening group. Homicidal protest can take differing forms" (cited in Grover and Soothill, 1999, p. 5).

Ultimately, the structural perspective of Leyton implies that serial murderers are not the product of biological or psychological abnormalities, but instead are a consequence of a society that, due to its intensely competitive nature, cannot reward the efforts of all. Likewise, Mitchell (1996) theorises that serial murderers are in fact individuals who are incapable of meeting the standards, goals and values of the society in which they inhabit and consequently turn into outcasts (cited in Pokel, 2000). Mitchell also proposed that Merton's (1938) "Strain Theory", within the context of serial murder, assists in explaining multiple murder as the behavior of "strained" individuals who are unable to achieve success in society and, as a result, resort to murder as a means of self-accomplishment (cited in Pokel, 2000).

With regard to Leyton's homicidal protest, there have been substantial changes in the socio-economic background of murderers and their victims between the historical eras identified. In general terms, Leyton argues that the socio-economic background of the serial murderer has dropped from that of upper classes in the pre-industrial period to upper-working class and lower middle class in the modern era. In contrast, the socio-economic background of the victims has escalated from peasantry in the pre-industrial period to that of the middle classes in the modern era. Through the concept of "homicidal protest", Leyton proposes that in each of the historical periods identified, the structure of the social hierarchy was in such a way that some individuals, when challenged in regards to their position, respond to those encounters through the "protest" of killing members of the hostile group.

While Leyton's theory of homicidal protest was successful in moving attention away from the individual and instead towards the wider societal context, there are apparent limitations to his theory. First, the focus of how and where Leyton's theory is applied is somewhat confusing. Leyton draws from examples of multiple murderers in the USA and Canada to test his hypothesis. While Leyton achieves some success within the context of the USA, he loosens his focus when he attempts to apply his theory at an international level. Second, as noted by Grover and Soothill (1999), Leyton's description of the three historical periods can be described as being both too broad and, at the same time, too rigid.

In regards to the first point of criticism, a number of researchers have tested Leyton's theory in different societal contexts, including Britain.

Grover and Soothill (1999) and Wilson (2007) have taken Leyton's structural approach to multiple murderers and applied it within the socio-economic context of Britain. Grover and Soothill (1999) offer one of the earliest examples of other researchers adopting the "structural tradition" to serial murder. In this study, it is evident that they do not consider Leyton's structural analysis as reflecting Britain's experience with serial murder especially, as noted earlier, Leyton only generating his theory based on circumstances in the USA. However, Grover and Soothill do recognise the important role of Leyton's structural analysis to "understanding the meaning of serial killing at a societal level" (1999, p. 13). In order to test Leyton's theory, Grover and Soothill collected information on all known British serial murderers since 1960. This included background information, such as occupations, on not only the serial murderers, but also victims. Grover and Soothill state that post-1960, otherwise referred to as the "modern era", serial murderers originated from the upper working class and lower middle class, and that victims were primarily from the middle classes. With this information, Grover and Soothill conclude:

"Considering the Leyton framework, it becomes evident that paradoxically the experience of Britain since the 1960s both supports and refutes his claims concerning the perpetrators and victims of serial killing" (Grover and Soothill, 1999, p. 8).

In concluding their argument, Grover and Soothill ultimately argue that Leyton's structural explanation cannot, in its entirety, be applied to Britain. Instead of finding working class and lower middle class individuals murdering members of the middle class, they discovered that an overwhelming number of victims were in fact from "relatively powerless and vulnerable groups" (Grover and Soothill, 1999, p. 9). Grover and Soothill (1999) argue that homicidal protest cannot simply be described as class frustration, as it is simply too "narrow" (p. 10). Instead they propose that factors such as patriarchy also need to be taken into account when explaining the British experience of serial murder. Here feminist approaches to murder offer an enhanced understanding of how "homicidal protest" may be applied to Britain in an adapted form. Feminist advocates have, for many years, refuted the notion that violent crimes against women and children, members of this "vulnerable" group outlined by Grover and Soothill (1999), are simply a result of class frustrations (Kelly and Radford, 1987; Walby, 1990; Cameron and Frazer, 1987). As a result of this, Grover and Soothill (1999) recognise that Britain has to be seen as "both a capitalist and a patriarchal society" (p. 10).

Wilson (2007) takes Grover and Soothill's (1999) observations regarding the social position of the majority of known serial murder victims and has explored this further. Wilson, too, moves away from the individualistic, clinical discourse of the medical-psychological tradition and attempts to create a sociological rationale as to why serial murderers exist. In common with Grover and Soothill, he asks whether Leyton's "homicidal protest" fits Britain's experiences of serial murder. Similar to their conclusions, Wilson both supports yet refutes the theory of homicidal protest by incorporating Young's (1999) theoretical discussion on the transformation of Britain from an "inclusive" to an "exclusive" society. Young's (1999) *The Exclusive Society* argued Britain was, at one stage, a society that placed great emphasis on community, locality and employment. This, according to Young, changed during the 1980s where Thatcherism's antisocial welfare policies de-emphasised these very principles. As a result of the more "exclusive" society, which emphasised materialistic consumption, individualism, anonymity, and less about "traditionalities of community and family" (Young, 1999, p. 6), certain groups became increasingly marginalised in society. With Government policies that have, over a period of time, weakened the economic and social protection of the elderly, gay men, runaways and throwaways, children, and women involved in prostitution (Wilson, 2007).

Wilson takes Young's theory of the "exclusive society" and uses it in an attempt to understand serial killing patterns beyond victim selection. Wilson's research suggests that, of the 326 victims murdered by 19 identified serial murderers between 1960–2006, the majority were indeed part of this marginalised group; a result of a society that "moved inexorably from production to consumption" (Wilson, 2007, p. 184). Wilson further reinforces his argument by incorporating the work of Jenkins (1994), who states that there were no serial murderers during the 1920s and 1930s, a period before society became "exclusive", and seven confirmed active serial murderers in the 1980s — the height of Thatcherism.

Jenkins (1988; 1994), takes a sociological approach to argue that the popular assumption, principally throughout the 1980s, that the threat of serial murder was abundant and rapidly growing and that it required the knowledge and direction of a federal agency such as a the FBI to control it, was in fact grossly exaggerated and misinformed. He argues that the responses of law agencies, government, mass media, and various interest groups far outstripped serial killing's actual lethality. While Jenkins utilises a sociological approach, he takes a somewhat different perspective from the researchers previously described. Instead of focusing on the socio-economic climate of a society, Jenkins organized his work into three main areas. The first addressed the reasons for the rising public concern for serial murder and the role that political and bureaucratic interests played in defining and "nurturing" the issue. Second, he looked at the prevalent cultural imagery as portrayed principally in the mass media and how "mythic" the image of the serial murderer became, and how it was influenced by the various law agencies. The third discusses how the issue was used by political interest groups to legitimise their ideological perspectives (Jenkins, 1988; 1994). In order for Jenkins to validate his hypothesis, he employed a "contextual constructionist" perspective. This approach not only scrutinises the claims made by various groups attempting to define an issue, but also attempts to measure the relative reliability of the claims. To do this Jenkins examines archival, newspaper and secondary accounts of multiple murders over the last hundred years, selecting periods such as 1911–1915 and 1935–1941. As such, he discovered that, while Germany had 12 cases of serial murder during the 1920s and 1930s, Britain had no reported cases (Jenkins, 1988). While critics may highlight the possibility that any serial murderer(s) active in this time period were simply not identified or apprehended, Wilson (2009) offers support for Jenkins (1988). In examining public documents on murder in 1935, he explains:

"Of the forty-seven people who faced a criminal trial: three were discharged; one died while on remand in prison; six were found to be insane; six were acquitted; fourteen were found guilty but insane; eight were executed; seven had their death sentences commuted to life imprisonment; one was sent to Broadmoor; and the final defendant had his conviction quashed at the Court of Appeal" (Wilson, 2009, p. 86).

Wilson expands, stating that "these statistics give an appearance of certainty, finality and order" (p. 86) in Britain at that time. While he (2009) entertains the possibility that many cases of reported suicide during the inter-war period may have actually been murders, the socio-economic climate and Home Office records suggest that "any serial killer active at the time would not have escaped detection for long" (p. 92).

The case of Harold Shipman has also been discussed within the structural tradition (Soothill and Wilson, 2005). Soothill and Wilson, for example, discuss "Britain's most prolific serial killer" (Batty, 2005), and attempt to employ sociological reasonings to better understand why Shipman was able to kill so many people. This is significant in two key areas. Firstly, it further reinforces the need to look beyond the "usual individualistic explanations of serial killing" (Soothill and Wilson, 2005, p. 685). Secondly, this study offers an insight into the potential significance of the occupational background of the offender. Of note, Soothill and Wilson (2005) reference Simpson (1980), a pathologist who deliberated on another famous murder case involving a doctor who was ultimately acquitted of the charges (Soothill and Wilson, 2005). Soothill and Wilson pay close attention to Simpson's description of his occupation:

"Doctors are in a particularly good position to commit murder and escape detection…'Dangerous drugs' and powerful poisons lie in their professional bags or in the surgery. No one is watching or questioning them, and a change in symptoms, as sudden 'grave turn for the worse' or even death is for them to interpret" (Simpson, 1980, p. 235).

They argue that taking a more sociological, as opposed to psychological approach, helps to understand why certain serial murderers can "remain hidden for so long" (p. 692). They also utilise a secondary source, this time Freidson (1970), to establish that a solo medical practitioner had unique freedoms and lack of "control by outsiders" (Wilson and Soothill, 2005, p. 692).

This study again brings Leyton's theory of "homicidal protest" to the forefront of the argument, reintroducing Grover and Soothill's statement that Britain may be more akin to the "industrial period"; during which members of the middle class, including doctors, "preyed on members of the lower orders, especially prostitutes and housemaids" (Leyton, 1986 cited in Soothill and Wilson, 2005. p. 694). Soothill and Wilson (2005), in this instance, use the case of Harold Shipman to challenge this hypothesis by suggesting that, if this was the case, then Shipman would have targeted those who threatened "industrial discipline" and who lived outside the "new moral order" (p. 694), and not the "elderly, vulnerable women who formed the main constituency" (p. 695) of his victims. Similar to Grover and Soothill (1999), Soothill and Wilson (2005) support the concept of moving beyond class structure by including such social relations as patriarchy to better understand the British experience of serial murder. With this wider critical analysis of Leyton's theory, they entertain the possibility that Shipman did not murder his victims as a form of "revenge" due to class frustration but instead because they were perceived as "living outside the moral order of competitive capitalist society" (p. 696). To support this argument, they draw upon their previous works to identify that the general trend in serial murder victims, be they sex workers, runaways, throwaways and the elderly, can be interpreted as being a "socio-economic 'burden' on society" (p. 696). This, they argue, is potentially why Shipman, regardless of his respected occupation, was ultimately able to "continue killing his patients over two decades" (p. 696). All of this shares similarities with Wilson's book previously discussed, in that the primary reason that allowed not only Shipman, but also other British serial murderers, to repeatedly kill was a lack of "social and economic protection for the poor and vulnerable" (p. 697). While Soothill and Wilson offer a compelling argument with regards to how particular groups are more vulnerable to serial murder due to their social status and, in the case of sex workers, profession, this same level of attention is not given to the serial murderers themselves. For example, the discussion concerning Shipman raises important questions regarding how serial murderers' social standing and occupation may perhaps place them in proximity, and provide access, to these already socially isolated and vulnerable victim groups.

To summarise, the structural tradition seeks to offer a different theoretical perspective to that of the "medical-psychological" tradition. The relatively small amount of literature regarding this tradition conveys how it is still in its infancy and that it has limitations. Firstly, as noted by Soothill and Wilson (2005), the "structural" approach is unable to offer a "complete explanation" (p. 693) to the phenomenon that is serial murder. Secondly, another limitation is the risk of attempting to find a "universal" sociological explanation of serial murder. As illustrated by Leyton, when attempting to apply his hypothesis to Britain, UK based researchers encountered a series of factors that dramatically weakened his "structural" explanation. Instead, as demonstrated by Grover, Soothill and Wilson, it is vital that researchers take into account the socio-economic and cultural differences before applying, for example, Leyton's theory of "homicidal protest" that was designed to fit North America, a continent with its own sociological, economic and cultural identity separate to that of Britain and many other countries.

While the medical-psychological tradition has not been critically discredited, the current literature that has been generated within Britain strongly supports a more "structural" standpoint when it comes to understanding the existence of serial murderers within the UK. This is further reinforced by Grover and Soothill (1999), who state that, over the past 30 years, advocates of the "medical-psychological" approach have become much more willing to "recognise the importance of the social context" (p. 4) of the offender. They further reinforce their "structural" argument by highlighting a "paradox" (p. 4) that the opposing tradition has been unable to rectify. This paradox involves how psychiatrists explain deviance as a result of psychiatric abnormalities, but that in actuality "few offenders are so psychiatrically disturbed as to be termed mentally ill" (p. 4). Furthermore, Mitchell (1996) declared that the link between genetics and serial murderer behaviour has not been established and that it is "not possible to make a general statement that all serial murderers as psychopaths" (cited in Pokel, 2000, 41).

With regard to how the "structural tradition" relates to serial killing in Britain, the increase of reported cases of serial murder can, according to Grover (1999), Soothill (1999; 2005), Wilson (2005; 2007) and Mitchell (1996), best be understood through the awareness of the socio-economic changes that began in the 1960s. The gradual erosion of community, family, and job security has given way to a market society driven by free enterprise, individualism and competition. All of this, it has been suggested, has marginalised particular groups and filled others with intense hate and a disposition to kill. Taking into account Wilson's (2007) observations that the highest number of serial murderers emerged, and were active, during a period of extreme socio-economic collapse which witnessed a substantial number of people become unemployed, a rise in poverty, and a decline in earnings only strengthens the hypothesis that environmental and societal influences caused the increase of serial murderers in Britain.

The points raised do not necessarily discredit the "medical-psychological" approach to serial murder. In fact, this more individualistic approach to serial offending behaviour is able to tackle questions sbout serial murder that the "structural tradition" may struggle to answer.

The Medical-Psychological Tradition

While the "structural tradition" takes a more sociological stance on how, and why, certain individuals become serial murderers, the "medical-psychological" tradition instead takes a more intimate viewpoint. By doing so, it examines the potential biological, psychological and, to a lesser degree than the structural tradition, sociological factors that may lead to better understanding why people commit multiple murders.

Biological and neuropsychological perspectives

Offenders who have been classified as serial murderers are very limited in numbers and are difficult to study (Lundrigan and Canter, 2001). Despite this, it has not stopped researchers from investigating the potential factors that led these individuals to repeatedly kill (Lester, 1995; Egger, 1998;

Schlesinger, 2004). A great deal of attention has been given to discovering possible biological influences, and the neurological structure of these offender's brains, that may have influenced their behaviour.

One notable example that highlights this perspective in action is Silva et al's (2002) study that examined the American serial murderer Jeffrey Dahmer. This specific research is of interest because Dahmer was demonstrated as being a "considerabl[e] influence" with regards to "on-going dialogue concerning serial killing behaviour" (p. 1347). Silva et al, utilising a "developmental and neuropsychiatric perspective" (p. 1347), suggest that Dahmer's behaviour before, during and after he committed his offences was primarily due to his suffering from "pervasive developmental disorders" (p. 1348). Specifically, they state that Dahmer suffered from a "form of high functioning autistic psychopathology, namely Asperger's disorder" (p. 1347). The researchers, further reinforcing their biological argument, pay considerable attention towards the subject's parents. They discuss in detail how both parents suffered from a variety of conditions, such as "disabling protracted nausea" (p. 1348) for his mother, and that his father's similar social introversion may suggest that Dahmer inherited his Asperger's disorder from him (p. 1351). While this study attempts to provide a biological reasoning as to why Dahmer became a serial murderer, the researchers have only biographies and accounts from family members on which to base their conclusions. This is not a direct criticism of the study; more that the question has to be asked whether they would have come to the same conclusion if they had been able to interview Dahmer, who had been killed by a fellow inmate in 1994 (Masters, 2007). It is also important to stress that pervasive developmental disorders are not exclusive to biological perspectives, but have also been associated with social, behavioural, and psychological perspectives (Allely et al, 2014). Others have criticised this posthumous diagnostic approach to Dahmer, with Palermo and Bogaerts (2014) stating that "the case of serial killer Jeffrey Dahmer is a typical example where a somewhat facile and almost syllogistic application of perhaps over-inclusive criteria may have contributed to the legend of solitary murderers as possibly suffering from an autism spectrum condition" (p. 1). They also note that Dahmer's father, whose recollections regarding his son were considered and used as data for Silva et al (2002), may have been displaying signs of "recall bias". Specifically, they argue that, "because of his own circumstances and his son's behaviours, and given what he, and the public, knew of the nature and modus operandi of his son", his father's "impressionistic interpretations" were perhaps influenced — resulting in potentially unreliable data.

Gao and Raine (2010; see also Raine, 2013 for a more general biological analysis of murderers) have also suggested a neuropsychological perspective to assist in answering why certain individuals repeatedly kill. Their study suggests that psychopaths will have a decrease in prefrontal and amygdala volumes, and that these individuals will have problems with the hippocampus (p. 203). These are the areas of the brain that help people to perform tasks such as decision-making and fear processing (p. 203). More specifically, the researchers compare what they label "successful" psychopaths, individuals who show psychopathic tendencies but yet have never been incarcerated, to "unsuccessful" psychopaths, people who also show these traits but have been imprisoned. Gao and Raine (2010) conclude that "successful" psychopaths have "intact or enhanced neurobiological functioning...which in turn helps them to achieve their goals using more covert and non-violent methods" (p. 194). This is in stark contrast to "unsuccessful" psychopaths, whose "brain structur[e] and functional impairments together with autonomic nervous system dysfunctions... [lead] to more overt violent offending" (p. 194). Whilst the researchers offer a multitude of examples of psychopaths in a variety of contexts, the significance of the study here lies in the fact that they specifically examine cases of serial murder and the potential link between these unique offenders and neurobiological influences. Gao and Raine (2010) describe serial murder as being "inevitably linked" to psychopathy (p. 202), and deducted that, in general terms, individuals who are, or become, serial murderers fall in between the two forms of psychopaths identified, and are thus labelled as being "semi-successful" psychopaths. This was deducted through a somewhat generalised description of serial murderers:

"First, they have the capability to identify vulnerable and passive victims...second, some use their superficial charm and glibness to win the affection of the victim by being apparently loving and considerate … third, they have the capability to dispose of the bodies in the remote and undetectable locations (Gao and Raine, 2010, p. 202).

As Gao and Raine (2010) illustrate, certain serial murderers, it would seem, appear to share traits associated with the "successful" psychopath. It should be noted, though, that there is "limited evidence and mixed findings" regarding the hypothesis of there being "successful" and "unsuccessful" psychopaths (p. 203). Despite these limitations, there is a considerable body of literature surrounding the potential biological influences on individuals who become serial murderers. Another significant limitation of this study is the noticeably small sample size, and a biased population that resulted in other groups and individuals being neglected — potentially influencing the study's findings.

Psychological and personality perspectives

When compared to the relatively recent emergence of the "structural tradition", studies that have focused upon the psychological explanations for serial murder date back to the late 19th Century with the works of Krafft-Ebing (1896) especially his text *Psychopathic Sexualis*. Krafft-Ebing provides examples of serial murderers from Germany who are drawn to "sadism, lust murder, and sexual violence" (Myers et al, 1993, p. 444). While more contemporary literature has moved towards the understanding of fantasy and its influence upon serial murder, the concepts of sadism, lust, and sexual violence are prevalent amongst most of the literature relating to serial murder and psychodynamics.

It is important to take into consideration that much of the literature that will be presented focuses predominantly on "serial sexual" murder. Whilst published over 20 years ago, Liebert (1985) offers one of the most significant examples of research in this area. Liebert suggests that there are two types of serial murderer: the sexual and non-sexual serial murderer. The sexual serial murderer, it is argued, is the result of very primitive emotions, and that vicious and impulsive sexual action is the systematising power behind the offender's personality and behaviour. Liebert (1985) recognised that psychodynamic influences are important in the etiology of a sexual serial murderer. He also suggested the importance of considering the "pleasure principle" (Freud, 2003) in a sexual serial murderer's "multicidal behaviour". The psychodynamic perspective, as Liebert (1985) contests, is a key piece of the puzzle when attempting to understand serial murder and therefore these factors need to be considered in any overall explanation for this unique form of offending behaviour.

So too, Turco (2001) states that genetics, biological and neurological perspectives do not have all the answers, and that, in the case of "malignant narcissism" (p. 331) for example, it should not be "viewed as a disease but as an aspect of personality structure" (p. 331). Turco (2001) further elaborates by stating that the underlying "psychopathology and personality" of the serial murderer is necessary in understanding the "repetitive drive to kill" (p. 332; Liebert, 1985). Turco (2001), and Liebert (1985), attempt to provide the "clinical foundation" (p. 332) of the psychodynamic approach by declaring that narcissistic and borderline conditions assist in understanding an offender's personality and behaviour. Turco (2001) in addressing the subject of malignant narcissism, describes it as being an extreme variation of narcissistic personality disorder and as an "intermediate form" of character disorder between narcissistic and anti-social personality disorders (p. 335). He explores the potential impact of the offender's childhood, specifically the relationship between child and mother and suggests that a serial sexual murderer's "parental and other objects were experienced as cruel, attacking, destructive and oppressive of any self-development" (p. 335).

With regards to more contemporary research into the psychological reasonings behind serial murder, attention has shifted more to the labelling and categorising of particular behaviours. For example, Bennell et al (2013) re-examined the classification system first introduced in 1999 by Keppel and Walter. Their classification system of serial sexual murder/murderers offered a more refined classification system for rape than which was originally developed by Groth et al (1977). Keppel and Walter (1999) argued that, similar to rape, sexual murderers are "motivated by either anger or power" (Bennell et al, 2013, p. 7). Where Keppel and Walter (1999) differed from Groth et al (1977) was in their attempt to objectify the classification system by "indicating what specific crime scene behaviours and background characteristics would be present in each theme" (Bennell et al, 2013, p. 7). The sample used within Bennell et al's study had been used previously by Godwin (1998) and it recorded the "crime scene behaviours and background characteristics of 96 serial sexual murderers" (Bennell et al, 2013, p. 10). The authors' findings, which offered the first empirical test of Keppel and Walter's (1999) model, failed to validate it as statistically viable. This particular finding has further reinforced the seemingly impossible goal of empirically validating typological models that are concerned with sexual murder/murder—including models generated by Hazelwood and Douglas (1980) and Holmes and Holmes (2002). This is due to, as Bennell et al (2013) state, the complex and ambiguous nature of human emotions and behaviours that prevent them from being "neatly" placed in specific categories or typologies. Due to these findings, attention has now moved away from the categorising of behaviours and motivations, and instead to identifying "themes" (p. 20). For example, Jones et al (2012) found recurring trends across both criminal and non-criminal domains for offenders for a variety of expressive crimes. These "themes" were demonstrated in other, similar research such as Canter et al (2003) and Bennell et al (2002). They, Bennell et al (2013) argue, are even more relevant when taking into consideration that "similar sorts of themes have been reported in other forms of interpersonal violence, such as rape and child sex abuse" (p. 20).

To summarise, the psychodynamic approach proposes that serial murderers are the product of either one, or more of the following: an absence of psychosis; psychopathic/narcissistic personality assemblage; a history of maternal overprotection, coupled with paternal detachment or mistreatment; and a history of early childhood suffering. As witnessed in Bennell et al's (2013) study, there is a danger when seeking causative factors to oversimplify these offender's motivations and subsequent actions, with other potentially equal or more important factors, such as, for example, their society's structural condition.

Behavioural and learning theories about criminal behaviour, unlike the arguably more intrinsic nature of the psychodynamic perspective, can be more objectively scrutinised and tested through scientific means. Watson (1925) asserted that human behaviour is in fact formed by environmental and social dynamics, particularly when it comes to gaining knowledge, which is defined as a change to previous behaviour or intellectual processes as a consequence of gaining experience (Cassel and Bernstein, 2007). Operant conditioning, first proposed by Skinner (as cited by Hergenhahn and Olson, 2007) is a principle founded on the influence of reward and punishment. Using the basis of such theories similar to this, it is advocated that a serial murderer is sculpted by their environment through social learning experiences and reinforcements.

Social learning theory, which was derived from the work of Bandura (1977), results in behaviours that are assimilated through modelling, or by means of rewards and punishment (Wright and Hensley, 2003). With regards to serial murder, social learning theory would propose that these offenders learned to commit murder by observing others, or through a gradual process of being rewarded for homicidal behaviour. In reviewing the literature on serial murderers, it was not possible to find any evidence of an identified serial murderer who had a serial murderer as a parent, caregiver, or who was in an authority role. As this seems to rule out modelling as a social learning perspective of serial murder, attention must then turn to whether serial murder may be influenced through reward situations. By studying the childhoods of serial murderers, a "graduation hypothesis" has been suggested (Wright and Hensley, 2003) to explain how previous experiences may have been rewarded and created an escalation of behaviours that in due course resulted in the creation of a serial murderer.

In viewing the "graduation hypothesis", there is usually an emphasis on the role of animal cruelty and its influence regarding similar violence towards humans. Mead (1964) was one of the earliest researchers to suggest a link between childhood animal cruelty and adult aggressive behaviour towards other people; stating that animal cruelty "could provoke a diagnostic sign" (p. 22) that, if identified, could lead to the prevention of adult violent behaviour. One of the most thoroughly documented cases from this perspective is Jeffrey Dahmer. As a child, Dahmer reported that he captured and tortured animals for curiosity but this later turned into a source of pleasure for him (Wright and Hensley, 2003). Martens and Palermo (2005) explore this notion of animal cruelty and escalation. In their study, the researchers state that Dahmer spoke at length about his development into a serial murderer and how experimentation with animals in early life led to later experimentation with human victims. Of major interest in this case is the fact that Dahmer used acid to strip the flesh from the bones of animals and later repeated this behaviour when he was murdering humans (Martens and Palermo, 2005). In explaining this experimentation, Ressler and Shachtman (1997) state that it was Dahmer's primary motivation to create "zombies" to satisfy his sexual desires without the need for emotional bonding and caring that is normally associated with relationships.

Again reinforcing the "graduation hypothesis", Edmund Kemper, another serial murderer from North America, also had a history of killing animals as a child and developed a strong fantasy of carrying out these same actions toward humans (Ressler and Shachtman, 1992). Kemper's childhood experiences involved the decapitation of animals and then bringing the heads back to his room as a trophy (Ressler and Shachtman, 1992; Martens and Palermo, 2005). Later in life, Kemper progressed to decapitating humans and bringing their heads back to his room, where he would engage in sexual acts and then place the heads on a shelf as a trophy (Ressler and Shachtman, 1992). When the police apprehended Kemper and searched his home, they found his mother's head mounted in his room. Kemper explained that the act of killing his mother was a "cleansing" moment that fulfilled his homicidal cravings (Hickey, 1997).

Taking into account the two examples described above, there may be a potential connection between childhood animal cruelty and later re-enactment actions resulting in murder. In a study conducted by Wright and Hensley (2003), 354 serial murderers were examined. It was discovered that 21 per cent of these offenders had a history of animal cruelty as a child. In another study by Ressler et al (1988), it was found that out of a sample of 36 subjects, 36 per cent reported a substantial history of animal cruelty. Although a notable percentage of serial murderers reported acts of animal cruelty, a far greater number of incarcerated serial murderers do not have, or at least have not recounted, such acts against animals (Wright and Hensley, 2003). Consequently, from a social learning standpoint, more evidence is necessary to support a causal relationship between animal cruelty and serial murder.

Returning to the social learning theory, it has been suggested that military experience may contribute to the development of serial murder dynamics (Castle and Hensley, 2002). Grossman (1996) coined the term "killology" to describe the psychological effects of training humans to kill others. From this theoretical standpoint, it is believed that the idea of killing humans is learned during military training or real acts during a time of war. For the serial murderer, this develops into a satisfying experience and is sustained with the instigation and continuance of criminal offences. Again, there is limited support for this hypothesis since there is not a large sample of serial murderers with military experience. In a study conducted by Castle (2001) of 354 serial murderers, it was discovered that 25 American serial murderers had military experience—some seven per cent. Taking into account these findings, it is hard to accept learning to kill through military experiences is a strong explanation for the development of serial murder.

To summarise, behavioural and social learning theories traditionally rely greatly upon behavioural modelling and conditioning. Compared to the more "inward" looking psychodynamic perspective, this particular approach instead focuses upon the external factors and influences that may potentially contribute in the creation of a serial murderer. Although some of the literature presented here seems to support serial murderer development on a limited basis, from a purely social learning theory perspective these arguments appear weak. Only limited research has been done in this area, and none of the previously mentioned social learning perspectives have been strongly supported by the research so far conducted. Certainly there are possible connections that may exist, but there is stronger support from the psychodynamic perspective to explain serial murderer development and processes.

Summary

This chapter has sought to provide the reader with both an historic and theoretical overview of how researchers have attempted to examine and understand the unique phenomenon of serial murder. In doing so, the paradigmatically opposed "structural tradition" and "medical-psychological tradition" were presented. Whilst it is acknowledged that both of these theoretical perspectives have contributed much to the understanding of serial murder at both an innate and societal level, it must be stressed that both traditions tend to overlook the potential significance of occupational choice for serial murderers. Specifically, the "medical-psychological" tradition tended to examine serial murderers within a "vacuum". As such, attention was primarily given to these offenders' behaviour when engaged in offending—and less to do with their lifestyles as a whole. With particular reference to the Holmes and Holmes typology checklist, in which a serial murderer is largely categorised depending on their reported motivation, it became apparent that much scholarly attention is focused on these individual's behaviour and less their everyday habits, including their employment. While it is accepted that sexually motivated offenders predominately target women, including sex workers, in an effort to fulfill their offending fantasies, the question as to whether these offenders' lifestyles somehow provides access and, more importantly, opportunity is rarely touched upon or explored in much detail.

With regard to the "structural tradition", whilst Leyton's concept of "homicidal protest" labelled both the offender and victim according to their social standing depending on the historical epoch they belonged to, there was no further examination as to what specific roles these individuals would or may have held within these social standings. Advocates of the "structural tradition", especially Wilson (2007; 2009), draw attention to those victim groups that are most vulnerable to being targeted by serial murderers within Britain. This particular structural approach highlights how these individuals' social status and, in the case of sex workers, their occupation, put them in harm's way. This book acknowledges and agrees with Wilson's thesis, but also recognises that it raises a question: If particular occupations and social statuses can place individuals in a vulnerable position to being targeted by serial murders, are there particular occupations that provide status, proximity and access for these offenders to these particular individuals?

Moving forwards, attention will now shift towards current academic understanding of the transient serial murderer. Will this more specific examination into the geographical movement of serial murderers shed light on the importance of occupational choice for serial murderers? Or will the pattern of ignoring this potentially significant aspect of these offenders' lives and daily behaviour again be present?

CHAPTER THREE

The Transient Serial Murderer: Current Understanding

In this truck is a man
Whose latent genius if
Unleashed would rock the
Nation, whose dynamic energy
Would overpower those
Around him: better let
Him sleep?

Note written by Peter William Sutcliffe aka "The Yorkshire Ripper" found in his truck

With a more holistic understanding of the various theoretical components that have laid the foundations for understanding serial murder, focus now shifts towards the understanding of the spatial behaviour of serial murderers—and the role occupational choice may have in this.

Serial Murder and Transience

There are a multitude of rationales and explanations regarding the spatial patterns of serial murderers. There is, according to Hickey (1991 cited in Snook et al, 2005), a general public perception that serial murderers are "unconstrained spatial decision-makers, who drift across national landscapes selecting victims at will" (p. 148). Snook et al state that this apparent image has caused an increase in:

"…the perception of serial murderers as a special breed of offender whose decision-making is not bound by the same financial, social, and cognitive constraints as other types of criminals" (Snook et al, 2005, p. 148).

This, as it turns out, is indeed a myth with no basis of academic support. For example, Godwin and Canter (1997) showed that victim and offender meeting locations were, on average, two kilometres from the offender's home or base, and the victim's body retrieval sites was 23 kilometres from the offender's base. Rossmo (2000) found that North American serial murderers commonly "run into" victims at a typical distance of almost 22 kilometres and subsequently dumped their bodies approximately 34 kilometres from their home or base.

There have been other studies that have again attempted to disprove this generally held view on transient serial murderers. Lundrigan and Canter (2001) for example carried out a cross-culture comparison between serial murderers in Britain and North America. Their findings determined that the average distance from the offender's base to crime scene was 15 and 40 kilometres in North America, while in Britain nine and 18 kilometres. While there appears to be a significant difference between these two sets of results, it is important to consider the environmental differences between these two countries. These results do suggest that the serial murderer is, in fact, far removed from the general public's perception of a "drifter".

Holmes and De Burger (1988) analysed approximately 400 cases of serial murder through the use of interview data. They proposed that there is a clear distinction between transient serial murderers and geographically stable serial murderers. Specifically, transient serial murderers travel continuously from one location to the next and dispose of their victims' bodies in distant locations. In contrast, the geographically stable serial murderer resides in one location for an extensive period of time and not only kills their victims in this same area, but also disposes of the victims' bodies in this same location or region. As Lundrigan and Canter (2001) highlight, these findings regarding the transient serial murderer suggest that the decision to travel a significant distance to offend is significantly influenced by the need to evade detection. Relating to the theoretical concept of rational choice, in which individuals "weigh up" the costs and benefits of committing a crime (Cornish, 1993), Lundrigan and Canter state that this very desire to not be caught suggests "rational consideration" (p. 426) on the part of the offender. Lundrigan and Canter elaborate further, proposing that:

> "Were this risk not present then these offenders would remain within a familiar environment. In other words, it may be an external influence that prompts serial murderers to travel large distances" (Lundrigan and Canter, 2001, p. 426).

The points raised by Lundrigan and Canter raises the question: could these "external influences" include their occupation and work environment?

Lundrigan and Canter discuss the potential factors that may contribute to the spatial patterns of serial murderers, arguing that factors such as the age of the offender; their intellectual ability; their motivation[s]; employment status; marital status and mode of transportation all may have a part to play in these offender's spatial movements. It is important to take into account that, while these factors have been examined in other types of offenders, "most of them have not been directly examined with regard to serial murder" (Snook et al, 2005, p. 149). While research has been conducted in cases of murder (see Groff and McEwen, 2005), most serial murder studies have described the age of the serial murderer "without examining how it relates to their spatial decisions" (p. 150) (see also Ansevics and Doweiko, 1991; Canter et al, 2000; Jenkins, 1988; Prentky et al, 1989). Due to little direct evidence and the conflicting results from previous research, a definite answer as to the influence of serial murderer age and spatial decisions and patterns has yet to be recognised. According to Snook et al (2005) "a number of researchers have published IQ scores of serial murderers but have not evaluated the relationship between intelligence and spatial decisions" (p. 150).

Despite this seemingly sparsely researched area, Ressler et al (1986) examined the crime location patterns of sexual serial murderers and determined that "organized" offenders have an average to above average intellect and are expected to offend far from their base or place or residence. On the other hand "disorganized" offenders have generally lower than average intellect and commit their crimes near to their base or location of employment. Ressler et al's study does not examine the significance of occupation for the "organized" offender. For example, could an "organized" serial murderer choose an occupation, which permits them to travel far from their base and place of employment in order to give them a valid reason to be in the location where their victim[s] were abducted or killed?

Holmes and De Burger (1988) examined the association between offender motivation and serial murderers' spatial patterns. Through their generation of offender typologies which included Visionary, Mission-Oriented, Hedonistic, and Power/Control-Oriented, Holmes and De Burger analysed the crime scenes of each of these typologies of serial murderers in regards to whether or not they were closely or widely located comparative to one another. According to Holmes and De Burger, serial murderers categorised as Visionary, Mission-Oriented, Hedonistic-Lust and Hedonistic-Comfort were found to have concentrated crime locations, while serial murderers categorised as Hedonistic-Thrill, Power/Control-Oriented and Opportunists were seen to have scattered crime scene locations. These constructed typologies, a by-product of the "medical-psychological" tradition, again demonstrates how the majority of serial murder oriented research is conducted within a "vacuum", more concerned with the relatively short offending period that these individuals "engage" in, and less concerned with the activities these offenders "re-engage" in after committing each consecutive murder. Based on this study's results, motive seems to be related to serial murderers' spatial decisions, though more research would need to be conducted outside of Holmes and De burger's typology classification due to researchers criticising the validity of their model (Canter et al, 2004).

With regard to the significance of employment status, Snook et al (2005) state that:

> "The conceivable effect of employment on spatial decisions is somewhat paradoxical–employed offenders may have more financial resources avail-

able to aid travel, but they may also lack freedom of mobility due to job commitments" (Snook et al, 2005, p. 151).

While this is plausible, these assumptions regarding the "lack of freedom" with job commitments demonstrate the need to more closely examine not only the types of occupations chosen by these offenders, but also whether in fact these occupations actually provide a freedom of mobility as opposed to lack of it. Hickey (1991), for example, discovered that those serial murderers that had regular employment stayed within the general area they lived in. Specifically, Hickey argued that employment is an indication of spatial stability within a city that may limit, and reduce, the spatial decisions and patterns of serial murderers. While some occupations may indeed restrict the geographical movement of a serial murderer, there are occupations, such as long-distance lorry and delivery drivers, which would result in the instability of spatial behaviour. Again, Hickey's observations raise interesting questions and highlight the need for more research regarding the significance of occupation choice and serial murder. Nor has there been research conducted on the importance of marital status on spatial patterns for serial murderers, with only Jenkins (1988) and Snook et al (2005) providing the only substantial examples. Jenkins (1988) stated that 6 of the 12 British serial murderers he examined were married, had a steady relationship with their partner, and lived in the same home for numerous years. Building on these observations, Snook et al (2005) state that "marriage conceivably acts as a social control" (p. 151), consequently making it less viable for a married serial murderer to carry out extensive and expensive searches for suitable victims or body disposal sites. With regard to transportation, Ressler et al (1986) reported that 85 per cent of "organized" sexual serial murderers used a vehicle compared with 62 per cent of "disorganized" sexual serial murderers. Ressler et al also determined that the organized offenders committed their crimes a greater distance from their base location compared to the disorganized offenders. These results suggest that serial murderers who use or own transportation, such as a car or van, may display larger home-to-crime distances than those who walk or who are dependent on public transport. "Hence, as one would intuitively expect, the mode of transportation a murderer uses may be an important factor in spatial decision-making" (Snook, et al, 2005, p. 152).

Serial Murder and Driving as an Occupational Choice

There has been little academic interest in the significance of driving as an occupational choice and its potential influences on those who commit serial murder. Attention has, for the most part, been given to those serial murderers who operate in a medical and healthcare profession. Most notably, Ramsland (2007) notes how a number of healthcare serial murderers "enter the profession as predatory angels of death, alert to the opportunities for murder" (xii). This line of thought regarding the health-care serial murderer will be explored to see if it can be translated to those serial murderers who drove as part of their occupation later in this thesis. While attention has been limited outside of the domain of healthcare serial murderers, this does not mean that the "geographically transient" offender has been completely neglected. McClellan (2008) for example offers the most recent example of the relationship between driving and serial murder. She examines 22 North American serial murderers, four European and one Chinese, whom she identified as being "employed as regional or long distance truck drivers" (p. 171). McClellan's research draws attention to why exactly some serial murderers choose occupations that involve driving:

> "Modus operandi in instances where the offender is a truck driver clearly indicate the use of a professional means of transportation (long haul and delivery) to expand the hunting grounds, familiarisation of routes, habits of travellers who do not engage in risk-taking behaviours (drugs or prostitution specifically), and truck stop/truck plaza operations (legal and illegal)" (McClellan, 2008, p. 174).

Here, McClellan offers an explanation as to why these types of occupations are prevalent amongst serial murderers and strikes a similar theme as Ramsland (2007) with regards to these individuals taking advantage of certain unique opportunities made available by these professions. While she does not attempt to provide motivational insight behind those serial murderers that drive, the instrumental, or practical, advantages that are available to these offenders is clearly highlighted. While McClellan does draw attention to an increased "hunting" zone and the "familiarisation" of road networks, and the use of cars and lorries to "lure their potential victims to their death" (p. 181), further analysis into how serial murderers use vehicles to instrumentally influence their offences is absent. Instead, McClellan explores preventive measures that could be implemented in what she calls a "truck stop culture" (p. 187) in North America. As such, McClellan draws attention away from the serial murderer and towards the victims, and comes to the conclusion that hitchhikers and prostitutes formed the majority of known victims and that in the case of Europe "all the victims were described as known prostitutes" (p. 181).

Taking McClellan's observations into consideration, it is arguable whether the type of serial murderer attracted to transient occupations falls under the "sexual serial murderer" classification described previously. While McClellan focuses more on prevention as opposed to exploration into the motivational and instrumental rationale as to why serial murderers choose occupations that involve long periods of driving, she clearly identifies that awareness of this "30-plus year phenomenon" (p. 189) regarding this unique form of serial murder needs to be raised.

Mott (1999) shares similarities with McClellan's research regarding the significance of mobile serial murderers, but is much more broad in his focus on the potential differences between solved and unsolved cases of serial murder. More specifically, Mott's attention is aimed towards not only transience, but also the rate of killing, victim vulnerability, body disposal, and lastly the location of body disposal. Interestingly, while Mott refers to the recurring issue of "linkage blindness", and hypothesises that "more inter jurisdictional offenders will exist within the set of un-solved cases than among the solved cases" (p. 244), the results gathered were less "clear-cut" (p. 249) than the other variables tested. Mott's findings, in fact, contradicted the hypothesis previously outlined, with a larger ratio of mobile offenders in the solved cases group than the unsolved group—consequently invalidating the predicted outcomes. Mott explores these unexpected outcomes, referring to the work of Hickey (1997) who suggested that urbanisation "may be one explanation for this decrease in travelling offenders" (cited in Mott, 1999, p. 245). To elaborate, the increased space taken by the urbanisation of certain areas increases the availability of potential victims and, at the same time, also increases anonymity subsequently making the detection of these offenders much more difficult. Mott challenges Hickey's argument and, while acknowledging the unexpected results, he argues that "these results do not exclude linkage blindness as a hindrance to investigations, but instead the results may further support the prevalence of it" (p. 251). In an attempt to further explain the findings, Mott suggests that the reason why there are more solved cases of inter jurisdictional offenders than unsolved cases was because the offenders may be "killing victims using a travelling pattern" (p. 252) and thus easier to detect. Mott does not expand upon this point and, as a result, there is no indication or discussion into what exactly is this "travelling pattern". Is this pattern a direct result of the offender pursuing victims, and independent from other aspects of their lives? Or is the offender's travelling pattern perhaps influenced or shaped by some other facet of their day-to-day lives such as, for example, their occupation?

Quinet (2011) examines the significance of occupational choice and transience not for the offender, but of the victim. Despite this divergence, Quinet's analysis regarding the nature of serial murder victims may, in turn, enhance the understanding of the nature of the transient serial murderer. From a theoretical standpoint, Quinet's research appears to adopt a "structural" approach—stating that "marginal victim populations such as drug users, prostitutes, migrant workers, and other transients—suggests that some victims matter less than others" (p. 80). Quinet expands on this statement, declaring that this transient lifestyle inherent within those occupations and lifestyles previously stated "may facilitate longer killing periods and higher numbers of victims" for serial murderers (p. 81).

Taking Quinet's observations into consideration, this is evidently an important factor to consider in regards to mobile serial murderers, which is that there is a clear, common denominator in relation to both this type of serial murderer and this particular category of victims—roads. Individuals who engage in prostitution, along with other lifestyles lacking a stable place of residence, are drawn to the streets and roads for a number of reasons. As Opack (2000) explains, roads act as a literal and metaphorical path away from "the abyss of the social, economic, and personal impoverishment of the 'throwaway' world" (p. 65). Drawing from research conducted by Salfati (2009) who documented cases of prostitutes who were murdered in Britain, Quinet (2011) determined that factors such as "availability; opportunity; [and] expressive motivations" (p. 82) are the primary reasons why certain groups, such as prostitutes, are recurring victims of serial murder. Due to the focus of the research being predominantly fixed on the victims as opposed to the offenders, Quinet does not attempt to explore the potential influences of the offenders' occupational background. This is rather unexpected as Quinet, in reference to decreasing the risks of victimisation to transient groups, draws upon a distinct occupational context: "the serial murderer who operates primarily in medical settings can be most effectively prevented by focusing our resources in this setting (e.g., death surveillance systems)" (p. 93). While not overtly referring to the occupation of the offender, Quinet's example of a "medical setting" carries with it certain connotations that the serial murderer is, in some way or form, associated professionally within the setting provided. The example provided by Quinet also reinforces the factors previously raised, specifically access and opportunity within specific environments. So while Quinet's research successfully draws upon the significance of occupation, or lack of it, for victims of serial murder, it is important to also understand the occupations of the offenders, and the level of access and opportunity that it provides them when committing their offences.

Finally, Roach (2012) has been at the forefront of scholarly work that draws attention to occupation and transience with regard to murderers who go undetected for a considerable amount of time. Roach focuses his attention on what he labels as "under the radar offenders", and how these offender's "behaviour and personal characteristics" may have impacted the investigation to apprehend them (p. 1). Specifically, he identifies that these offenders worked in only "unskilled jobs" and that they "moved around the country" (p. 10). Roach (2012) identifies that these under the radar offenders appear to be mobile and maintain low skilled jobs which suggest little or limited responsibility in their work environment. Whilst Roach's research does not specifically examine serial murder, three questions are still raised: firstly, what exactly are these "unskilled jobs"? Second, is it the occupation itself that facilities this transience? And, finally, does the occupation have a role in aiding their offences? These are questions that, so far, have yet to be answered and which this book will ultimately address.

Closing Comments

With a more in-depth understanding of the theoretical approaches to transient offender behaviour, existing scholarly literature related to the spatial patterns of serial murderers has been presented. While various facets have been analysed to explain the spatial patterns of serial murders, it is clear that the influence of employment has been considerably under researched. We will now move on to examine a psychological theoretical model that will inform how particular personality types "seek out" particular work environments. In doing so, this book will attempt to determine if serial murderers who choose an occupation that involves significant amounts of solitary driving have a particular personality type which, if recognised, could help to better understand the nature and behaviour of the transient serial murderer. Specifically, such findings may provide a valuable insight into whether these individuals consciously sought out these occupations in order to offend, or were in fact driven by other factors, and that their crimes were more a by-product or consequence of their occupationally-influenced lifestyle.

CHAPTER FOUR

Occupational Choice or Necessity?

Holland's research shows that personalities seek out and flourish in career environments they fit and that jobs and career environments are classifiable by the personalities that flourish in them.

Committee on Scientific Awards on the work of John L. Holland

During the course of researching the significance of driving as an occupational choice for British serial murderers there was one question that repeatedly came up but would prove almost impossible to answer: "Do these individuals deliberately choose an occupation in order to kill?" Did Peter Sutcliffe, for example, know he wanted to repeatedly kill sex workers and think to himself that being a lorry driver would allow him to do this? Or was it more to do with opportunity, and that such offending behaviour was influenced by other psychological factors, and the environmental stimuli provided by their occupation acted as a catalyst to these more subconscious forces? These are difficult questions and, given the infamous unreliability of serial murderers when interviewed (Wilson, 2009), may never be truly answered. Despite these obstacles, though, there are a number of psychological and criminological frameworks that may assist in shedding some light on these challenging questions.

Holland's RIASEC Model

In attempting to ask whether individuals either deliberately select occupations in order to kill, or instead kill due to factors that emerge once employed in particular occupations it is important to consider psychological models that examine the relationship between personality and occupation selection. Whilst there a multitude of personality models such as, for example, the HEXACO model of personality structure (Lee and Ashton, 2012) and the Colour Code Personality Profile (Hartman, 1987), Holland's RIASEC was chosen due to its longevity and reliability in providing insight into an individual's personality based on their occupational history.

John L Holland is an American psychologist who generated a model in which he grouped occupations and interests in a particular way — the so-called RIASEC categories of personality traits. During his work as a career counsellor, Holland became aware that among his clients, partiality and curiosity for particular categories of work tended to "co-occur" (Woods and West, 2010, p. 322–323). These observations led Holland to generate a hypothesis that argued that individuals actively search for occupations that match with their interests. When this "pairing" between individual and job environment match, the individual is more likely to be psychologically satisfied. Holland further argued that when this "pairing" does not necessarily match, the individual is less likely to be fulfilled, resulting in the individual looking outside their current work environment in search of an occupation that better fits their personality (Spokane and Cruza-Guet, 2005, p. 47). This hypothesis subsequently led to Holland identifying a set of distinctive occupational interest types, which he would come to label as personality types (Low and Rounds, 2006). Below is a brief explanation of what exactly Holland's model is designed to identify in regards to an individual's personality:

> "The theory consists of several simple ideas and their more complex collaborations. First, we can categorise people by their resemblance to each of six personality types: Realistic, Investigative, Artistic, Social, Enterprising and Conventional" (Woods and West, 2010, p. 323).

According to Holland (1973) these personality types are "the product of characteristic interaction among a variety of cultural and personal forces" (p. 2). These "forces" include the influence of peers, biological conditions, parental influence, social class, cultural context and the literal context. The second stage would involve characterising the environment in which people live and work in, and this is also identified through six model environments: Realistic; Investigative; Artistic; Social; Enterprising; and Conventional. The third and final step would be to "pair" the individual and environment that will ultimately lead to outcomes that could be predicted and understood, such as a particular personality type and their choice in work environments (Feist and Feist, 2006). Holland described six professional personality types and six subsequent work settings. This suggests that an individual's most prominent personality type will give a clue as to their ideal work environment (Shackleton and Fletcher, 1984, p. 140). The image below (Fig.2.) represents the RIASEC model in visual form:

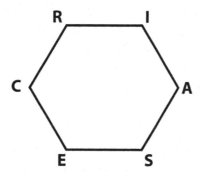

Adapted from Woods, S. A. West, M. A. (2010) *The Psychology of Work and Organizations*, Hampshire: Cengage Learning p. 328

This visual representation of Holland's model displays the empirical correlations between each personality type. With this model configuration, the types (RIASEC) that are adjacent to each other are thought to be more alike than those that are more distant (Holland, 1973). Holland's RIASEC model argues that individuals are drawn to work environments that fit with their interests. For example Realistic personality types are considered as individuals who are practical, conforming, and prefer to work with objects. In regards to occupations, this particular personality type is attracted to those such as being a mechanic; labourer; and driver (Holland, 1997).

The Investigative personality, in comparison, is regarded as someone who is observational, analytical, independent and intellectual. This personality type is drawn to often scientific; technical; and engineering career backgrounds (Holland, 1997). The Artistic personality type, similar to the Realistic personality, prefers to work with objects. The difference between these two personality types is that the Artistic personality takes pleasure in the manipulation of these objects. In regards to a preferred work environment, an individual with an Artistic personality is drawn to an occupation with little to no rules and would choose surroundings with a less structural and hierarchal order. With regard to the kinds of occupations that this particular personality type is attracted to, jobs such as a painter; interior decorator; journalist; and writer are the most prominent (De Fruyt and Mervielde, 1997). An individual with a Social personality type, compared to either the Artistic or Realistic types, prefers to work with people instead of objects. The Social personality type is arguably the most altruistic (McKay and Tokar, 2012), choosing professions that require a greater level of interaction and understanding between other individuals. The Social personality covers a wide range of occupations, but all are concerned with offering help and a service to others. The primary occupations that attract this personality type include teacher; counsellor; waiter/waitress; nurse; and tour guide (Holland, 1997).

In contrast to the Social personality, the Enterprising personality type instead prefers being in charge of other individuals (Woods and West, 2010). The main driving force behind this personality type is the desire of organizational and personal economic gain. An Enterprising personality is often drawn to a competitive work environment that also requires a risk taking attitude. These work conditions require an individual who is self-confident, ambitious, and assertive. The sort of occupations that this personality type is drawn to include a sales person; a manager within a company; a lawyer; a chief executive; and a recruitment consultant.

The sixth personality type, when compared to Enterprising, tends to prefer taking orders as opposed to giving them. An individual with a Conventional personality is described as being conforming, careful, disciplined and diligent. A Conventional work environment involves a series of set procedures and a well-planned routine that governs the day-to-day running of an occupational role. In contrast to the Artistic personality type, the Conventional personality is more comfortable when given information and data to work from, as opposed to actually generating original ideas and building upon them. Again, when compared to the Artistic personality, who is attracted to a more unconventional and less authoritative work setting, the Conventional personality is drawn to a work environment with a clear "line of authority" (p. 324). The array of professions that this particular personality type is largely found in includes accountancy; office clerk; cashier; auditor; secretary and administrator.

Testing the Validity of Holland's RIASEC Model

While Holland's RIASEC model has been widely acclaimed and considered popular within the academic community (see, for example, Farh et al, 1998; Furnham, 2001), this has not stopped researchers from testing its validity. First, a number of researchers have focused upon Holland's use of the hexagon as a basis for his model, as with the diagram earlier in this chapter. This hexagonal shape is the foundation of Holland's theory as it utilises both individuals' personalities and environments which are grouped into six categories. This model, as previously discussed, was developed to demonstrate the association between personality and occupational environment. Tinsley (2000) argues that the current research conducted demonstrates that the hexagonal congruence is not associated to satisfaction or other significant vocational results, and that Holland's (1997) model lacks validity. Tinsley elaborates further, stating that the lack of support for Holland's theory is not a product of design errors involving the sample volume, the soundness of the instruments used in the investigations, or the validity of the fit index used, but instead "a lack of commensurate measurement in research investigating Holland's theory may be a contributing factor" (Tinsley, 2000, p. 147). Tinsley also suggests that the advantages of implementing a particular structural representation such as a hexagon to signify the associations between sets of occupations and types of people has not been confirmed. Tinsley proposes that, in order to fix this issue, an explanatory two-dimensional illustration of the data is necessary and that the best solution is to "base conclusions on the skilful integration of descriptive and inferential information" (Tinsley, 2000 cited in Prediger, 2000, p. 200). While Tinsley insists that Holland's model lacks any valid credibility due to a lack of coherent measurements, Prediger (2000) challenged these findings — suggesting that Holland's theory instead lacks "perfect validity" (p. 201). Prediger draws upon the Hexagon itself, but in its two dimensional form:

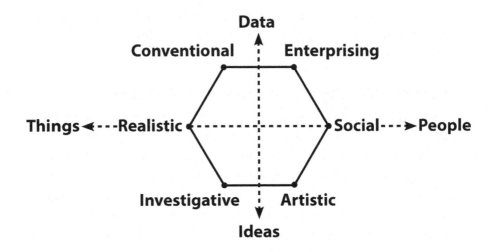

Adapted from Prediger D. J. (2000) 'Holland's Hexagon is Alive and Well — Though Somewhat out of Shape: Response to Tinsley', *Journal of Vocational Behaviour*, Vol. 56, pp. 197–204

The two-dimensional model depicted above illustrates Holland's personality types along with the corresponding work task dimensions. For example, the Realistic personality type prefers to work with objects and things as opposed to the Social personality who would prefer working with people. Prediger continues in his support of the hexagonal shape by incorporating a previous study (Prediger and Vansickle, 1992), in which they examined 3,612 college students who had participated in a RIASEC personality test eight years beforehand. Upon implementing the hexagonal shape associated with Holland's model, the researchers discovered that the vast majority of participants who were now employed were indeed "located near the Holland type to which they belonged" (Prediger and Vansickle, 1992 cited in Prediger, 2000, p. 202). Holland (1997) also responded to criticism regarding his use of the hexagonal shape, stating that "if these attributes did not hold most of the time, the research about the [personality] types would not support the expected similarities and differences" (p. 159–160). Holland (1997) continues, arguing that if his model was of poor design, then these consistencies found regarding similarities and differences would not exist. Consistency, Holland states, "is clearly related to direction of choice" (p. 160).

Taking the above into consideration, it is suggested here that such a model may prove useful in better understanding whether these serial murderers select their occupation in order to offend, or in fact are driven to such occupations due to the psychological "pull" of their personality. Before we apply this theoretical model to the serial murderers in this book, we will examine how Holland's model has been applied before to a criminological context.

The Application of RIASEC in a Criminological Context

With regard to the implementation of Holland's RIASEC to offenders, the literature to date has been somewhat sporadic with different researchers focusing on distinct criminological contexts. For instance, Shrewsbury (2008) implements Holland's model in an attempt to understand why many of North America's black prison population have a lack of employment. The crux of Shrewsbury's argument is that an individual's environment at a young age is important when predicting their likely future occupation. Specifically, Shrewsbury states that:

> "This researcher contends that youths entering the correctional system, especially as juvenile offenders, never go through the developmental or decision-making stages needed to make career decisions or to develop career maturity" (Shrewsbury, 2008, p. 4).

Shrewsbury's hypothesis supports the research of Tracey et al (2005; see also Tracey et al, 2006), in that those adolescent years in which juvenile offenders are in a correctional facility are vitally important in terms of their occupational interest development. Ultimately, Shrewsbury argues, these juvenile offenders become "part of a need-driven, group-survivor lifestyle" (p. 4). In terms of the significance of Holland's model to this book, it is used to examine the career development of "Black male criminal substance abusers" (p. 5) in regards to their interests, skills, individuality, and work record. Shrewsbury does not rely solely on this model, though, with various other psychological tests such as the Rorschach test as such, Shrewsbury determined that prisoners with an increased quality and quantity of work within their respective community will have considerably improved "profiles in ability, interest, and personality" (p. 5) than individuals with a less mature development over a period of time.

Ameen and Lee (2012) implemented Holland's model within the context of juvenile detention centres with the "posit that juvenile detention centres may be most efficacious by serving as both place and process to create career opportunity through vocational training" (p. 98). This comes in contrast to Shrewsbury's (2008) study, in which a prison-like setting in fact impedes an individual's occupational interest development. Ameen and Lee (2012), while not disagreeing with Shrewsbury's observations, do argue that a juvenile detention centre, when properly managed, may in fact provide young offenders with the necessary environment required for them to stop reoffending. While the authors draw upon other psychological factors that may influence repeat offending in adolescents, it is the inclusion of career theories, such as Holland's RIASEC, that the researchers argue may help lower recidivism rates.

Glaser et al (2003) also incorporated Holland's model when examining adolescent offenders. Whereas Ameen and Lee's (2012) study attempted to improve the occupation interest development of young offenders, Glaser et al (2003) instead compare the mean RIASEC personality measurements of 28 adolescent offenders, with non-offending high school students. The researchers determined that the mean Artistic score of the "adjudicated" (p. 73) group was considerably greater than the high school sample, though the investigative personality score was highest in this group. In addition, when compared to the high school sample, the "adjudicated sample showed poor differentiation and significantly higher inter-correlations among the Holland codes" (p. 73). Glaser et al's results raise interesting questions regarding the general personality type of young offenders and highlights, along with Ameen and Lee's (2012) study, the most recurrent research environment for Holland's model and offenders. Of course, taking into account the sparse literature so far published and the model's relative infancy when applied to a criminological context, this may well change over the coming years.

A number of other studies are also relevant. Railey and Peterson (2000), for example, examined the career thoughts and patterns of three distinct groups of subjects. These included: First-time Offenders; Probationers; and Repeat Offenders. The participants were 92 female offenders aged 18 to 54 and housed, at the time, within a correctional facility in North America. These three groups were compared in "terms of dysfunctional career thoughts and career interest structure" (p. 119). Despite clear differences between this particular study and Shrewsbury's (2008), Railey and Peterson's (2000) study shares the assumption that a lack of development in regards to career interests and a young age may be a significant contributor to the lack of ability certain individuals face when attempting to put together vocational goals and suitable occupational interests. Railey and Peterson's study focuses on the issue of "Commitment Anxiety", and its relation to offender's ability to not only find employment, but also remain employed. The variables that were tested included potential dysfunctional career thoughts. These include such factors as decision-making disorder, commitment concern, and external conflict outside of the participant's control. Another important variable was the career interest structure, which included aspects such as congruence, frequency of employment, differentiation between occupations, and stability. With regards to their findings, there were considerable differentiations between the three groups of offenders, with "Commitment Anxiety" within the Repeat Offender group indicating notably less anxiety than First-time Offender or Probationer groups. The factor of coherence was also raised as a varying facet between the groups. Coherence was recorded as being highest with the Probation group, though only 13 per cent of that particular group were documented as having high levels of coherence. In regards to Holland's RIASEC and this book, it is evident that it was implemented with very different rationales than Shrewsbury's (2008) study and within this work—arguably showcasing the validity and flexibility of the model.

Finally, Harrison's (1998) study which implemented Holland's model to characterise the occupations of drink driving offenders resonates the most with this research. The study's central aim was to assist authorities in identifying similar characteristics of drink drivers through the uncovering of their occupations. In doing so, Harrison states that:

> "Such groups could then be utilized in the development of targeted public education campaigns in the Victorian (Australia) context where there are already high levels of enforcement and mass-media publicity" (Harrison, 1998, p. 119).

Here it is worth noting that of each study so far discussed, none were conducted within Britain. This is a clear indicator of the model's infancy in regards to implementation to a criminological context. Referring back to Harrison's study, the results identified two possible groups, which were responsible for 58 per cent of the male drink-drivers. These groups were recognised as being notably different from other male drink drivers in a variety of ways, "underlining the potential for their use as targets in future campaigns" (p. 119). According to Harrison, one occupational group was responsible for 42 per cent of the male drink drivers. These occupations included roles such as "carpenter, electrician, chef, mechanic, gardener, and labourer" (p. 119). These occupational roles fit neatly into the realistic personality type of Holland's model and suggest that these offenders are asocial, compliant, introverted, methodical, and prefer to work with objects rather than people. The latter occupational group accounted for 16 per cent of the male drink drivers and consisted of occupations such as "business manager, company director, public servant, and sales representative" (p. 119). These occupational roles are more consistent with the Enterprising personality type and propose that such individuals are energetic, adventurous, confident, dominant, and enthusiastic. Through analysing Harrison's findings, it is apparent that, in the context of the study, the Realistic personality type is the most common and dominant type in regards to drink-driving offences. This is an interesting finding and raises questions regarding the general personality type of offenders who commit multiple murders with the aid of a vehicle.

Holland's RIASEC Model: Closing Comments

To summarise, it is apparent that Holland's RIASEC continues to generate interest since its original conception. The model, despite receiving some criticism, has found a valid position within the occupational psychology community, suggesting a valid and widely accepted longevity. While it has been applied to a vast number of different cultural contexts and to a large, though seemingly incomplete, number of work environments—how has this model been so far applied to offenders? In answering this question, it is evident that since Holland's conception of RIASEC over 40 years ago, there has been little research conducted in terms of its relevance to offenders and offending behaviour. The context of juvenile correctional facilities has seen the most application. With a large amount of research conducted on the significance of childhood and adolescent experiences and its impact on future occupational choices, it is reasonable for researchers to naturally be drawn to the issue of youth offenders and their occupational interest development. Nevertheless, it is apparent that, apart from Harrison's (1998) study of Australian drink-driving offenders, research attempting to identify traits of a particular type of offender, such as general personality patterns, is still in its infancy and requires further study. With this in mind, this particular examination into the role of driving as an occupational choice for serial murderers provides a new channel in which to apply this psychological model within a criminological context. In applying this personality model, the subsequent case studies of those serial murderers identified as holding driving-oriented professions (*Chapter Six* to *Chapter Twelve*) will carefully chart the occupational histories of these individuals. Taking into account Holland's stance that occupational choice is an expression of personality, if there is a consistency in these individual's work environments as they move between jobs, then this would suggest that these individuals were indeed drawn to such professions outside of their desire to kill.

CHAPTER FIVE

Serial Murder, Occupational Choice and Offending Behaviour: An Overview

We serial killers are your sons, we are your husbands, we are everywhere.
And there will be more of your children dead tomorrow.

North American serial murderer Ted Bundy

Before we proceed, let's take a brief moment to reflect upon Bundy's words in the above quote. In his reference to sons and husbands there is a striking normality to his words, and this in essence is what this book is attempting to draw upon. In our consumption of serial murder through films, television shows and true crime books, we sometimes forget that such individuals lead very much normal lives outside of their crimes. When serial murderers are not out looking for victims they have hobbies, families, and jobs. In order for us to gain a deeper and more holistic understanding of serial murder, we need to keep in mind this important piece of information, and not fall into the trap of sensationalising and mystifying serial murder. More importantly, by examining the daily activities of serial murderers, in which employment, or lack thereof, heavily shapes, we can potentially uncover how and why particular serial murderers are more successful in evading capture than others.

Prior to examining the significance of driving as an occupational choice for British serial murderers, it is important to determine just how "popular" this form of employment is within the sample of known serial murderers. In doing so, it is also advantageous to determine what other forms of occupations these individuals held whilst they committed their offences. With the occupations of known British serial murderers established, attention will shift to examine if those serial murderers in the same occupational grouping shared any offending characteristics, and how occupational choice may assist in serial murder. For example, establishing patterns in offending motivation, victim selection, and length of offending prior to being arrested in relation to occupation may increase our understanding as to why particular work environments are selected by such offenders. The rationale for recording and including such factors is the belief that they could, in some shape or form, assist in building a more holistic picture and understanding into how the occupations of serial murderers may impact or influence their offending behaviour, and shed light into whether serial murderers who work within similar occupations share other traits that seep into their offending activities. It is also important to acknowledge that those serial murderers that were not recognised as holding an official occupation have been included. The basis for this is that important distinctions may be made between those serial murderers that were employed, compared to those who were not.

Identified British Serial Murderers

It is important that we establish how many cases of serial murder have taken place within Britain. The table below illustrates the history of serial murder in Britain, starting with the case of Thomas Neil Cream, to the more contemporary example of Levi Bellfield, who was found guilty of the murder of a third victim, 13-year-old Milly Dowler, on 23 June 2011 (Davies, 2011), thus confirming him as a "serial murderer" in 2011.

Known British Serial Murderers

Name	Years Active	Victims	Number
Thomas Neil Cream	1877–1892	Sex workers	3

Name	Years Active	Victims	Number
George Chapman	1897–1902	Women	3
George Smith	1912–1914	Women	3
John Haigh	1944–1949	Indiscriminate	6
Reginald Christie	1943–1953	Women	6 (possibly more)
Peter Manuel	1956–1958	Indiscriminate	8 (possibly more)
Michael Copeland	1960–1963	Gay men	3
Ian Brady and Myra Hindley	1963–1965	Children and young people	5
Patrick Mackay	1974–1975	Elderly women and priest	3
Donald Neilson	1974–1975	Young people and Men	3
Trevor Hardy	1974–1976	Young women	3
Archibald Hall and Michael Kitto	1977–1978	Acquaintances and employer	5
Peter Dinsdale	1973–1979	Indiscriminate	26
Peter Sutcliffe	1975–1980	Sex workers and women	13
Dennis Nilsen	1978–1983	Gay men	15
John Duffy and David Mulcahy	1985–1986	Young people and women	3
Kenneth Erskine	April 1986–July 1986	Elderly people	7

Name	Years Active	Victims	Number
Beverly Allitt	February 1991–April 1991	Children	4
Colin Ireland	March 1993–June 1993	Gay men	5
Steve Grieveson	1993–1994	Young people	4
Robert Black	1981–1986	Children	4
Fred West and Rosemary West	1967–1987	Family and young people	12
Peter Moore	September 1995–December 1995	Gay men and Indiscriminate	4
Harold Shipman	1975–1998	Elderly People	215
Mark Martin	2004–2005	Homeless women	3
Steve Wright	October 2006–December 2006	Sex Workers	5
Colin Norris	2001–2002	Elderly	4
Levi Bellfield	2002–2004	Young women	3
Peter Tobin	1991–2006	Young women	3 (possibly more)
Stephen Griffiths	2009–2010	Sex workers	3

Adapted from Wilson, D (2009) *A History of British Serial Killing*, London: Sphere, pp. 8–9

The number of serial murderers included in this study derives from the work of Wilson (2009), who meticulously charted each confirmed case of serial murder within Britain. The above table demonstrates that there have been 30 separate and identifiable cases of serial murder, with four of these involving two offenders, in Britain since 1877. A number of themes emerge about the nature of serial murder in Britain, most notably the type of victim a serial murderer is likely to attack. The most predominant victim type of a serial murder in Britain is the elderly. While Patrick Mackay, Kenneth Erskine and Colin Norris targeted the elderly, with a total of 13 victims between them (Mackay's third victim, a priest, is not included), it was Harold Shipman, otherwise referred to as "Dr. Death", who made the elderly the most predominant type of victim, killing 215, though found guilty in court of far fewer (Wilson, 2009). Whilst it is acknowledged that Shipman tended to target elderly women (Wilson, 2007), it is important to note that young women have also continually been the targets of serial murderers. George Chapman, George Smith, Reginald Christie, Trevor Hardy, Peter Sutcliffe (who, while murdering sex workers, killed at least two young women who were not), John Duffy and David Mulcahy, Mark Martin (his victims were homeless women), Levi Bellfield and Peter Tobin all targeted women with a combined total of 29 victims of serial murder. Gay men also appear to be targets of serial murder with Michael Copeland, Dennis Nilsen, Colin Ireland and Peter Moore each targeting gay men. In total, 25 gay men have been victims of serial murder in Britain. The final type of victim that features predominantly in the above table is sex workers, and it is important to note that this category of victim is classified not by age or gender, but by a profession. Thomas Neil Cream, Peter Sutcliffe (who murdered eleven prostitutes along with two women who were not), Steve Wright and Stephen Griffiths targeted sex workers, with a combined total of 22 victims.

The "structural tradition", as discussed in *Chapter Two*, contends that victims of serial murder are often members of society who are margin-alised and insufficiently supported by those in power (Wilson, 2009, p. 19–20), thus becoming a more viable target for serial murderers. While there are indeed other forms of victims, such as young children and arbitrary victims to serial murderers, the categories of victims previously highlighted raises an interesting question: do the types of victims often associated with serial murder indicate potential occupational choices for individual serial murderers? For example, a number of true crime authors

(Bilton, 2003; Wansell, 2011) have drawn attention to the importance of cars, lorries and more generally driving as an under-researched issue. Even so, within an analysis of serial murder, there has been no systematic attempt to look at British serial murderers through the lens of occupational choice. With this in mind, we will now begin to examine the professions of these individuals by first determining how many of these serial murderers actually held jobs whilst committing their murders.

The Occupations of British Serial Murderers

	N	%
No. Cases	34	100.0
Employed	20	58.8
Unemployed	14	40.2

No. of employed and unemployed serial murderers (%)

The above table illustrates that 20 out of the 34 known British serial murderers were employed in the time period in which they committed their murders. Now we will examine the occupational backgrounds of these known British serial murderers in more detail. Analysing the data presented in the following table, it was clear that there are four principal types of occupations that appear to be chosen. These primary occupational roles are driving and transitory dependent work/business/public and personal service/and finally healthcare. These terms were generated and selected due to their generalised meaning in which a variety of occupations could be accommodated, but were also specific enough to separate two distinctly different occupations. For a more detailed breakdown of the following table, please refer to the work of Lynes (2015; see also Lynes and Wilson, 2015).

Employment Details of 34 Known British Serial Murderers

	Driving and Transitory Dependent Work	Business	Healthcare	Public and Personal Service	Unemployed
	Peter Sutcliffe Robert Black John Duffy David Mulcahy Fred West Steve Wright Levi Bellfield Peter Tobin	John Haigh Ian Brady Myra Hindley Peter Moore	Thomas Neill Cream Beverly Allitt Harold Shipman Colin Norris	George Chapman Reginald Christie Archibald Hall Dennis Nilsen	George Smith Peter Manuel Patrick Mackay Trevor Hardy Michael Kitto Kenneth Erskine Colin Ireland Mark Martin Peter Dinsdale Steven Grieveson Rosemary West Stephen Griffiths Donald Neilson Michael Copeland
No (%)	23%	12%	12%	12%	41%
No (%) of Serial murderers employed	40%	20%	20%	20%	N/A

Adapted from Wilson, D. Yardley, L. and Lynes, A. (2015) *Serial Killers and the Phenomenon of Serial Murder*. Hook: Waterside Press, p. 116

From this attempt at categorising the means and methods of 34 convicted UK serial murderers, it is evident that a substantial number lacked any form of recognisable employment. While it is apparent that the "driving and transitory dependent" category is the principal occupational choice for British serial murderers, these statistics presented also consider those who were not in legitimate employment. By removing the "unemployed" category, the results offered an even more dramatic representation of occupational choice. In disregarding this category, of the remaining 20 convicted serial murderers, 40 per cent were classified as having a driving element to their work. With the occupations of known British serial murderers established, attention will now shift to examine if those serial murderers in the same occupational grouping shared any offending characteristics.

Offending Period

Offending Period	Healthcare	Business	Driving and Transitory Dependent Work	Public and Personal service	Unemployed
Min	0.16	0.33	0.25	1	0.33
Max	24	5	20	10	6
Average	10.4	2.4	6.9	5.3	2.1

Offending Period (Years) of Known British Serial Murderers in Relation to Occupation

From examining the above table, it is evident that discernible differences can be found between the various occupational groups of known British serial murderers. Out of the four categories that contain employed serial murderers, those who worked within a business-oriented profession and/or environment appeared to have the shortest average offending period at 2.4 years. John Haigh had the longest known offending period out of those serial murderers that belong to the "business" grouping, committing his known murders over a five-year period. With regards to "public and personal service", Archibald Hall, the butler who targeted his employers, had the shortest offending period at one year. Reginald Christie, who provided a much more public service as a wartime special constable, murdered his victims over a ten-year period. With the inclusion of those other serial murderers that held occupations of a similar nature, the average offending period was 5.3 years—a significant increase from the "business" grouping.

Whilst the case of Harold Shipman may be considered an extreme example of serial murder and thus an "outlier" (David and Nagaraja, 2003) when compared to other cases, the significance of his occupation in relation to both his number of victims and offending period cannot be ignored and, as a result, has been included. Shipman, a GP who would frequently make home visits to his patients, was active for approximately 24 years before being apprehended. Conversely, Beverly Allitt, another serial murderer who worked within a "Healthcare" capacity, was active for significantly less time at only 59 days. The average offending period, when analysing all known British serial murderers that worked within a "Healthcare" environment, is 10.4 years—the highest average of any occupational grouping.

With regards to the final occupational grouping, "Driving and Transitory Dependent Work", the average offending period, 6.9 years, is greater than that of both "Business" and "Public and Personal Service" with only "Healthcare" yielding a longer average offending period, although the latter is heavily skewed by Shipman. The serial murderer with the shortest period of offending is Steve Wright, who murdered five women over 40 days. Odd-job labourer Fred West, along with his unemployed wife Rosemary, murdered his known victims over a 20-year period, becoming Britain's second longest offending serial murder behind Harold Shipman. Interestingly, this particular occupational grouping also contains the third longest offending serial murderer—Peter Tobin, who is known to have murdered three women over the course of 15 years.

The "Unemployed" category, when compared to those serial murderers that were employed, presents some interesting findings. In particular, the average offending period for this group is lower than each of the four employed groups at 2.1 years. It is important to note that both Rosemary West and Michael Kitto were not included in this analysis due to them engaging in criminal behaviour with the aid of another employed serial murderer. With regards to the shortest offending period, two serial murderers, Kenneth Erskine and Colin Ireland, both committed their offences over the relatively short period of approximately four months.

Peter Dinsdale had the longest known offending period of six years before being apprehended. Patrick Mackay, Donald Neilson, Steven Grieveson, Mark Martin and Stephen Griffiths were all active for approximately one year prior to being arrested, suggesting that those serial murderers with a lack of official employment appear to be caught, on average, much sooner than those with steady employment in a variety of professions.

With regards to offering possible explanations for these findings, it would appear that those serial murderers who held some form of legitimate employment were able to engage in their criminal behaviour longer than their unemployed contemporaries. Apart from the "Business" grouping, in which the average offending period was only slightly higher than the "Unemployed" category, those serial murderers belonging to "Healthcare", "Public and Personal Service", and "Driving and Transitory Dependent Work" were, on average, active far longer — at 10.4, 5.3, and 6.9 years respectively. It would appear that legitimate employment provides some form of protection, or "shielding", with regards to being identified as an offender. If we were to apply theories related to environmental criminology, namely routine activity theory, which argues that you need a motivated offender, a suitable victim, and a lack of capable guardians in order for a crime to occur, the three necessary factors for a crime to occur appear to coincide in time and space at a higher frequency than for those serial murderers who were employed. Not only do these three components appear to occur more often, the fact that they are generated more naturally, or fluidly, within the contexts of these offenders' day-to day lifestyles, which are influenced by their occupations, appears to also provide them with a legitimate and valid reason for being in close proximity to their victims. For example, with regards to those serial murderers who held an occupation within the "Healthcare" environment, their position afforded them access to their victims, whilst also ensuring that there was a lack of capable guardians to prevent them from being murdered. Whilst Beverly Allitt was apprehended relatively quickly, it is important to take into account that she suffered from a personality disorder (Ramsland, 2007) and that, in comparison to both Shipman and Norris, targeted children. These two factors arguably resulted in her identification and eventual apprehension. For Shipman, despite also working within the same field as Allitt, his status as a GP, the fact that he was the only doctor to make house visits in the area (Bunyan, 2001), and that he targeted elderly people resulted in him only coming to police attention after 24 years of murdering his patients.

"Public and Personal Service" also share similarities with "Healthcare" in that, in the cases of Reginald Christie and Dennis Nilsen, their positions would have given them authority and respectability. In the case of Christie, for example, he attained authority through volunteering to keep the peace during a time of war and had been, at one time, a soldier. Nilsen, despite leaving the army, still held somewhat authoritative or respectable positions in both the police and as a civil servant. Whilst George Chapman and Archibald Hall also fall under this occupational grouping, their more personal oriented service of pub landlord and butler, respectively, would see a reduction of perceived authority and both men targeted individuals known to them. Taking this into consideration, it could assist in offering an explanation as to why Hall was apprehended within a year. On the other hand, with regards to Chapman, his method of killing his victims, which will be discussed later, may assist in explaining why he was active for five years prior to apprehension.

As discussed, those serial murderers that fall under the "Business" grouping were apprehended, on average, much sooner than their other employed equivalents. One explanation for this can be found in the context of their offending in relation to their employment. For example, other than John Haigh, who was active for five years, dissolved his victims' bodies in acid baths (Wilson, 2007), and often targeted those who were, in some way, connected to his entrepreneurial business (Ramsland, 2006), those serial murderers who held a business-oriented occupation often targeted victims that were not congruent with their employment. This could be due in part to the fact that, unlike the other occupational groupings listed, the "Business" category entails occupations that do not place those serial murderers within close proximity to their victims. Instead, these particular serial murderers, with the exception of Haigh who was motivated by money and whose victims were, as a result, accessed through his occupational status, had to search elsewhere for suitable victims. This can be witnessed with Brady, Hindley, and Welsh serial murderer Moore. All three were, in some way, sexually motivated and, as a result, searched for victims outside of their everyday employment environments. As a result of having to artificially create the circumstances needed for a crime to occur, the validity of proximity to victims afforded to serial murderers who held different occupations is lost. By adopting this environmental criminological perspective, the reasons as to why these particular serial murderers were more quickly apprehended may have been uncovered. Of course, such a rationale cannot be taken as fact, but this opens up the possibility for more research in this area.

For those serial murderers who drove or who relied on transport as part of their employment, their occupation afforded validity to be in close proximity to their victims. For example, Peter Sutcliffe would often drive through Bradford's red light district and select potential victims during the course of driving his lorry (Bilton, 2003). Similarly, Robert Black, who worked as a delivery van driver, was often in the general area where his victims were abducted as a result of making his deliveries. This "shielding" that his occupation awarded him during the course of his offending can be best demonstrated in the murder of Jennifer Cardy. Cardy, who was abducted in 1981, has only recently been linked to Black, who was found guilty of her murder in 2011 (McDonald, 2011). Such validity or justification for being in close proximity to their victims can also be witnessed in the case of Duffy and Mulcahy, who would often use Mulcahy's taxi, which he drove as a means to supplement his income as a plumber, to hunt for suitable victims (Clough et al, 2001). Similarly, van driver Steve Wright, wheel clamper Levi Bellfield, and odd-job labourers Peter Tobin and Fred West each targeted their victims whilst employed in occupations that required them to drive between various locations. Such occupational "cover" may further provide reasons as to why Moore and Brady and Hindley, who committed their offences with the aid of a vehicle but whose occupations lacked such necessities, were apprehended sooner than their driving oriented counterparts.

Also of note for these particular serial murderers, is that their occupation provides them legitimate means to cross police jurisdictions. For example, Black committed his offences in England, Scotland, and

Northern Ireland ("Robert Black Guilty of Fourth Child Murder", *The Telegraph*, 2011)—locations that he legitimately needed to visit due to his work commitments. Tobin, whose labourer-related skills would send him across the UK, committed his murders near Falkirk and Glasgow, and buried his victims' bodies at his home in Kent (Edwards, 2009). Such freedom to travel across a large geographical area without raising suspicion further demonstrates how these occupations can create some form of protection for these offenders, whilst also generating "linkage blindness" (Newton, 2006) between their offences.

With the exception of Dinsdale, whose method of setting fire to peoples' homes made the task of identifying the individual responsible more difficult for the police (Sagar, 1999), the majority of unemployed British serial murderers were on average apprehended sooner than their employed equivalents. All other cases, with the exception of Michael Copeland, who was active for three years prior to arrest, and Smith, Manuel and Hardy, who each committed other offences within a two-year period, were apprehended within a year of committing their first known murder. In comparison to the majority of employed serial murderers, in which their occupations appeared to generate the necessary components of routine activity theory for a successful crime to occur, these serial murderers would have needed to artificially create such circumstances, without the protection that particular occupations appear to provide. For example, MacKay and Erskine both targeted elderly people—often breaking into their homes and stealing valuable possessions that belonged to their victims. However, unlike Shipman, who had legitimate reasons to have been in the homes of his victims, both MacKay and Erskine had to violently enter their victims' homes in order to gain proximity and access (Wilson, 2007). Such inability to provide a legitimate reason for being in close proximity to their victims may have impacted these serial murderers' ability to avoid detection by the authorities.

Victim Selection

With the offending period of known British serial murderers in relation to their occupation established, attention will now shift to whether certain victim types are repeatedly targeted by those serial murderers that share similar working backgrounds. The table below demonstrates how the various reported victim types are generally associated with serial murderers belonging to particular occupational groupings.

Victim Type in Relation to Occupation	Healthcare	Business	Driving and Transitory Dependent Work	Public and Personal Service	Unemployed
Elderly people	219	0	0	0	10
Children/Young people	4	5	4	0	4
Sex workers	3	0	16	0	3
Women	0	0	21	6	5
Homeless women	0	0	0	0	3
Gay men	0	3	0	15	5
Men	0	1	0	0	5
Acquaintances/ employer	0	6	0	5	0
Partner	0	0	0	3	3
Random	0	0	0	0	34

Victim Selection in Relation to Serial Murderers' Occupational Grouping

It is evident that particular victim types are predominantly targeted by those serial murderers holding specific occupations. For example, out of the 229 victims who were described as being "elderly", 96 per cent were associated to a serial murderer that worked within the "Healthcare" profession. It is important to note that Shipman was responsible for the majority of these victims. Colin Norris was the only other "Healthcare" serial murderer that targeted the elderly, administrating fatal overdoses to four of his patients during his time working as a nurse. Interestingly, the remaining ten victims who were considered as being "elderly" were murdered by unemployed serial murderers — Erskine and Mackay.

With regard to victims who were described as being "children/young people", discernible differences between the various occupational groups proved to be difficult to establish. Serial murderers in "Healthcare", "Business", "Driving and Transitory Dependent Work" and "Unemployed" have been found guilty of murdering this victim type. Approximately 24 per cent of these victims can be associated to "Healthcare", due to nurse Beverly Allitt who administered fatal overdoses to her young patients. Twenty-eight per cent of this victim group were murdered by serial murderers who worked within a "Business" environment. The serial murder "team" of Brady and Hindley differ from Allitt in that they carried out their crimes outside the context of their occupations. Twenty-four per cent can be attributed to the Parcel Delivery Services (PDS) delivery driver Robert Black, who is known to have murdered four young girls whilst he was making deliveries across the UK. Similar to Allitt, Black undertook his offending behaviour whilst under the pretence of engaging in legitimate employment duties. Unemployed Steve Grieveson was found guilty of a fourth murder in 2013, with all of his victims being teenage boys whom he murdered due to a fear that his sexuality may become public knowledge (Armstrong, 2013).

Sex workers can be linked predominantly to one occupational grouping — "Driving and Transitory Dependent Work". Out of the recorded 22 victims of serial murder who were reported as sex workers, 72 per cent were targeted by those who held a profession that relied extensively on transport. For example, 11 out of Sutcliffe's known 13 murder victims worked as sex workers in Leeds, Bradford and Manchester. Interestingly, Sutcliffe would often travel through the red light districts of these locations whilst carrying out duties related to his occupation, then later return in his own vehicle, pick up, and eventually murder a sex worker he selected earlier (Bilton, 2003). Steve Wright, a van and fork-lift driver, murdered five sex workers in 2008 and, similar to Sutcliffe, used his own vehicle when engaged in criminal activities. Fourteen per cent of murdered sex workers can be attributed to a serial murderer that worked as a healthcare professional. Thomas Neil Cream, whilst targeting a starkly different demographic than other healthcare oriented serial murderers, still administered lethal overdoses to his victims under the guise of a medical practitioner. The remaining 14 per cent of sex workers who were victims of serial murder can be linked to Stephen Griffiths, who was officially unemployed at the time of his murders.

The next reported victim type, "women", includes those victims who were female but had no other discernible traits such as occupation, social status, or age. Similar to the "sex worker" victim type, this particular group appear to be predominantly targeted by those serial murderers that reside within the "Driving and Transitory Dependent Work" grouping. Out of the 32 confirmed victims that fall under this category, 66 per cent were victims of a serial murderer whose occupation was transient in nature. Fred West, an odd-job labourer who, at one time also owned an ice cream van, murdered ten women over a 20-year period. He would often pick up women who would be walking along roads that he and his wife Rosemary would be driving along. Similarly, odd-job labourer Peter Tobin murdered three women over a 15-year period, burying his victims in his back yard prior to moving under the pretence of new work opportunities. With regards to those women who were murdered by serial murderers who were not employed in a transitory oriented occupation, 19 per cent were attributed to Reginald Christie. Christie's occupation as a war-time constable provided him with a level of authority that may have been vital in gaining trust from his victims, who willingly entered Christie's home prior to being murdered (Oates, 2012). The remaining 15 per cent of women were murdered by serial murderers that did not hold any recognisable form of employment. For example, Trevor Hardy, who had an extensive criminal career prior to committing his known murders, murdered three women and Donald Neilson murdered two women in pursuit of monetary gains. Three women who were targeted by a serial murderer were described as being "homeless" at the time of their murder and, as a result, were categorised independently from those victims described above. All three were murdered by Mark Martin, who was unemployed at the time of committing his known offences and was also described as having "no fixed address" (Post, 2013).

Gay men have been repeatedly targeted by serial murderers from a variety of employment backgrounds. In particular, 65 per cent of the victims of Dennis Nilsen were gay. As discussed, Nilsen had a tendency to be drawn to occupations that held a level of authority, such as the army and police service, which also offered a form of service to others. So too, Moore, who would drive along country lanes in pursuit of victims, murdered three gay men (13 per cent) (Wilson, 2007). What is of note is that both of these offenders appeared to have engaged in their offending independently of their occupation—instead targeting and ultimately murdering their victims outside of their working hours. The remaining 22 per cent of gay men were targeted by unemployed serial murderer Colin Ireland. Ireland, when compared to Nilsen and Moore, was not gay himself and was instead driven by a desire to become famous (Wier, 2011).

The victim group "men", similar to "women", are those victims who were male and lacked any other discernible characteristics. This particular victim group can be attributed almost exclusively to those serial murderers who were unemployed. Michael Copeland, and Donald Nielsen, each targeted men for variety of different reasons, which will be discussed later in this chapter. The only other victim to fall under this category was murdered by cinema owner Peter Moore.

Moving on to those groups that were targeted on rare occasions, the victim category classified as "acquaintances/employers" can be attributed to only two particular cases of serial murder. Haigh, driven by the desire for money, murdered, as Wilson (2007) notes, indiscriminately and often had prior relationships with his victims. For example, Haigh murdered his former employer before targeting acquaintances he met during his time at the Onslow Court Hotel in Kensington—all the while using his business persona as a means to manipulate his victims and gain their trust (Ramsland, 2006). Hall, and by association Kitto, also sought targets that were perceived as being high value with regards to potential monetary rewards. Specifically, Hall used his position as a personal butler to members of the British aristocracy (Nicol, 2011) to gain access to such targets prior to (with the aid of Kitto) murdering them. Similar to war-time constable Christie, Hall offered a service to others that was vital in gaining access to victims without raising suspicions.

The victim group "partners" were those victims that were reported as being in a relationship with their murderer prior to their death. George Chapman, who worked as a publican during the period in which he committed his murders, killed his partners by poisoning them (Wier, 2011). The remaining three victims to fall under this category can be attributed to George Smith who was unemployed at the time of committing his known offences and already a career criminal (Wilson, 2007).

The final victim group, "random", contains those victims who were killed by a serial murderer who appeared to lack any consistency in the targeting and selection of victims. Of note, the entirety of those victims who fall within this category were murdered by a serial murderer that did not hold any form of official employment. Dinsdale and Manuel both appeared to target victims with a lack of consistency, although with regard to Dinsdale this may be attributed to setting fire to residences, which would contain a variety of victim types (Wilson, 2007). Interestingly, this particular victim group is similar to the elderly for "Healthcare" and sex workers and women for "Driving and Transitory Dependent Work", in that it is closely allied to those serial murderers that were unemployed.

Shipman's occupation as a doctor may assist in explaining why he was able to murder so many elderly people. Amplifying the concept of occupational "shielding" introduced previously, Shipman's ability to target and murder at least 219 patients further demonstrates how his work afforded him both access to his victims and the necessary protection from being perceived as a threat. Environmental criminology helps to explain why particular victim groups are repeatedly targeted. For example, with the exception of Cream, all "Healthcare" related serial murderers targeted either elderly patients or, in the case of Allitt, children that have been admitted under their care. For these serial murderers, they have been granted access but are also seen as being a carer or, in the words of routine activity theory, a supposedly capable guardian to these individuals. Proximity has also been created between those serial murderers who relied on transport as part of their occupation, and the victim groups that they predominantly targeted. For example, those women who worked as sex workers would have been situated near roads, in order to demonstrate their "availability" to potential customers (Ditmore, 2006, p. 432). With regards to those women who did not engage in such activity, the extensive hours that these serial murderers would have covered whilst travelling on the road would have increased the likelihood of these women being perceived as suitable victims, due to an increased probability of there being a lack of capable guardians. So, whilst the general victim types repeatedly targeted by these two occupational groupings differ, the particular environments these offenders inhabit as a result of their employment is also often shared by their victims. This again demonstrates how, by applying routine activity theory, particular occupations appear to facilitate the necessary components for a crime to be committed.

The "Unemployed" grouping presents the most discrepancies between victim types, with victims ranging from elderly people to gay men. In comparison to "Healthcare" and "Driving and Transitory Dependent Work", in which proximity is naturally created between offender and victim, those serial murderers who were unemployed lacked such advantages. With a lack of consistent work environments or lifestyle generated by employment, a particular victim group could not be repeatedly targeted by unemployed serial murderers. This is perhaps best illustrated with the "random" victim group, which only unemployed serial murderers appeared to target. For example, both Manuel and Dinsdale were reported as having no particular victim type, with Dinsdale indiscriminately setting fire to peoples' homes and Manuel targeting both men and women. Again, through an environmental criminological perspective, it could be argued that these serial murderers lacked any consistency with regards to victim type due to a lack of stable work environments, which may have afforded them proximity and access to a particular demographic.

Reported Motivations

During the course of analysing the victim types that serial murderers belonging to particular occupational groupings tended to target, the reported motivations of these offenders were considered. For example, whilst both Peter Sutcliffe and Steve Wright targeted sex workers, did they do so under similar motivations? The table below examines the reported motivations of known British serial murderers by way of their occupational grouping:

Reported Motives	Healthcare	Business	Public and Personal Service	Driving and Transitory Dependent Work	Unemployed
Sexual gratification		17	11	44	28
Money		17	17		66
Wanted to be famous					100
Unclear	50		50		
Power and control over life	100				
Arsonist					100
Munchausen's Syndrome by Proxy	100				
Fear of sexuality becoming public					100

Reported Motivations in Relation to Occupational Groupings (%)

The motive "sexual gratification" consists of all cases in which some form of sexual motivation or reasoning was reported when attempting to explain the offender's behaviour and actions. This particular motivation was, by far, the most frequently reported one, with a total of 18 cases. Of note is that, despite being the most common motivation behind serial murder in Britain, there are no subjects within the "Healthcare" grouping to have been motivated in such a way. From the 18 cases identified to have been sexually motivated, nearly half shared a similar work environment in the form of being transport dependent. Similar to how all serial murderers belonging to "Healthcare" shared similar methods of killing their victims, "Driving and Transitory Dependent Work" contains serial murders that all appear to share similar motivations with regards to their known offences. Whilst such inferences were initially made upon analysing the victim types often targeted by those serial murderers who fall under those occupational groupings all cases, including Black, who was the only serial murder in this group to not target women or sex workers, appeared to be sexually motivated in some way. It is important to stress that this form of motivation manifested in different ways across these offenders. For example, Sutcliffe did not have sexual intercourse with his victims but it is accepted that his crimes fit Brooks et al's (1988) description of serial murder in that they "reflect[ed] sadistic sexual undertones" (cited in Castle and Hensley, 2002, p. 455). In comparison, the sexual nature of Black's offences was more overt, with news articles noting that there were signs that his victims had been "sexually assaulted" ("Child killer Robert Black's past revealed to Northern Ireland jury", *The Guardian*, 2011). With regards to motivation, "Driving and Transitory Dependent Work" presents the only occupational grouping in which all offenders appeared to act upon similar motivational driving forces.

With regards to providing a rationale for these findings, the fact that all those serial murderers who fall under the "Driving and Transitory Dependent Work" were in some way sexually motivated could further explain why these serial murderers overwhelmingly targeted women. The concept of proximity has been employed. However, this proximity also brings with it occupational "exposure" to particular individuals or groups. Here another environmental criminological approach, Crime

Pattern Theory, will be applied. Crime Pattern Theory operates on the assumption that crime is structured, and that criminal opportunity is tied to the everyday movements, or routine activities, of both offenders and victims — including occupational influences (Brantingham and Brantingham, 2008). With those serial murderers that relied on transport as part of their employment, their awareness and activity space would have arguably increased to cover a larger geographical space, as opposed to those serial murderers that had fixed work locations or lacked employment. Taking this into consideration, the probability that the awareness and activity spaces of their victims, who predominantly included sex workers and isolated women, would intersect with that of these offenders would have greatly increased. For example, a motivated offender such as Levi Bellfield had the occupational freedom to travel across a large geographical space due to working as a wheel-clamper. This would have increased his opportunities in overlapping his own activity space with that of isolated and vulnerable young women — such as Marsha McDonnell ("Levi Bellfield defence was a charade driven by hatred, victim's family claims", *The Guardian*, 2011). Similarly, Black, whose activity space would be greatly influenced by his occupation as a van driver, would have had more opportunities to overlap with the activity space of young girls, who were often abducted in the course of moving from one location to another in their respective towns. Such an example can be found in the murder of Jennifer Cardy, who was abducted by Black as she made her way to visit a friend in the Lisburn area — a location that Black's occupation sent him to at the time of her disappearance ("Cardy family 'do not hate' child killer Robert Black", *BBC News*, 2011). In comparison to those serial murderers who worked within healthcare, where victims were initially brought to them as patients, those who worked within a transient oriented profession instead gained more opportunities to offend due to an increased "exposure" to certain victim groups — in this case vulnerable women and young girls.

"Driving and Transitory Dependent Work" serial murderers all engaged in their offending as a result of being, in some form, sexually motivated. However, there were other serial murderers belonging to different occupational groupings who also appeared to be similarly motivated. Within

"Business", Brady and Hindley were reported to have acted upon sexual motivations, with Brady introducing sadomasochistic sex to Hindley prior to committing their offences (Murray, 2009). Peter Moore offers another example of a sexually motivated serial murder to have also worked within a business capacity. For example, Wilson (2007) notes that there were signs of sexual activity on Moore's first victim's body which likely occurred prior to death, and that his trousers were pulled down with visible stab wounds on his buttocks. With regards to "Public and Personal Service", Christie and Nilsen, who both worked with members of the public, appeared to be sexually motivated. Christie, who used his position as a war-time constable as a means to lure women to his home, would engage in sexual acts with his victims—including necrophilia (Oates, 2012). Nilsen, who targeted other gay men, would also often engage in sexual acts with his victim both prior to, and after, their death (Masters, 1995). The "Unemployed" grouping contains the second highest amount of serial murderers who were sexually motivated after "Driving and Transitory Dependent Work". Cases such as those of Manuel, Copeland, Hardy, and Erskine were all reported to have either sexually assaulted their victims or, similar to Sutcliffe, their crimes contained sexual overtones.

British serial murderers that were reported as being financially motivated can be predominantly attributed to the "Unemployed" grouping. Chapman, Smith, Mackay and Neilson all lacked legitimate employment and, it would appear, turned to crime as a means of achieving financial reward. Each of these offenders had a criminal history prior to committing their known murders. Similar to the motive of sexual gratification, this financial motivation manifested in different ways. For example, Chapman drowned his partners in order to receive money from their will, and Neilson murdered his victims in the process of committing armed robbery (Wilson, 2007). Only two employed serial murderers that were also financially motivated could be identified. Businessman and entrepreneur Haigh is known to have forged documents in order to gain approximately £4,000 belonging to Donald and Amy McSwan, whom he murdered shortly after murdering their son, William (Wier, 2011). Lastly, personal butler Hall and, through association, the unemployed Kitto, murdered their employers prior to stealing their high value possessions and money (Nicol, 2011). Of note is that both of these employed serial murderers also had histories of petty crime, with Haigh and Hall both serving prison sentences for financially motivated offences (Wier, 2011; Nicol, 2011).

The remaining reported motives can each be exclusively attributed to one occupational grouping. For example, each serial murderer who was recognised as committing their offences in an effort to gain some form of "power and control" over their victims held an occupation within a healthcare environment. Shipman and Norris were both reported to have used their position within the healthcare profession as a means to exercise power and control over their vulnerable patients. For example, during Shipman's trial, the Crown stated that "he clearly enjoyed exercising power over life and death … and that it was important to him to be in control of the process" ("The Secret world of Harold Shipman", *BBC News*, 2001). For Norris, who also targeted elderly patients, a similar motive was reported, with news articles stating that he seemed to relish the powers his position awarded him and that, in the words of one of his victim's relatives, "it gave him the power to give life and take life" (Stokes and Britten, 2008). With regards to the remaining healthcare serial murderers, Cream and Allitt, the former's motivation proved to be difficult to determine due to having committed his offences in the late 19th century (Wilson, 2007). No specific motive has been settled and speculations range from financial gain, power over life, and a deep rooted hatred of women (Mellor, 2012; McLaren, 1995). This issue of ascertaining a clear motive proved to also be difficult with another Victorian serial murderer — publican George Chapman, in which a myriad of potential motives have been put forth but no definitive conclusion reached (Wier, 2011). For both Chapman and Cream, the fact that they committed their murders over a century ago suggests that definitive answers to why they carried out their crimes will not be found. For Allitt, while there is still a level of uncertainty as to why she carried out her offences, one prevailing theory is that she suffered from Munchausen Syndrome by Proxy (Clothier, 1994 cited in Wilson, 2007). This personality disorder supposedly causes the individual to fake illness, or cause illness in others, in order to receive attention (Ramsland, 2007). Allitt is the only British serial murderer to have been reported as suffering from such a disorder, and it is the most prevalent explanation for her offences.

Ireland, Martin, and Griffiths were all reported to have committed their offences with a desire to gain notoriety and fame. Ireland targeted gay men and became increasingly frustrated with how the police were handling the investigation. For, as Wier (2011) highlights, "he wanted to be famous, he wanted to be remembered for ever as a serial killer" (p. 402). So too Martin, who targeted homeless women in Nottingham, was quoted as saying that he "wanted to become the city's first serial killer" ("Murderer made serial killer boast", *BBC News*, 2006). Griffiths, who was in fact a PhD student at Bradford University researching serial murder, appeared to treat the status of "serial murderer" as aspirational, with Griffiths informing a psychiatrist that he "would be infamous — not famous" prior to committing his offences (Dixon, 2011, p. 50). Interestingly, each of these serial murderers were unemployed during the course of their offending, with only Ireland holding some form of past employment, as a manager at a homeless shelter.

The remaining two reported motives exclusive to the "Unemployed" grouping demonstrates how this particular occupational category contains the most discrepancies between serial murderers in relation to their respective motivations to offend. Dinsdale, for example, was an arsonist whose murders were a result of setting fire to various buildings (Wilson, 2009). On the other hand, Grieveson was reported to have been concerned about his sexuality becoming public. Having engaged in sexual activities with one of his victims, Grieveson is reported to have stated that he panicked about anyone finding out and that he "got scared, I started shouting at him not to tell anyone … I flipped out and started strangling him" (Armstrong, 2013).

Closing Comments

Lynes (2015) established the occupational backgrounds of British serial murderers, which revealed that there were indeed particular forms of employment that were repeatedly selected by British serial murderers. Out of these frequently selected occupations, those that involved periods of driving and transience were determined to be the most "popular".

So too were there commonalties between these individuals' offending behaviour–namely that they were all sexually motivated and targeted predominately similar victim types. Whilst this particular occupational group is the central focus of this book, it is important to also acknowledge that similar relationships between offending behaviour and occupational choice can be traced to the group "Healthcare". It was also established that, in comparison to the other occupational groups, these individuals were capable of engaging in their offending whilst also supposedly carrying out work-related duties. This demonstrated that particular occupations and work environments do in fact provide the necessary status and/or access to suitable victims without the need to physically "disengage" from their everyday activities. This ability not to physically remove themselves from their work-related awareness and activity space has afforded these serial murderers a number of key advantages that are not available to those individuals who work in professions that do not create the necessary access and opportunity to their victims, along with those that lack employment entirely. This has been illustrated by the fact that those serial murderers belonging to either "Healthcare" and, more importantly, "Driving and Transitory Dependent Work" were, on average, identified and apprehended after longer periods of offending. So whilst these offenders do, in the manner of the "medical-psychological tradition", psychologically "disengage" from their everyday activities, their employment provides a means to not physically "disengage" and consequently make them more susceptible to being identified and apprehended quicker. This was most obviously demonstrated by the cinema owner Moore and those serial murderers who were unemployed. On the other hand, Black, for example, was making, and continued to make, deliveries pre- and post-abducting his victims, and Sutcliffe continued to engage in his work-related activities whilst searching for suitable victims. These cases illustrate just how significant an offender's occupation may be in the aid of their offending.

Whilst this chapter sought to explain these findings in relation to the each of the identified occupational groupings, attention will now be given exclusively to the central focus of this book—those offenders who drove, or relied on driving, as part of their occupation. This will be achieved by presenting a series of case studies of those eight serial murderers that were identified as holding transient oriented occupations. We will begin with Peter Sutcliffe: the lorry driver.

CHAPTER SIX

The Lorry Driver

The women I killed were filth–bastard prostitutes who were
littering the streets. I was just cleaning up the place a bit.

Peter Sutcliffe in Jane Caputi, *The Age of Sex Crime*
(1987; Bowling Green state University Popular Press)

Name: Peter William Sutcliffe (aka the "Yorkshire Ripper")
Born: 2 June 1946
Location: Yorkshire
No. of victims: 13
Victims: Sex workers; women
Motive: Sexually motivated
Offending period prior to arrest: 5 years

Occupational Background

Sutcliffe had an extensive history of working in either labour intensive or transient-orientated occupations that tended to more solitary and technical in nature. He was described as being shy as a child who was "withdrawn and passive" (Wilson, 2005), and he appeared to carry on this trend of being isolated and removed from others into adulthood. After leaving school, Sutcliffe's first known employment involved a short period working as a grave-digger, which consisted of mainly menial labour-oriented tasks and duties (Bilton, 2003). It was during this time Sutcliffe appeared to demonstrate a rather dark and macabre sense of humour (Keppel and Birnes, 2003). He also appeared to enjoy the solitary nature of the job. Interestingly, it was during Sutcliffe's time working as a gravedigger that he said God first spoke to him and subsequently ordered him to murder sex workers (Bilton, 2003, p. 621). Sutcliffe subsequently moved from his grave-digging profession towards more factory-oriented work at Baird Television Ltd, in which he worked on a packaging line (Burn, 1984). Again, Sutcliffe appeared to be drawn to work environments that oriented around physical and labour intensive activities. This trend towards working in such occupations continued, with Sutcliffe leaving Baird when asked to become a travelling salesman and subsequently began to work nightshifts as a factory worker for Anderton International (Cross, 1981). In 1975 Sutcliffe was made redundant, and he used the redundancy money to acquire a heavy goods vehicle licence. As noted by Cross (1981), Sutcliffe in fact passed the HGV test Class 1 at Steeton Driving School on June 4 — two days after his 29th birthday. After obtaining his HGV licence, he became employed as a lorry driver. This vocation, which consisted of "short and medium-distance hauls all over the North and the Midlands of the UK" (Burn, 1984, p. 134), would play an instrumental part in Sutcliffe's increasing awareness of Britain's road networks:

> "…He used the experience to familiarise himself with the network of motorways and trunk-roads linking his destinations to each other and to West Yorkshire. He also became an authority on the best access routes to many town and city centres, to some of which he was already less than a stranger" (Burn, 1984, p. 135).

After leaving this particular job, Sutcliffe continued to make use of his HGV licence and took up employment as a lorry driver for T and W H Clark (Holdings Ltd). This was situated on the Canal Road Industrial Estate in Bradford ("Did the Yorkshire Ripper murder five women in the Midlands?", *Birmingham Mail*, 2014). It would be whilst employed here that Sutcliffe committed the majority of his known offences. All of his occupations: grave-digger; factory worker; heavy-goods driver; and finally lorry driver all fall within those professions aligned with the Realistic personality type (List of Occupations by RIASEC Interest Area, n.d.). With reference to Holland's notion that occupational choice is an "expression" of an individual's personality, it is evident that Sutcliffe was continually drawn to professions that demanded the same or similar skill sets. In examining Sutcliffe's employment history, it is apparent that he appeared to be drawn to occupations that consisted of either labour or transient-oriented occupations. So too his movement between occupations appeared to have a consistency, despite changing between a variety of fields and environments.

Offending Background

Whilst the motivation behind Sutcliffe's murders are widely acknowledged as being sexual in nature, little is known about his offences prior to holding his position as a lorry driver. By analysing both his crimes and behaviour prior to committing his known murders, it is evident that he was, in some shape or form, setting the template for his future murders. Sutcliffe's first recorded offence involving a sex worker would do this. For Sutcliffe, who was known as a regularly visitor to the red light district of Bradford along with his friend Trevor Birdsall, appeared to commit his first known offence after an altercation with a sex worker in 1969—six years prior to committing his first murder (Keppel and Birnes, 2003). Sutcliffe, whilst in the company of his friend Birdsall, assaulted and attacked a sex worker with a rock that was placed within a sock (Keppel and Birnes, 2003). In this particular instance, Sutcliffe, supposedly angered by the sex worker, left Birdsall alone in his car and, on his return, informed Birdsall that he had tried to attack the sex worker (Wilson, 2007, p. 80). He also displayed signs of sexual deviancy whilst employed as a grave-digger. Many of his co-workers were concerned about Sutcliffe's constant comments about necrophilia when around dead bodies (Greig, 2012). Sutcliffe's history of violence towards women clearly set a template for his future offences, which were in turn heavily influenced by the environmental conditions, or cues, that his occupation positioned him within close proximity of (Brantingham and Brantingham, 1978).

The Ripper's Hunting Grounds

Sutcliffe did not commit any of his murders until gaining his position as a lorry driver — a position that greatly increased his geographical flexibility. This, it would appear, was an important factor in his ability to access a much larger geographical canvas in which to hunt for potential victims. In his formal statements to the police, Sutcliffe acknowledged that he would travel to a number of different locations in search of potential victims, thus enabling him to access areas that would otherwise be inaccessible without the use of a vehicle. This ability to see the "bigger picture" has its advantages, and Sutcliffe touched upon the primary benefit of being able to travel across a wide geographical area. For example, he stated that "I realised things were hotting up a bit in Leeds and Bradford. I decided to go to Manchester to kill a prostitute" (Bilton, 2003, p. 703). With access to a vehicle, Sutcliffe was consequently able to continue feeding his desires to kill women without the fear of raising any suspicion in one particular area. Sutcliffe not only visited Manchester, but also "the red light districts in Leeds, Bradford, Halifax, and York" (p. 742). This seemingly sporadic selection of locations not only kept the police a step behind the offender in terms of when and where the next attack would be, but this range of locations also crossed a number of police boundaries. This ability to gain access to different areas and committing murder makes the task of connecting these offences to the same offender difficult, creating "linkage blindness" (Keppel and Birnes, 2003, p. 3) between the various police services involved. It is arguable that this advantage of being able to access a wider geographical area was one of the many established reasons why it took so long for the police to finally apprehend Sutcliffe.

Time to Hunt

Sutcliffe's use of a vehicle whilst engaged in offending also provided him with the ability to spend more time with his victims, and also gave him the capacity to remove himself as a suspect. Particular attention will be given here to how Sutcliffe's occupation lacked much in the way of managerial oversight and control. This is important to consider as it influenced this serial murderer's offending behaviour in some rather interesting ways. For instance, Sutcliffe had periods in his employment where he had managerial control of others, which he ultimately resented and strived to be free from. Whilst the level of managerial control would differ between occupations for Sutcliffe, the use of vehicles in his offences clearly provided some form of instrumental advantage—namely that it afforded him the time to physically remove himself from abduction, kill, and disposal sites.

Here we will be applying Eck's (1994) "problem analysis triangle". This examines how the presence, or absence, of particular factors makes a crime either difficult or "feasible" (Felson, 2008, p. 74). With regards to the offender, the lack of a "handler", who is an individual who can exert some form of control over them, such as their parents, siblings, or spouse (Eck, 1994), is an important factor that may assist in preventing a crime from occurring. With regards to their occupation, this control can extend to supervisors and superiors. In relation to Sutcliffe and those other British serial murderers relevant to this book, it demonstrates how a transient-oriented occupation places these particular offenders out of the managerial sight, and subsequently the control of their superiors. This results in a weakening in an ability to exert control and influence over the behaviour of these individuals.

Whilst Sutcliffe committed his murders outside of his official working hours, the level of managerial oversight within his job impacted on his ability to travel across particular areas that he would later revisit when seeking potential victims. Outside of these occupational factors, the use of a vehicle during his offending afforded him more immediate advantages. For example, the ability to remove himself from the scene of the crime and ensure there was no physical evidence that linked him to his victims. The most apparent advantage that Sutcliffe discussed in his police interviews was the ability to flee the scene of the crime, with Sutcliffe often noting how he "jumped into [his] car...and drove home" after each murder (Bilton, 2003, p. 704). This capability to "getaway" offers an immediate important benefit for the offender. In being able to quickly leave the crime scene, Sutcliffe had time to return home, or to a place he considered "safe", and remove any trace of physical evidence that could place him at the scene of the crime. While Sutcliffe did not explicitly state that he would return home in order to remove any potential evidence, he would occasionally make comments in his police interviews such as, "I found that I didn't have any blood on my clothes" and "I looked at my clothes at the garage I saw that I had blood on the bottom of my jeans … I took my jeans off and rinsed them under the cold tap" (Bilton, 2003, p. 695–698). Remarks such as these convey the importance of being able to leave the scene of the crime, and to offer the offender an opportunity to compose himself, assess the conditions of his clothes and appearance, and thus conceal any apparent signs that they were the guilty party.

At an occupational level Sutcliffe went through periods where he clearly resented the presence of managerial oversight and, on one occasion, having managerial duties for others. Sutcliffe worked at the Water Board (Bilton, 2003, p. 730), and as a lorry driver (p. 710), and it would appear he not only consciously chose jobs that required an individual who was practical, conforming, and preferred to work with objects, but also one that provided him with a legitimate way for him to be alone and away from outside interference. When this ability to be alone was interrupted or threatened, Sutcliffe stated that he was "deeply upset" (Bilton, 2003, p. 730). During one of his police interviews, he explained how he could not "concentrate at work" due to working with an assistant who "didn't fully understand the mechanics of the job". As a result Sutcliffe was consequently demoted and "got a steady number at the Waterworks base at Gilstead". What is interesting here is that Sutcliffe did not appear to be upset by the fact that he was demoted and lost responsibility over other individuals. Apparently the pressures of working with others, especially those with less experience than Sutcliffe, left him feeling he had lost the freedom that originally attracted him to the job. Sutcliffe's demotion and his choice of the word "steady" to describe his new position implies a sense of renewed freedom in a job he feels comfortable doing. With this renewed freedom, Sutcliffe was able to take time examining the suitability of potential victims whilst supposedly engaging in work-related activities:

"One day I had to make a delivery in Huddersfield in the afternoon. I noticed a few girls plying for trade near the market area. Two or three nights later I decided to pay them a visit" (Bilton, 2003, p. 710).

As can be observed from the above statement, Sutcliffe relieved of any managerial responsibility, and physically removed from being under the oversight of others, was able to take time to engage in criminally-oriented thoughts and behaviour without raising concerns from those who either worked under or above him. This lack of managerial oversight and ability to access a much larger geographical space may shed some light as to why it took the authorities five years before finally apprehending him.

Learning on the Job

Serial murderers who held some form of transient occupation often, as we will come to see, applied occupationally gained knowledge into their offending behaviour. These include, for example, victim hunting locations; attack sites; and, victim disposal sites.

Whilst Sutcliffe is known to have picked up his victims prior to murdering them outside of his work-related activities, he appeared to "educate" himself with regard to suitable hunting grounds and even the selection of victims that he would later return to after finishing work:

"Before Yvonne was found I had committed another murder in Huddersfield Helen Rytka. I did not know the Huddersfield Red light area but…the urge inside me to kill girls was now practically uncontrollable I drove to Huddersfield in my Red Corsair one Evening" (Bilton, 2003, p. 710).

As noted above this was as a result of his earlier recognisance whilst working in Huddersfield. Due to Sutcliffe's occupations often requiring him to travel over a large geographical space in order to make deliveries, his awareness and activity space would also increase. As a result he gained more intimate knowledge of other towns and cities that he otherwise would not have visited. So, whilst he was officially in these locations due to his occupation, Sutcliffe was in fact analysing his surroundings as places to offend. He used this prior knowledge to quickly return to these suitable hunting locations. All of this is reinforced in Sutcliffe's account of his murders in Leeds, where he stated that, "I drove off Lumb Lane into Church Lane I knew this was a prostitute area" (Bilton, 2003, p. 696). Taking this into consideration, it is obvious that his occupation brought him within close proximity to those individuals whom he repeatedly targeted and, as a result, informed him of the exact locations to which to return when actively engaging in his offending. Sutcliffe "worked for Bradford-based T and W H Clark (Holdings) Ltd as a lorry driver delivering goods to and from a number of Black Country destinations" ("Did the Yorkshire Ripper murder five women in the Midlands?" *Birmingham Mail*, 2014), as a result he would have gained extensive knowledge of Britain's road networks including "the M1 and routes across the Midlands" (Ibid.). He may have also been able to use this occupationally gained information in order to return home quickly after each successive murder. For example, Sutcliffe would often note that he would "drive straight home" (Bilton, 2003, p. 695) after murdering his victims and, on some occasions, would describe the exact route that he took when leaving the crime scene:

> "I remember that I backed out of the street into Bowling Back Lane facing towards the city. I drove along Bowling Back Lane towards the general direction of the city centre and drove home to Garden Lane" (Bilton, 2003, p. 702).

As this shows, not only did Sutcliffe's occupation offer him the ability to gain intimate knowledge of where his victims were located, it also provided him with an extensive knowledge of road networks—affording him the means to return home in a relatively short period of time. With his access to a vehicle, an occupation that lacked much in the way of managerial oversight, and his extensive knowledge of road networks, Sutcliffe was a dangerously well-informed and equipped serial murderer.

Hidden in Plain Sight

As noted previously, Sutcliffe's occupation provided him a means to gain a variety of skills, or knowledge, which influenced his offending.

The most prominent feature of this was his victim hunting sites and the subsequent disposal of his victim's bodies. One significant factor that afforded him such close proximity to these locations and individuals was the validity and status his occupation as bestowed upon him. However, it is also important to note that this particular instrumental advantage extends beyond just his occupation, and the more immediate advantages of using a vehicle to offend. It also extends to the use of his vehicle to hide weapons, and by inference his true intent re his victims.

Sutcliffe, for example, was required to travel across a large geographical area — including locations such as Bradford, Leeds, and Manchester (Bilton, 2003). Due to this occupational prerequisite, he was able to stake out potential hunting sites whilst driving his lorry — effectively hiding in plain sight. As Kind (cited in Canter, 2004) notes, "if he had a vehicle, he probably also had work: something that would have taken him into these different cities. His visits there would not seem unusual" (Canter, 2004:165). During the period in which the investigation into Sutcliffe's murders was taking place, cars similar to those that he would drive at night actively looking for victims were under intense scrutiny. At this time, Sutcliffe was approached and interviewed by the police given that his car was spotted in the red light districts of Bradford, Leeds, and Manchester (Bilton, 2003). Whilst these interviews proved fruitless, they also highlight the types of vehicles that the police were looking for in relation to the murders. With this in mind, using his work lorry enabled Sutcliffe to travel repeatedly through these ever-increasingly monitored areas relatively free from scrutiny. In effect, his lorry acted as a form of "occupational camouflage" which made him "above suspicion". Sutcliffe, also spent many hours in his own garage fixing and tweaking his cars (Bilton, 2003, p. 750), he may have therefore been in a good position to know the best place to position his weapon(s) for concealment and for easy access. Sutcliffe described this in his formal statement:

> "I had picked up the hammer which I had put near my seat for that purpose…I had taken the screwdriver with the hammer in the well of the driving seat (Bilton, 2003. 695).

While he was "working on" his cars, Sutcliffe not only made changes in order to improve the performance of his vehicles, but he also made adaptations that would ultimately improve his own "performance" when committing murder. Similar to how he would "pull engines out" and replace them in order for his car to perform better (Bilton, 2003, p. 748), placing his hammer tactfully and discreetly under his seat would have allowed him to be more efficient in attacking his victims and crucially gave him an element of surprise.

Waiting Until Dusk

Sutcliffe's occupation as a lorry driver brought him within close proximity of his preferred target group. However, unlike other serial murderers who held transient-oriented occupations who took direct advantage of a similar occupationally generated proximity, Sutcliffe committed his murders after his work-related activities were finished. He predominantly targeted sex workers, and as such the evening and night would have been a more suitable time frame in which to successfully commit an offence. It would presumably have been perceived by Sutcliffe as advantageous to target and select victims at night. After all, stopping to pick up sex workers in a highly recognisable work lorry during the day would have increased the risks of being identified and apprehended. Sutcliffe also lacked the extensive occupational freedom to travel across an even larger geographical space, as evidenced by other British serial murderers, and this may have further prevented him from engaging in criminal behaviour whilst supposedly undertaking work-related activities. So, whilst Sutcliffe held an occupation which provided him with close proximity to his preferred target group, the type of victims he targeted and the greater managerial control over his employment may have contributed to him not taking immediate advantage of the opportunities his work provided.

With Sutcliffe we have a serial murderer that personifies the rise of the transient serial murderer. It is little coincidence that Sutcliffe's murders were committed in the 1970s, the decade in which vehicles had become much more accessible to the general public. The wide-ranging locations that he targeted his victims in also appeared to coincide with road networks expanding in order to meet the increase in car ownership, with more and more locations becoming accessible that were previously difficult to reach (Donnelly, 2005, p. 31). Sutcliffe, unfortunately, would not be the last British serial murderer to make use of these ever-expanding road networks, with the case presented in the next chapter occurring only a few years after Sutcliffe's arrest.

CHAPTER SEVEN

The White &Van Man

I just saw her and got her into the van. I tied her up cos I wanted to keep her until I delivered the parcels to Galashiels ... I wanted to keep her until I went somewhere like Blackpool so I could spend some time with her.

Robert Black at Armagh County Court, 7 October 2011

Name: Robert Black
Born: 21st April 1947
Died: 12th January 2016
Location: Grangemouth, Scotland
No. of victims: 4
Victims: Young girls
Motive: Sexually motivated
Offending period prior to arrest: 5 years

Occupational Background

Robert Black, the Scottish delivery driver who would go on to abduct and murder four young girls, was placed into care by his mother when he was a baby and was described as being a loner, and had few friends and a fiery temper (White and Cooper, 2011). He also appeared, similar to the "Yorkshire Ripper", to be continually drawn to occupations and work environments that were more labour-oriented and often solitary in nature. Black left school at the age of 15 and became a delivery boy in Scotland (Hilliard et al, 2011). During this time he committed criminal offences that shared characteristics similar to those of his later known murders:

> "Black first tried to rape a girl when he was 12 and later spent a year in juvenile detention for a sexual attack. He later admitted having molested up to 40 girls after he got a job as a delivery boy in Glasgow, Scotland, when he was 15" (Hilliard et al, 2011).

Black was also found guilty on one occasion of the sexual assault of a young girl during this period, and received a caution for "lewd and libidinous behaviour" ("Robert Black: profile of a serial killer", *The Herald*, 2011). After leaving his job as a delivery boy, Black moved to Musselburgh, where he subsequently found employment as a swimming pool attendant and lifeguard (Ibid). Whilst it is unknown whether Black committed any crimes during this period of employment, it is interesting to note that his third victim, Caroline Hogg, was abducted in Edinburgh — not too far from the pools he once worked at. It was also reported that Black had a young girl's swimsuit in his possession when he was later arrested (Tozer, 2011). In 1976 Black obtained his driver's licence and relocated to London, where he gained employment at Poster, Dispatch and Storage Ltd (PDS), a London-based delivery firm (Tozer, 2011). In many ways he had therefore returned to a similar occupation to the one he had held in his youth. However, instead of a bike, he now used a van to make his deliveries, and these would become instrumental in his offending. Examining Black's occupational history through the "lens" of Holland's theoretical framework, it again shows a consistency that would suggest an expression of a particular personality-type. In accordance with the List of Occupations by RIASEC Interest Area (n.d.), Black's role as a delivery boy, swimming pool attendant and delivery driver again respectively fall under occupations affiliated with the Realistic personality type. Examining Black's occupational history, it again shows a consistency that would suggest an expression of a particular desire to work in professions that were more labour-oriented, solitary in nature, and removed from much in the way of managerial oversight and control. While this book is mindful to separate speculation from fact, it is arguable that Black's selection of work environments, while on the surface rather distinct and removed from each other, were not only a result of the nature and type of work they required but also the close proximity and access they provided to him in relation to his preferred victim-type—young girls. This line of enquiry will be explored in more detail when investigating Black's history of offences prior to gaining employment with PDS.

A Pattern Emerges

In examining Robert Black's criminal history, it became apparent rather early on that this is a serial murderer with a very specific type of victim in mind when on the hunt for potential targets. For example, his earliest recorded offence shares striking similarities to his later known sexual assaults and murders. At the age of 12, along with two other boys of approximately the same age as Black, he attempted to rape a young girl in an isolated field (Tozer, 2011). While Black was unable to complete the act of penetration, the police were alerted to Black's behaviour and, as a result, he was moved to the boys-only Red House Care Home at Musselburgh (White and Cooper, 2011). It was here where he was reported to have been sexually abused by a male staff member (Adams, 2011). His next known offence occurred at the age of 16 shortly after leaving the care home. Black lured a seven-year-old girl to an abandoned air raid shelter under the pretence of seeing a box of kittens. He sexually assaulted her and "chocked her within an inch of her life" (White and Cooper, 2011). Black only received a caution for lewd and libidinous behaviour for this offence (Adams, 2011). This targeting of pre-pubescent girls would continue as Black grew into adulthood—firmly setting the template for his future murders. He spent the next three years sexually assaulting and molesting young girls (White and Cooper, 2011). It was also later revealed that, whilst working as a lifeguard, he would collect young girl's swimming costumes (Ibid). Unlike other serial murderers that are discussed in this book, in which their template for committing murder evolved over a period of time before becoming more established,

Black's appears to show a consistency from as far back as age 12 and his first recorded offence. Looking at these early crimes, it is clear that he was drawn to particular environments such as those already described. This template is replicated in his known murders, in that each victim either lived in, or was subsequently found, in rural locations. Black's history of occupations appeared to have placed him within close proximity to not only his victims, but also to the environmental conditions that provided the situational context that informed him that a potential target was "good" (Andresen, 2010) — consequently resulting in him carrying-out a series of murders that spanned over the course of five years until he was finally apprehended.

The Whole Country as a Hunting Ground

Black, who had access to a van due to his occupation as a poster deliveryman, killed four young girls between 1981 and 1986 and was eventually apprehended in a failed attempt to abduct another young girl in 1990. His modus operandi included snatching "his young victims off the streets as they played, or walked to and from their homes" (Wilson, 2007, p. 150). On first inspection it would appear that he sporadically selected the locations in which he attacked his victims. For example, Jennifer Cardy was abducted in County Antrim, Northern Ireland, while his second known victim — eleven-year-old Susan Maxwell — was abducted near the village of Cornhill-on-Tweed, on the English side of the English/Scottish border, as she walked to play a game of tennis across the border. A little under a year later in 1983, Black's third known victim, five-year old Caroline Hogg, left her home in Portobello, an eastern suburb of Edinburgh, to play in the nearby playground. She never returned home. Black's final victim that we know about — ten-year-old Sarah Harper — was abducted almost three years after Caroline. Sarah lived in Morley near Leeds; Black kidnapped her as she made her return trip home from the corner shop. The case relating to the murder of Jennifer Cardy went unsolved until 2011. The investigation into her abduction and murder was left open for 28-years and was reviewed again in 2005 (McDonald, 2011). This led to the prosecution of Black (*R v. Black*, 2011), which took place in County Armagh, Northern Ireland, and during this time Black's modus operandi was described in detail. This involved the use of his work delivery van, and it was noted that the van, and by association his occupation, was integral to his abduction of his victims (Court Transcript, Crown Court, 8 December 2011). Throughout the five-week trial, it became clear that, while the van proved to be an invaluable tool for Black in order to commit his crimes, his occupational requirements to be in the area at the time of Jennifer's abduction would also ultimately lead to his down-fall and conviction for her murder. The prosecution in particular drew attention to key evidence that proved that Black's delivery van was close to the area in which Jennifer's body was found, thus implicating Black in her abduction:

> "The Crown has also argued that petrol purchases made on the day after the murder demonstrate that Black was in Northern Ireland the previous day" (Court Transcript, Crown Court, 8 December 2011).

It is apparent that the use of his occupational vehicle was not only one of the most important aspects of Black's modus operandi, but also the most important element of building a case against him. Through an analysis of the evidence used against him during his trial, we are offered an insight into this.

With his ability to travel across the length and breadth of the UK and seemingly not operating from an "anchor point", a location to which he must return after committing his murders such as, for example, his home (Canter, 2005), he posed potential challenges to the authorities. Whilst Sutcliffe, for example, travelled to different areas in search of victims, due to him often leaving his home and quickly returning after committing an offence (Bilton, 2003), his geographical "anchor point" was accurately determined by the work of Stuart Kind. Whilst Kind's work had little impact on the investigation, Sutcliffe's need to search for victims and return home clearly demonstrates what is referred to as the least effort principle of journey-to-crime:

> "Kind plotted the dates and times of the attacks on a map, with the aim of determining their 'centre of gravity'. He realised the killer needed darkness

to cover his crimes and was trying to mislead the police as to the base of his operations. But Kind also knew that the Ripper had to return to his home as soon as possible afterwards to avoid capture near the scene of his crime. He therefore deduced that the earlier in the evening an attack happened, the further away from home the killer was" ("Professor Stuart Kind", *The Telegraph*, 2003).

In comparison to Sutcliffe, Black's occupation took him across the United Kingdom, with offences committed in England, Scotland, and Ireland. Due to this occupational influence in Black's use of geographical space, Black was not as susceptible to the same pressures with regards to travelling the minimal distance required in order to commit a crime. He also lacked the same pressures to quickly return to his "anchor point" — which in most cases is the individual's home. Here it is important to stress that this anchor point, or base, does not have to be a static location. Specifically, as Canter (2004) argues, this base can take "various forms", such as a van, for example, which allows the offender to "bring his victims" as he travels but, more crucially, also "helps shape the scale of his activities" (p. 11). In the case of Black, his base was arguably his occupational van, which allowed him to travel across a large geographical space, whilst also providing a means to engage in his offending in relative privacy.

The issue of "linkage blindness" was also apparent in the case of Black, with no better example than that of the murder of Jennifer Cardy. Not only did his trial take considerable time to establish a connection between Black and Cardy, but it also showed how Black's occupation further increased the difficulties in establishing connections between his other known murders:

Susan Maxwell was abducted from the roadside in Coldstream, Scotland. Her body was eventually found two weeks later dumped behind a layby in the English Midlands. Caroline Hogg went missing from a seafront promenade in Portobello, Scotland. Her body was found ten days later in a ditch in the English Midlands. Sarah Jane Harper was abducted as she walked home from the corner shop in Morley. Her body was found three and a half weeks later in the River Trent near Nottingham (Court Transcript, Crown Court, 8 December 2011).

"Due to Black's victims having lived in different parts of the UK, and their bodies being subsequently found many miles from their homes, the police's ability to link these murders to the same individual was compromised. It was later revealed that Black's occupation at PDS required him to return to the company depot situated in London once all the items had been delivered [Court Transcript, The Crown Court, 8 December 2011] and, due to this, he would drop his victim's body in locations along this route back to London. Again, due to the nature of Black's occupation, he was not constrained by the influential psychological factors prescribed by a stationary 'anchor point'. Instead, Black's murders were a consequence of his day-to-day activities that were heavily shaped by his employment and, as a result, rooted in his journeys pertaining to his occupational requirements."

A Mobile Murder Site

Black made use of the time-saving advantages afforded to him due to using a vehicle. He was able to successfully leave the scene in which he abducted his victims, with one of his victim's parents noting how their daughter had seemed to be playing safely before "she vanished" (*The Telegraph*, 2011). It was Black's use of a van that afforded him this time with regard to his offending behaviour. This can also be observed in Black's statement during his trial for the murder of Jennifer Cardy in 1981:

"I just saw her and got her into the van. I tied her up cos I wanted to keep her until I delivered the parcels to Galashiels."

The detective then asked Black whether he had touched the girl. "'It just happened so quick," he said. 'I only touched her a little. I wanted to keep her until I went somewhere like Blackpool so I could spend some time with her'" (Court Transcript, 7 October 2011).

In the above statement—which was shown to the jury when Black's offending history was revealed to them for the first time—there is evidence of the premeditation with regard to what he was going to do once he had abducted his victim. This premeditation and planning starts from the abduction of his victims, and only ends when the fantasy of committing the act is complete—an act that required considerable time. At this point, as Black states, he would "Just let her go, drop her off", though, of course, there is a deeper, more sinister, meaning to this statement. Black did not simply "drop them off". Instead he would kill his victims before dumping their bodies in an often-remote location. In the case of Jennifer Cardy, for example, "in a dam behind a roadside lay-by 15 miles away at Hillsborough" (Rayner, 2011). Indeed, he went as far as not only using his transport as a way of moving his victims from the scene of their abduction, but also incorporated it as part of his "fantasy space" (Wilson and Jones, 2008, p. 107). It was in his van that Black felt most comfortable in exploring and developing his fantasies. However, he has rarely spoken about his crimes (and also pleaded not guilty to Jennifer's murder), and so it is difficult to be too precise about what actually took place in his van and when he had total control over his victim(s). However, we can gain some insight into what actually took place through the simple description given at the Cardy trial of how Mandy Wilson was discovered:

> "Mr Hedworth told the silent courtroom that when Black, who worked as a poster delivery driver, was arrested in Stow, the six-year-old girl was found stuffed into a sleeping bag in the back of his van" (Court Transcript, 7 October 2011).

Mandy—who survived this attack—was being kept alive so that Black could spend more time alone with her and indulge his fantasies. In many respects his van became his home—a private space where guests were abducted, rather than invited into it. For Black, his vehicle not only provided him the means to access a large geographical space, but also a considerable amount of time to engage in his offending behaviour within the confines and safety of his van. This ability to abduct his victims into his own private world that happened to also be mobile proved to be a significant instrumental advantage to the Scottish serial murderer, and might go some way towards explaining why he was able to repeatedly offend over a substantial period of time prior to his arrest.

Taking in the View

Black's continual travelling through both the major road networks that connect the UK, along with the more rural back roads that are dotted across the country, would have resulted in him gaining extensive knowledge of the areas in which he targeted his victims, and the locations in which he disposed of their bodies. This, it goes without saying, was heavily influenced by his occupation, which would have greatly expanded both his awareness and activity space (Rossmo, 1999). This proved vital in his ability to find and select suitable disposal locations for his victims' bodies. This was further reinforced at Black's trial for the murder of Jennifer Cardy, where he also said "that on outward journeys when the van was full [he] would stick to motorways but when homebound [he] would use A and B roads to alleviate the boredom" (Court Transcript, the Court of Appeal, 27 June 2013). However, Black would also have learned during the course of his work the ideal situations and opportunities in which to successfully abduct vulnerable and isolated young girls. Jennifer Cardy, for example, who lived in the relatively small "Antrim village of Ballinderry" ("Robert Black jailed for murder of Ulster schoolgirl Jennifer Cardy", *Belfast Telegraph*, 2011), would become the template for Black's subsequent murders. The locations of his other murders are described earlier in this chapter.

With reference to rational choice theory, whereby offenders who successfully engage in criminal behaviour seek out other, similar, opportunities (Wortley and Mazerolle, 2008), it could be argued that Black sought out similar environments and conditions that were present during the abduction of Jennifer Cardy — whilst also engaging in work-related tasks. This is also apparent in the disposal sites Black chose. For example, at the Court of Appeal it was noted that "each victim was carried in the direction of Robert Black's return to London" (Court Transcript, Court of Appeal, 27 June 2013). In reviewing Black's previous convictions at the Court of Appeal, the case of Caroline Hogg conveys how his occupation seemed to inform, or "educate", him with regards to the careful selection of victim disposal sites:

> "Her body was found ten days later in a ditch in the English midlands. Her underwear had been removed. The Appellant was on the Scotland run on the date of the abduction and his deliveries would have taken him near Portobello. Furthermore, the body was found ten miles from where Black had re-fuelled in Stafford on his journey back to London" (Court Transcript, Court of Appeal, 27 June 2013).

It is evident that Black's awareness and activity space was significantly influenced by his occupation, and this provided him with a wealth of suitable conditions in order to successfully abduct young girls, along with the necessary environmental conditions to dispose of their bodies post-mortem. Jennifer Cardy, was found in McKee's Dam (Court Transcript, Court of Appeal, 27 June 2013), which is described as a beauty spot and is situated ten miles away near Hillsborough, County Down ("Child killer Robert Black's past revealed to Northern Ireland jury", *The Guardian*, 2011). It is possible that he sought out similar environmental conditions informed by this occupationally-shaped activity and offending space. As Wortley and Mazerolle (2008) note, opportunity is an important cause of crime, and that "Criminally disposed individuals will commit greater numbers of crimes if they encounter more opportunities" (p. 179). For Black, whose occupation took him across the UK and through relatively small towns and villages, his employment provided him the means to take advantage of environmental conditions that would have generated more "organically" than if he lacked such a transient lifestyle. As a result, he identified that the best opportunities to commit his offences were tied to his occupation, and it should be noted that Black has yet to be linked to any similar offences outside of it (Court Transcript, Court of Appeal, 27 June 2013). What makes Black an even more dangerous serial murderer is the fact that not only was he able to gain this important environmental information, but that he was able to do so without raising suspicion.

"Can you fix engines?"

Black's occupation as a delivery driver provided him with proximity and access to the locations in which he abducted his victims. For Black, whose occupation offered extra monetary incentives for long distance deliveries to both Scotland and Ireland of up to £77.50 (Court Transcript, Court of Appeal, 27 June 2013), he was provided with the necessary legitimacy to travel over a large geographical area without others questioning his activity, or his reasons for it. Of interest, due to the nature of Black's occupation, the vehicle he used, a white Datsun van, would become an integral factor of his offending and a literal manifestation of a "collision" between employment and murder (Tozer, 2011). As previously mentioned, he would note that he tended to drive down more secluded and rural roads on his journey back to London in an effort to "alleviate the boredom" (Court Transcript, Court of Appeal, 27 June 2013). Whilst there may be some truth to this statement, it also harbours more insidious undertones. Black's van was a fundamental means to make deliveries but, once these were made, he was then free to use it within his offending without losing any of the validity and legitimacy for being in those areas in which he abducted his victims. This can be observed in Black's modus operandi when abducting, or attempting to abduct, Teresa Ann Thornhill. She recalled the moments leading up to the event:

> "I saw the driver get out and open the bonnet of the engine…then he shouted 'Can you fix engines?'…I suddenly felt the man grab me from behind…I think he said something like 'Get in you bitch,' as we were struggling" (Wyre and Tate, 1995).

In Teresa's case, due to her looking younger than she actually was, she was able to fight Black off and escape (Wilson, 2007, p. 157). From her account it is evident that not only did he use his work vehicle as a means to abduct his victims, but that he was also aware of the apparent perceived legitimacy his occupation and vehicle provided him. It is also important to stress that if it was not for a witness being present at his last and ultimately failed attempt to abduct a victim, Black could have easily continued his hunt for targets whilst hidden behind the legitimacy of his white delivery van.

An Opportunity Presents Itself

Black is the epitome of a serial murderer who chose driving as an occupation. In comparison to Sutcliffe and Wright, Black lacked a strong managerial presence that may have influenced his behaviour and conceivably could have prevented him from offending whilst undertaking work-related activities. Not only did Black lack the presence of a "handler", his targeting of young and isolated girls who often lived in rural towns and villages may have also influenced the time in which he chose to engage in his offending behaviour. Sutcliffe and Wright both had occupational bases situated close to their place of residence. They also lived near the red light districts they frequented in order to find and select a suitable victim. Black did not face the same concerns of being recognised or identified by locals due to his infrequency of travelling through the same location over a short period of time, and the validity of his presence due to his delivery commitments. His preference for and selection of victims was heavily informed and influenced by his "crime template". The time of day in which suitable victims would both be in public and alone would contrast greatly with the sex workers that Sutcliffe and Wright targeted. This may also have been a contributing factor as to why Black only appeared to commit his abductions and murders during the day. His victims lived in more rural locations, and would be less likely to be left alone in public at night, and be in the presence of those that could provide protection. Taking these factors into consideration, it is likely that Black's occupation acted as a means of propulsion towards locations that, with reference to routine activity theory, provided suitable targets that also lacked capable guardians. Black was also an offender who operated alone. He was therefore free to fully take advantage of the criminal opportunities presented to him, and committed all of his known abductions and murders whilst carrying out deliveries for his company. As noted in the Court of Appeal, he had significant freedom when making deliveries that covered a large geographical space:

"He said he would have made drops in Belfast, Dunmurry and Newry and would normally have been back in Belfast for about 12:30 pm in plenty of time for that evening's sailing back to Liverpool. He also said that on outward journeys when the van was full he would stick to motorways but when homebound he would use A and B roads to alleviate the boredom" (Court Transcript, Court of Appeal, 27 June 2013).

Black's description of his occupation certainly portrays a form of employment that lacked clear supervision so that, when making his deliveries, he had complete control over the route he would take and, as noted in the above statement, had a significant amount of time in order to engage in his offending.

Robert Black, it is hoped this chapter has demonstrated, was a serial murderer who made full use of his transient-oriented profession in order to successfully engage in his offending behaviour. By examining his occupational history, it is apparent that, similar to Peter Sutcliffe, he was driven to labour-oriented and solitary-natured professions that provided him with the means to fantasise in his own private, transient world. He also exhibited similar motivational and behavioural characteristics in his offending prior to gaining his infamous white van for PDS — setting his template for his targeting and selection of young girls. Unfortunately for the young girls that were taken by him, his profession provided him with a means and, more importantly, legitimacy to gain proximity to them without gaining suspicion, even in broad daylight.

CHAPTER EIGHT

The Railway Stalkers

It was only later that the criminals moved further afield, as they became more confident. The early rapes marked a vicious territory around North London, West Hampstead and Kilburn ... by the time the map was competed the extremities were marked by a triangle of murders.

David Canter, *Mapping Murder* (2005, Virgin Books)

Names: John Duffy and David Mulcahy
Born: Both in 1959
Location: London
No. of victims: 3
Victims: Women
Motive: Sexually motivated
Offending period prior to arrest: 4 years

Two Bodies One Mind

John Duffy and David Mulcahy were serial rapists and murderers who used railway stations as their hunting sites throughout the South-east of England including the North and West areas of London (Canter, 2005, p. 173). At work, both men appeared to be inseparable. "They worked at Westminster City Council, where Mulcahy was a plumber and Duffy a carpenter" and Mulcahy engaged in work outside of the council "moonlighting as a mini-cab driver" (Clough et al, 2001). Both of their respective occupations for the council, due to constantly changing work-sites, relied heavily on the need to travel. At the time when the attacks took place, the police and the media were unsure if the offences were being committed by one or two assailants. This led to the media dubbing the attacks as the work of the "Railway Rapist" (Canter, 2005, p. 174). Forensic psychologist, David Canter, who worked alongside the police to help apprehend the attackers, notes that not only did the offenders literally travel over a wide geographical area in search of potential victims (p. 174), but that those involved were also going through a much more personal, psychological journey:

> "This case showed a person on a vicious journey, starting with unplanned, opportunistic rape and leading to planned, brutal murder. What if this mental journey was reflected in the killer's journeys to his crimes?" (Canter, 2005, p. 175).

The case of Duffy and Mulcahy offers an interesting perspective into mobile serial murderers in regards to how the instrumental and psycho-logical factors of travelling are intertwined. Canter discovered that as time passed and more attacks were being reported, the locations of these horrific events seemed to change, spreading outwards like a "disease" (p. 175).

Occupational Background

Duffy and Mulcahy appeared to not only share a propensity for murder, but were also drawn to similar, labour-oriented occupations. They were described as being inseparable both as children and later as adults, although they seem to have had distinct and different character traits:

> "David Mulcahy was strong, outgoing, something of a show-off and always wanted to be the centre of attention, the court heard. By contrast John Duffy was small, quiet and introverted" (Hopkins, 2000).

Despite these apparent differences, both appeared to be drawn to labour and transient-oriented occupations. Duffy, after leaving school, was employed as a carpenter for British Rail (Jenkins, 1992). Mulcahy, on the other hand, became a plumber, which meant he travelled to people's homes in order to carry out work-related tasks (Clough et al, 2001). Thus, for this serial murdering "team", they both individually appeared to be drawn to occupations within the building trade (Harris and Wright, 2001) — and neither sought work in other forms of employment. With this in mind, it is evident that these British serial murderers shared not only criminally-oriented motivations, but also a similar desire to work in professions that relied on a particular set of skills that also did not require much in the way of social interaction. Again, with regard to the RIASEC model (*Chapter Four*), it is evident that they shared not only criminally-oriented motivations, but also a similar personality-type. For Duffy, whose occupational history solely consisted of carpentry work and Mulcahy, who worked as both a plumber and as a taxi driver, each of their respective forms of employment are again indication and expression of the Realistic personality type (List of Occupations by RIASEC Interest Area, n.d.), and this reinforces the notion that they were drawn to such professions other than just for the pursuit of victims.

From Petty Crime to Murder

For Duffy and Mulcahy, their history of sexually-motivated offending was formed through a shared history of criminally-oriented experiences. For example, it has been noted that both Mulcahy and Duffy were bullied as youths and, as a result, formed a close friendship that soon took a sinister turn (Pritchard, 2001). Their first known criminally-oriented behaviour shared particular hallmarks and characteristics with their later offences:

> "They played truant and indulged in petty crime. Gradually the bullied became bullies. On Hampstead Heath they terrified courting couples and homosexuals, jumping out from bushes wearing masks" (Clough et al, 2001).

Whilst their selection of targets would change as they got older, their selection of similar environments to search for victims and the wearing of masks would become a hallmark of their later offences. Mulcahy, who began to show signs of being the dominant of the two from an early age, was found covered in blood after bludgeoning a hedgehog to death — Duffy was reported to have been laughing next to a blood-covered Mulcahy (The "wicked soul mates", *BBC News*, 2001). Whilst they appeared to be developing a propensity towards more instrumentally-oriented crimes such as robbery, burglary, and car theft (Crace, 2004), Duffy's former wife provides an insight into the pair's growing penchants towards sexual deviancy. For example, she noted at his trial that he would tie her up and make her perform acts of bondage and strangulation (Clough et al, 2001). These were hallmarks of his and Mulcahy's modus operandi. Their development from instrumental to more expressive forms of crime seemed to be further propelled by Mulcahy's dependency on violence to get sexually aroused (Hopkins, 2000). So too Duffy's reported low sperm count appeared to fuel his anger towards women (Morris, 2001). Similar to Sutcliffe, it is apparent that Mulcahy's and Duffy's criminal and personal history prior to gaining employment assisted in creating a template that would emerge later in their lives whilst working in their respective occupations. Again, the environment which Duffy came into contact with during his time as a rail carpenter shared striking similarities to the settings in which he and Mulcahy used when attempting to scare couples in parks, demonstrating how, once a "crime template" is "established, it is relatively fixed and influences future criminal behaviour" (Andresen, 2010, p. 26).

Hunting London's Rail Network

The "Railway Papists" were able to traverse a large geographical space in an effort to identify and select appropriate targets. Duffy, who used his knowledge of the London rail network (Clough et al, 2001), would, along with his accomplice, Mulcahy, go on "hunting parties" in search of victims, which often covered a large geographical space. Specifically, the pair was identified as being responsible for a series of rapes prior to murdering any victims, with the majority of these women being attacked in areas around North London — especially Kilburn and West Hampstead (Clough et al, 2001). As the two offenders, who were often described as operating as "two bodies with one brain" (Harris and Wright, 2001), escalated their behaviour towards murder, so did they also appear to seek out new areas in which to offend. For example, the pair's first confirmed murder victim, 19-year old Alison Day, was killed in Hackney Wick in East London, which was followed by the rape and murder of Maartje Tamboezer, a Dutch teenager who lived in East Horsley, Surrey (Clough et al, 2001). Their final murder of Anne Lock (aged 29) took place in Brookmans Park, Hertfordshire, shortly after Anne got off a train ("Sex Killers Link to 20 more Attacks Police Quizzing Convicted Pair", *Birmingham Evening Mail*, 2001). In comparison to the majority of their earlier offences, in which the general area of North London served as a "hunting ground", Duffy and Mulcahy's, murders were situated further apart. David Canter, already mentioned, who was brought onto the investigation in order to create an "offender profile" of the assailant (2004), described the serial murdering "team's" geographical movements as:

"...moving outwards like a disease. It was only later that the criminals moved further afield, as they became more confident. The early rapes marked a vicious territory around North London, West Hampstead and Kilburn...by the time the map was completed the extremities were marked by a triangle of murders" (Canter, 2004, p. 175).

Again, similar to that of Sutcliffe and Black, this ability to access a large geographic space, which was often influenced by Duffy's time working for National Rail as a "rail Carpenter" (Putwain and Sammons, 2002), provided these offenders with a means to generate significant space between each of their murders. This space increased the numbers of potential suspects considerably (Ainsworth, 2001). As a result, traditional policing methods had to be re-examined, with the inclusion of Canter, an environmental psychologist, bringing with it new investigative techniques. Canter applied the principles related to journey-to-crime, a theory which hypothesis that the likelihood of an individual committing a crime decreases as they travel further away from their base or "anchor point", and determined that "the killer must have had a residence near the hub of criminal activities" (p. 173). With this information, Duffy was identified as living in this determined area and this subsequently aided in his arrest. Despite the aid of Canter's profiling techniques and the consequent arrest of Duffy, it would be a number of years before the other half of the "railway rapists" was brought to justice. Following his imprisonment, Duffy confirmed to a forensic psychologist the already held belief by the police that he committed his crimes with an accomplice — he consequently implicated Mulcahy in 1997 in their rapes and murders. With the advancements in DNA-profiling, a recourse that was not available during the time of their offences, Mulcahy was subsequently found guilty of three murders and seven rapes. Not only did these offenders have access to similar instrumental advantages to Peter Sutcliffe and Robert Black, but the fact that they worked as a team made the task of apprehending them that much more difficult.

Creating Temporal Distance

In both their occupations and their offending, the use of vehicles by Duffy and Mulcahy also provided them with valuable time to find and select a suitable victim; attack them; and, finally successfully leave the kill site. Similar to Sutcliffe, the immediate instrumental advantages of using a vehicle meant that the serial killing "team" were able to flee the scene of the crime immediately after committing their offences. This ability would again generate much needed physical space between themselves and their victims over a short period of time, especially in comparison to those offenders who lacked access to a vehicle. With this time, they were also able to remove any forensic evidence that may have linked them to the crime. For example:

> "They carried a rape kit of balaclavas, knives and tape. Matchboxes were stuffed with tissue so the matches would not rattle. The tissue was for wiping away body traces, the matches to burn the tissues" (Harris and Wright, 2001).

Taking these factors into consideration, Duffy and Mulcahy were able to use this afforded time to physically and forensically remove themselves. These particular serial murderers were also afforded time due to the careful selection of kill sites which were predominantly influenced and shaped by Duffy's occupation as a carpenter for British Rail. In particular, it has been noted that Duffy "used his knowledge of the rail network around London when planning his crimes" (Clough et al, 2001). This notion of "learning on the job" brings attention to another instrumental advantage that was afforded to these particular serial murderers that will be explored in more detail later in this chapter. Duffy's extensive knowledge further provided these offenders with areas in which they knew would have minimal risk of witnesses or suitable guardians being present. This is most notably illustrated in how they both had time to individually sexually assault their victims prior to, in three instances, murdering them:

> "Mulcahy told me to lie back on the bench, pushed me down and tried to have intercourse with me. He couldn't manage it and this made him very angry. The tears were pouring down my face by now. The beast made Valerie perform a sex act while Duffy stood close by, watching and waiting his turn. When they had both finished, Duffy told Valerie to stay perfectly still for 10 minutes while he and Mulcahy escaped. 'I was shaking uncontrollably,' she said. 'I couldn't believe it had happened.' Hysterical and terrified, Valerie scrambled in the dark for her clothes and staggered back to the road" (Oswald, 2001).

With Duffy's extensive environmental knowledge of the locations they targeted, the use of a vehicle in the escape from a crime scene, and the instrumental advantages of working in a pair, these particular British serial murderers were able to generate sufficient geographical and temporal distance from their victims.

Occupation and Offending Collide

For the serial murdering "team" Duffy and Mulcahy, it was the former's occupation as a carpenter for the rail network that ultimately led to them being labelled the "Railway Rapists". Specifically, during the period in which they sexually assaulted and murdered three women, it was noted how the offenders seemed to target isolated women as they left or walked past various rail stations:

> "The two men had created a new game, 'hunting'—cruising streets near railway stations in search of victims as they sang along to the Michael Jackson hit Thriller" (Clough et al, 2001).

Whilst such locations provided them with the opportunity to commit a prolonged sexual assault and later the murder of their victims, it was Duffy's general knowledge of these locations that is of interest. As has already been stated, he worked for British Rail and as a carpenter for Westminster Council ("where most remember him as a 'skiver' who repeatedly phoned in sick" (Harris and Wright, 2001)), would have gained intimate knowledge of the various routes and stations that the trains would pass through as he engaged in work-related activities. Others have also noted this, with Clough et al (2001) observing that "Duffy [was] known as the "railway rapist" because he used his knowledge of the rail network around London when planning his crimes". This can be demonstrated in the rape and murder of 29-year-old Anne Lock, who left her bicycle at Brookmans Park Railway Station in Hertfordshire. In preparation for her return, Duffy and Mulcahy hid the bike and, as she searched for it, "she was seized and taken to a field where she was raped and murdered" (Levin, 2001). According to Levin (2001) two months passed before her body was eventually discovered. This was in all likelihood due to Duffy's extensive knowledge of the areas surrounding the train stations and of what specific areas could effectively conceal a body over a long period of time. While Duffy's occupationally-gained knowledge of the locations used to commit their murders formed the geographical basis for the majority of their known offences, there were occasions where Mulcahy's job as a plumber also informed the locations for some of their less successful crimes. For example, Mulcahy's occupation would often result him changing work sites placing him in near proximity to a woman he intended to assault. This can perhaps be best demonstrated where Mulcahy got into an altercation with a woman who lived near a house he was at the time working on. Upon engaging with a heated argument with the woman, Mulcahy decided that she need to be "taught a lesson" (Clough et al, 2001) and broke into her home with the intention of sexually assaulting her upon her return. Fortunately, the woman failed to return and Mulcahy had to abandon his plans. Whilst this rape failed to transpire, what is of note is that Mulcahy's time engaging in occupational activities influenced the location and target of this particular incident in their offending lifespan. Despite both men committing their crimes together, their respective occupations ultimately influenced the locations they stalked and the victims that they targeted.

Disappearing into the Night

Several serial murderers used their vehicles as occupational camouflage. This is most apparent in the case of Sutcliffe, but can equally apply to Duffy and Mulcahy. This ability to hide in plain sight is demonstrated by Mulcahy's occupation as a labourer for the council. In particular, the nature of his employment would put him in direct contact with potential victims under valid circumstances:

> "The trigger is believed to have been a row with a woman for whom he did some building work. He planned to teach her a lesson, to break into her home with Duffy, and rape her. The pair made two attempts, but the woman was not there" (Levin, 2001).

Despite Mulcahy reportedly arguing with the homeowner, it is obvious that his occupation afforded him proximity and situational knowledge of potential victims, without the fear of raising suspicion. Out of the two, though, it is clear that Duffy, despite often being considered the weaker of the two (Pritchard, 2001), also used his occupation to gather intelligence for future offences under the guise of working as a rail carpenter. Whilst performing a variety of labour-oriented tasks along London's rail network, Duffy was able to gather important intelligence pertaining to prospective offences without his presence ever coming under question or scrutiny. This extensive environmental knowledge of London's rail network through Duffy's time working as a rail carpenter, along with Mulcahy's knowledge of the road networks gathered through his moonlighting as a taxi driver, would provide this serial killing "team" with an almost complete map of their hunting grounds—and a further means in which to quickly and successfully fade into the city's backdrop.

Similar to how Sutcliffe could drive freely throughout red light districts, the "railway rapists" were also able to gain legitimate access to future hunting grounds and potential victims under the guise of their occupations. They were also able to use transport as a means to move and hide instruments that they would use in their attacks. Specifically, these instruments would consist of a "rape kit of balaclavas, knives and tape" (Clough et al, 2001). This serial murdering "team's" use of transport provided them with the means to efficiently hide their true intentions as they stalked London by night—effectively blending into the backdrop of the city's road and rail networks. Whilst, as we will come to see with more recent cases of transient British serial murderers, the use of CCTV and other forms of surveillance is ever increasing the risks for such offenders to use transport in the commission of their crimes, the implementation of this technology was still in its infancy when Duffy and Mulcahy committed their rapes and murders. With the lack of such technology, they were able to travel across London in relative obscurity and, upon committing a crime, fall into the arterial-like road systems of their busy city and disappear into the night.

Night Stalkers

Despite the apparent wealth of instrumental advantages afforded to both of these serial murderers through their respective occupations, Duffy and Mulcahy in fact offended outside of their work-related activities. Arguably, the most obvious reason for this is the fact that both men tended to commit their offences, and in particular their murders, whilst in the company of each other. Whilst it is generally accepted that both men also committed a variety of sexual assaults separately, with police suspecting Mulcahy of having committed a series of rapes after Duffy was arrested, it is the fact that the three murders attributed to them were committed while both men were present that is of interest here. Both men worked for the city council but in different capacities and at different locations—with Duffy working on London's rail network and

Mulcahy tending to work on "odd jobs" for the council in a variety of different locations — these serial murderers were simply unable to commit their crimes in the same manner as, for example, PDS delivery driver Robert Black. Whilst both Duffy and Mulcahy's occupations afforded them the ability to be transient and, as demonstrated by Duffy, provided close proximity to the locations in which they committed a number of their assaults and murders, the fact that they were separated during these periods significantly impacted upon their ability to take advantage of such instrumental advantages. It is also important to consider their modus operandi and how this may have influenced the pair's decision to hunt and select victims at night. For example, the fact that both men would carefully plan their attack and both took turns to sexually assault their victims would require a substantial amount of time both leading up to the offence and during it (Clough et al, 2001). This rather significant and defining aspect may have deterred them from engaging in an offence whilst undertaking work-related activities, and while not within each other's company.

It is also important to discuss the importance of managerial control in their respective occupations. Mulcahy, whilst working as an "odd-job" labourer of sorts, was not self-employed and worked for the council (Clough et al, 2001). While still required to be transient for his occupation, Mulcahy lacked the level of autonomy and freedom that other labourers presented in this book held, and this may have further prevented him from offending during the hours he was engaged in work-related activities. Again, whilst Mulcahy's secondary occupation as a taxi driver also required him to be transient and arguably brought him within close proximity of individuals who would match his "crime template", he too lacked managerial freedom in this role as he worked for a taxi firm, as opposed to being self-employed (Shaw et al, 2001). Duffy's occupation as a carpenter for British Rail assisted him in selecting suitable locations in which to search for victims. However, it is important to note that he was considered as being the weaker of the two, and operated under the guidance and control of the more dominant Mulcahy (Pritchard, 2001). Not only was it this relationship between the pair that influenced Duffy's decision to commit his crimes outside of his work hours, but he too, due to working for the council, would have been under managerial pressures that may have further restricted his ability to commit crimes during these periods.

With Duffy and Mulcahy, we have two motivated offenders who have been bonded together through years of co-offending and criminal behaviour (Clough et al, 2001). Not only did this provide them with a number of distinct instrumental advantages in the commission of their sexual assaults and murders, the fact that both held transient dependent occupations provided them with further means to successfully commit a series of horrific crimes prior to being apprehended. Specifically, with Duffy's profession as a rail carpenter, these "Railway Rapists" were able to seek out and select future locations in which to hunt for victims whilst all along engaging in work-related tasks. Similar to how Peter Sutcliffe would dive through red-light districts whilst making deliveries in his lorry, Duffy, and to a lesser extent Mulcahy, were able to hide in plain sight while on the lookout for suitable locations or victims to target at a later time. This ability to hide their true intentions extended beyond their occupation, with the simple use of Mulcahy's vehicle providing them a means to disappear into the backdrop of London's busy road networks. While this serial killing "team" had a number of instrumental advantages afforded to them, this need to commit their crimes while in the company of the other came with some drawbacks. Specifically, unlike the Scottish serial murderer Robert Black, Duffy and Mulcahy were limited in their ability to commit their offences whilst engaging in work-related activities due to being separated from each other, whereas being together was an integral component of their offending behaviour. What is also of importance is the fact that both men would have come under more managerial oversight, an important factor that may have played a part in the managing of their behaviour during their work hours.

With the present overview of Sutcliffe, Black, and Duffy and Mulcahy, we are starting to see common themes emerge regarding how transient-oriented occupations influence and aid these offender's criminal behaviour and activity. So too, are we beginning to uncover how, despite these advantages, committing serial murder with an accomplice, the targeting a victim-type, such as sex workers, that are not congruent with their occupation, and a stronger presence of managerial control or oversight, negatively impacts on how integral their profession is to their crimes. In continuing this examination into the significance of transient occupations for serial murder, we will now be moving attention to a serial murderer who presents a very different take on the "geographically transient" serial murder.

CHAPTER NINE

The "Odd-Job Man"

We are going to keep you in the cellar and let our friends use you and, when they have finished with you, we will kill you and bury you under the paving stones of Gloucester. There are hundreds of girls there ... the police haven't found them and they won't find you!

Fred West quoted by Former nanny Caroline Roberts, *Mail Online* (2009)

Name: Frederick Walter Stephen "Fred" West
Born: 29th September 1941
Death: 1st January 1995
Location: Gloucester
No. of victims: Ten confirmed
Victims: Young women
Motive: Sexually motivated
Offending period prior to arrest: 20 years

A History of Labour-oriented Professions

Born in 1941, West was the first of seven children born to Walter and Daisy West of Much Marcle, which is situated in the Forest of Dean in Gloucestershire (Woodrow, 2011). Like Robert Black (see *Chapter Seven*), West left school at a young age, leaving behind a poor record of bad behaviour and sporadic attendance (Newton, 2006). After school, he joined his father in the agriculture trade. He would bring in the crops during the harvest period, hunt for rats and other rodents, watch over the sheep and, at night, stop any poachers that happened to enter their land, (Woodrow, 2011). Whilst he appeared to enjoy this form of employment at first, he would later leave it and move to a more transient-oriented occupation.

In the early-1960s West was employed as an ice cream van driver located in Coatbridge, Scotland (Borland, 2013; Newton, 2006). According to Newton (2006), he used this occupation as a means to satisfy "his desires with young girls he met on his job as a driver of an ice cream truck" (Newton, 2006, p. 281). It was during this time that West hit and killed a young boy with his van (Kerr, 2011). Whilst he was not charged with the death of the young boy, he left his place of employment and subsequently moved to Gloucester, where he briefly worked at a slaughterhouse (Newton, 2006). It was while working here, Kerr (2011) argues, that West began to develop an unusual fascination with corpses and dismemberment—a hallmark of his later murders. West's time working at the slaughterhouse was brief, and by the time he met his future wife and serial murdering accomplice Rosemary, he was working as a delivery driver for a bakery (Kerr, 2011; see also Newton, 2006). Again, West seemed to be drawn to both manual labour-oriented and transient dependent occupations. By the time he moved to 25 Cromwell Street he had moved occupations yet again and become a self-employed odd-job labourer, which required him to travel continually to new locations in pursuit of work (Sounes, 1995). The nature of this work was varied, with West known for laying down patios (Bourke, 2006), and doing general "building work" (Bennett and MacDonald, 1995).

This particular form of occupation provided West with both an occupation that fulfilled his tendency to seek employment that required manual labour skills, whilst also allowing him the transient freedom that two of his previous jobs also afforded him. With reference to the List of Occupations by RIASEC Interest Area (n.d.) (*Chapter Four*), West's employment as a farm hand; ice cream van driver; slaughterhouse worker; delivery driver; and finally odd-job labourer all fall under those occupations ascribed to the Realistic personality-type. Whilst his occupation history appears mixed and varied in relation to work environment and job role, his jobs were each, according to Holland's model, attractive forms of employment for an individual with a Realistic personality.

A Learned Behaviour?

Similar to those serial murderers already presented in this book, Fred West also appeared to engage in sexually motivated crimes prior to committing his known murders. West's history of sexually deviant behaviour appears to have started at a very young age, and West's father appears to have been engaged in incestuous relations with his own daughters (Newton, 2006). West too would engage in incest when older (Murray, 2009). Outside of his own family, he is known to have sexually assaulted and impregnated his 13-year-old neighbour—and he was charged with "statutory rape" (i.e. of someone below the age of consent) at the age of 19 (Newton, 2006). His first wife, Rena Costello, complained about West's constant demands for sex, which also involved acts of bondage including tying her up and strangling her (Davis, 2005). It is evident that West's offences from when he was a young man and newly married shared similarities to his later murders whilst working as an odd-job labourer. During the time in which he worked as an ice cream van driver, for example, he appeared to spend a great deal of his time approaching and engaging in sexual activities with young women and girls (Newton, 2006). One of these girls was Anna McFall who became pregnant by West, who then murdered her and dismembered her body, taking as trophies her fingers and toes (Newton, 2006)—a hallmark of his future murders.

West's time working as an ice cream van driver may have assisted in forming his "crime template" with regard to understanding and interpreting the environmental cues and conditions that were necessary for a successful crime to occur. These were contextual signals, which would have been replicated during his time as an odd-job labourer. For West, his occupation as such provided him close proximity and access to those he desired. It also provided him with the occupational freedom necessary to engage in his propensity for committing acts of bondage and dismemberment of his victims, a predilection he developed prior to becoming an odd-job labourer.

Freedom Behind the Wheel

Fred West's occupation was more focused on labouring skills rather than specific driving-oriented tasks. Nonetheless it still required him to move from one location to another on a frequent basis, due to having no fixed and permanent work base. As a result of his need to travel between various locations in order to work, he too had access to a large geographical space that was used for his occupation, but also for offending purposes. It has been well established that West's wife, Rosemary, was heavily involved in most of their known murders, and her involvement altered how West used his vehicle. Bracchi and Wright (2011), for example, note how the Wests would use their vehicle as a means to find and select suitable and isolated young women:

> "Mr Leveson said that the Wests picked up a 17-year-old girl called Caroline Owens who was hitchhiking to Tewkesbury in the autumn of 1972. During the journey the Wests offered Miss Owens a job as their nanny and she accepted and moved into Cromwell Street. After a few weeks Miss Owen left but in December 1972 the Wests once again picked her up when she was hitchhiking…Mrs West then sexually assaulted Miss Owens and Mr West stopped the car. He then punched her in the face knocking her senseless and when she came round she was being tied up and gagged" (Bracchi and Wright, 2011).

Similar to Peter Sutcliffe, and even more so to John Duffy and David Mulcahy, given his use of an accomplice, West would often drive in search of victims after his work hours finished. Again, similar to Sutcliffe, these specific offences would have been susceptible to the psychological influences prescribed by journey-to-crime, in that Fred, and by extension Rose, would have sought to travel the minimal distance required in order to find and select a suitable victim. However, in comparison to these other serial murderers, it has been noted that West also appeared to behave in a similar fashion with regard to picking-up young women whilst alone and, more importantly, engaged in work-related activities. Felicity Nightingale, for example, recounted her personal experience on encountering West at a service station off the M5 motorway while she was hitchhiking across the UK. In comparison to the car used during the times in which both he and Rosemary searched for potential victims, Felicity observed that West was driving his work-related van at the time:

> "There was a slipway before the motorway started again and I noticed a blue van parked on it. The man leaning on it was looking over. 'You want a lift?' he asked, walking towards me ... It seemed odd he would offer to drive me, without being asked, but because I was caught off-guard I told him where I was heading. 'I'll give you a ride. Throw your rucksack in,' he said, 'motioning to the empty space in the back of his van'" ("My ride with a serial killer", *The Guardian*, 2009).

Similar to Robert Black, West appears to have actively employed the offending behaviour that he displayed when seeking suitable victims with Rose. Other similar instances were also reported in which West "enticed several of his victims into his van as they waited alone at bus stops" (Brunt, 2014). These particular instances would have altered in comparison to those crimes in which Rose was also involved, in that West's primary reason for travelling would not have been for offending-related purposes, but more for reaching work sites. These locations constantly changed, with West having to travel to different counties that surrounded his home city of Gloucester. One such example is the few days that he provided his labouring skills to a printing firm in Wiltshire, in which he was described as being a "totally ordinary guy" (Bennett and MacDonald, 1995). In comparison to the occasions that both he and Rose actively sought suitable victims, the instances that occurred during West's work hours were not operating under the same theoretical constraints proposed by journey-to-crime. Specifically, similar to the crimes of Black, instead of having to leave his home and actively seek suitable victims, the transient nature of West's occupations seemingly generated the necessary conditions for a crime to successfully occur while he was carrying out work-related routines and activities. This is perhaps best demonstrated by Felicity's account, in which West's occupation placed him within close proximity of young women who lacked the support of capable guardians. It is also important to note that there was "incontrovertible evidence of the bodies buried at 25 Cromwell Street" (Court Transcript, Court of Appeal, 2 April 1996). This facet of West's crimes not only indicates that West was able to use his vehicles as a means to transport his victims' bodies over a large geographical space, but also challenges another key theoretical aspect of journey-to-crime — namely that of the concept of "buffer zones". This concept postulates that offenders will not engage in offending behaviour in areas where they might be recognised, but West, being a builder, "could simply concrete over a victim" (Persaud, 1995) — thus reducing any suspicion and seemingly eliminating any area West could not, in some capacity, engage in offending behaviour.

Similar to Robert Black, a vehicle afforded a considerable amount of time to odd-job labourer Fred West when engaging in criminal behaviour. Whilst a van provided a means for Black to spend a significant amount of time alone with his victims, the majority of West's murders were conducted with the aid of his wife Rose and, as a result, West's work van was not used when trying to abduct victims. Instead, the use of their personal vehicle was employed as a means to transport their selected victims to their home at 25 Cromwell Street. Once West's victims were in his home, time would no longer be of concern. Since the Wests' arrest and, in the case of Rose, her conviction, it has been reported that, for the majority of their victims, they "were tortured over lengthy periods and raped before being killed" (Morris, 2014). This seems likely to have happened to Lucy Partington, who disappeared on the 27 December 1973:

"Records showed that just after midnight on the morning of January 3 1974, West appeared at the casualty department of Gloucester Royal Hospital with a serious laceration to the right hand. 'It seems only too possible that she was kept alive for several days,' writes one commentator. And yet the evidence remains entirely circumstantial. 'It is possible,' writes another, 'that [West's] wound occurred as a result of the dismemberment of a corpse'" (Amis, 2000).

Whilst the evidence is circumstantial the fact that Lucy's body was found "decapitated and dismembered, and her remains ... crammed into a shaft between leaking sewage pipes" (Amis, 2000) suggests that West did indeed have time to engage in his offending behaviour, and subsequently mutilate and hide the victim's body. It has also been reported that a number of West's victims were lured into his home under the pretence that work may be available as a nanny to his children (Murray, 2009). However, the van allowed him to traverse the areas involved for victims. For example, it has been noted that West "drove around alone following and sometimes assault[ed] girls and young women" (Bennett, 1995), and that he and Rosemary often offered lifts to isolated and vulnerable young women (Bracchi and Wright, 2011). In other words, Rose was his only "handler", and this provides another rationale as to why he was able to spend a considerable amount of time either torturing his victims or burying their bodies and removing evidence. Specifically, due to his neighbours' awareness of his occupation, and the fact that West had little in the way of supervisory oversight, he would not have been compelled to engage in his offending over a short period of time. Instead, West was able to take his time both in offending, and subsequently burying any evidence—sometimes in view of his neighbours.

Berry-Dee and Morris (2009) draw attention to this factor of time for West, in which his occupation as an odd-job labourer provided the necessary cover for him to in fact engage in offending-related activities hidden under the guise of work-related duties:

> "Its owner was a builder and was always busily at work, making improvements to the property—knocking down a wall here, concreting over a floor there. To the casual observer, there always seemed to be something going on inside 25 Cromwell Street" (Berry-Dee and Morris, 2009).

Thus it is apparent that the use of a vehicle, and the occupational guise provided to West due to his job as an odd-job labourer, afforded him abundant amounts of time to offend and, once finished, remove any evidence, all within the safety of his home at 25 Cromwell Street.

Burying the Evidence

As demonstrated by the serial murderer Peter Tobin (*Chapter Eleven*), certain transient-dependent occupations, such as those that also require construction-based knowledge beyond simply the need to drive, afford certain offenders with knowledge and skills that prove useful in the commission of murder. For example, for odd-job labourer and builder West, the most obvious knowledge gained during the course of his occupation is that of construction. This would consist of the building of private and public housing buildings, along with being responsible for undertaking all manner of renovations and maintenance work (Hislop, 1999). As a result, he would have the knowledge to quickly and efficiently remove and dispose of any victims' bodies, without the need of driving in search of suitable body disposal sites. West even provided his skills to the Probation Service. Whilst being held on less serious charges, he built patios, and undertook renovation work for various members of staff:

> "…A senior probation source has claimed that staff used the evil builder for unofficial work on their own properties—before his killings came to light. The source said: 'Staff at the Birmingham hostel took a liking to West who was a short, affable man who was very good with his hands. He started doing odd jobs around the hostel building and became a bit of a joey—someone who is being held on charges but helps around the unit. But then staff began using him to do odd jobs around their own homes. At least three took him out to build patios at their houses" (Bourke, 2006).

It would seem that West gained extensive knowledge regarding the building and construction of properties, and that these acquired skills would ultimately be used to assist in his offending. At the heart of this "collision" between his occupation and subsequent offending lie the nine bodies that were buried at his home. These included that of their 16-year-old daughter Heather, found beneath the self-built garden patio ("Sadistic Couple's House of Horror; Murder by Numbers: How Dennis Nilsen Shared his Bed with Corpses plus the Story of UK's most Notorious Address", *Daily Star*, 2013; Henderson, 1995). In fact West was always making changes to his house. His workshop was crowded with tools, electric saws and drills, but instead of making improvements, the police now suspected that he was in fact using these tools and the knowledge gained by his occupation as a means to carefully hide the bodies of his victims (Quinn, 1994). For West, unlike Sutcliffe, Duffy and Mulcahy, and Black, whose occupations provided them with environmental cues and stimuli which subsequently influenced their offending behaviour, West's role as a builder provided him with direct "hands on" knowledge which was ultimately used in the commission of his offences.

"You Want a Lift"?

West too had "occupational camouflage". The account given by Felicity Nightingale regarding her encounter with him illustrates just how effective such camouflage can be regarding a perceived level of threat:

> "There was a slipway before the motorway started again and I noticed a blue van parked on it. The man leaning on it was looking over. 'you want a lift?' he asked, walking towards me…he certainly did not seem to have any sexual motive. So when he opened the back of the van again, I relented, throwing my rucksack inside. In retrospect, I think he was very clever at manipulating me" ("My ride with a serial killer", *The Guardian*, 2009).

Fortunately for Felicity she was able to get out of West's van before any criminal events could transpire. Similar to Robert Black, West was able to use his vehicle as a means to create an unthreatening persona that could potentially lure victims as opposed to having to take them by force. The nature of his occupation also provided further "camouflage" when attempting to dispose of his victims' bodies. In particular, as noted previously, West was observed by his neighbours as constantly making "improvements" to house when in fact he was using these times to conceal and hide his victims' remains (Quinn, 1994). For West, who made sure to ask his neighbours how they were and whether they had "any jobs needed doing" (Quinn, 1994), his occupation provided him the necessary "camouflage" to successfully spend considerable amounts of time ensuring that his victims' bodies would not be found without his neighbours giving him "a second glance" (Quinn, 1994).

Similar to handyman Peter Tobin (*Chapter Eleven*) , West also lacked some form of managerial control and supervision due to being self-employed (Sounes, 1995). Whilst it has been demonstrated that West was known to pick up young women that would be of a similar age and build as his known victims whilst driving his work van during the day, the majority of his confirmed offences were committed outside of his occupation and, as demonstrated by Caroline Roberts, at night (Dagnell, 2012). Further demonstrating the significance of committing murder with an accomplice, West is known to have searched for potential victims whilst in the company of his partner Rose (Newton, 2006). Whilst West held the occupational freedom to spend a significant amount of time with his victims after getting them into his home in Cromwell Street, his tendency to use Rose as a means to lure his unsuspecting victims may provide a rationale as to why he actively searched for targets away from his occupation (Masters 2011). Felicity Nightingale's account of being offered a lift by the, at the time, lone West in his work van sheds light as to why he may have relied upon the support of his partner, when initially approaching and seducing young women:

> "I'll give you a ride. Throw your rucksack in," he said, motioning to the empty space in the back of his van. I told him I'd rather have it in the front with me, but he replied: 'It's perfectly safe, don't worry.' I tried to insist but he kept repeating that I had nothing to worry about. He even started to get a bit angry. I began to think I should turn down his offer, but I hadn't mastered the art of refusing a lift—it felt rude to say no and I had been brought up to be polite" ('My ride with a serial killer', *The Guardian*, 2009).

It was evidently beneficial for West to have Rose with him as he searched for suitable victims. This is one aspect of his offending behaviour that he could not employ whilst engaged in his work-related activities and thus may provide a reason as to why, despite the lack of managerial oversight, he committed the majority of his known abductions outside of his employment.

CHAPTER TEN

The Wheel-Clamper

When we started dealing with him he came across as very jokey,
like he's your best mate. But he's a cunning individual, violent.
He can switch from being nice to being nasty, instantly.

Detective Chief Inspector Sutton on interviewing Levi Bellfield

Name: Levi Bellfield
Born: 17 May 1968
Location: Isleworth, London
No. of victims: 3
Victims: Young women
Motive: Sexually motivated
Offending period prior to arrest: Two years

Bellfield: Night Club Bouncer Turned Wheel Clamper

In comparison to other British serial murderers, who had extensive and varied occupational histories, Levi Bellfield only held a couple of recognisable and known jobs. He left school in 1984 with no qualifications, and seemed to have turned to petty crime in his youth in order to receive financial reward. According to Wansell (2011), this included providing drugs, such as cannabis and ecstasy to his associates; assaulting other young men who threatened his friends; and, stealing and selling cars (Wansell, 2011). Bellfield's first known official employment was as a nightclub bouncer for Rocky's nightclub, which was located in Cobham (McShane, 2011). He would subsequently increase the number of night-clubs and pubs for which he would provide security (Edwards, 2010). He would remain in this profession until 2000, when he set up his own wheel-clamping business (Wansell, 2011). Whilst Bellfield's busi-ness appeared on the surface to be legitimate, his history of engaging in criminal behaviour would play a significant part in how his wheel-clamping firm was operated:

> "Bellfield continued to expand his wheel-clamping business. He would clamp cars at random, and then tell the frightened motorist that they had parked illegally, when clearly they had not. It was a perfect scam for a man who was prepared to back up his lies with the threat of violence" (Wansell, 2001, p. 147).

Bellfield used his position as owner of the wheel-clamping firm to hire his own friends as employees ("Emotional scenes as Levi Bellfield is convicted of Milly's murder", *The Independent*, 2011). This occupa-tion was characterised by complete managerial control and oversight, which resulted in occupational freedom to engage in whatever activi-ties he desired. Whilst Bellfield can only be recognised as holding two forms of occupation prior to being arrested for his murders, there again appears to be in relation to Holland's model (*Chapter Four*), a consist-ency in relation to personality-type and selected job roles. For example, Bellfield's occupation as a nightclub bouncer, which would have involved tasks and activities pertaining to security, shares similarities to that group identified as "security guards" under the List of Occupations by RIASEC Interest Area (n.d.). So too, does his time working as a self-employed wheel-clamper shares characteristics with the group identified as "parking enforcement workers", due to the nature in which Bellfield targeted and clamped parked vehicles — albeit under predominantly unlawful pretences. Both these identified occupation groups outlined by the List of Occupations by RIASEC Interest Area (n.d.) fall under the interest area of the Realistic personality type.

From Petty Crime to Sexual Violence

At first glance Bellfield appears to only have a history of instrumentally-oriented crimes. For example, he was convicted of carrying an offensive weapon and committing a string of burglaries in his youth (Davies, 2011). However, if we look more closely at his behaviour prior to becoming a self-employed wheel clamper we can uncover a history of alleged sexual offences:

> "After his arrest...the Metropolitan police investigated about 20 other offences of alleged rape, druggings and assaults. Some of the rape charges lie on file. On the other charges there was insufficient evidence to prosecute" (Davies, 2011).

The majority of these alleged offences were committed whilst Belfield worked as a nightclub bouncer. Wansell (2011) notes that Bellfield would use his occupation and position at the various nightclubs in which he operated in order to target and seduce young women—often spiking their drinks to prevent them from changing their minds. Through these acts of the sexual exploitation of young women, Bellfield demonstrates his predilections to target teenage girls in an effort to quell his "sexual obsession" (Wansell, 2011, p. 89). Whilst his targeting of young women and teenagers provide a target template for his future murders, his relationships with his former partners also sheds light on the origins of aggressive behaviour in relation to his murders. Fricker (2011), for example, notes that Bellfield had a history of "beating, raping, and terrorising his partners". One of his former partners, Johanna Collings, describes one of her more violent experiences with him:

> "He beat me and forced my face over the pictures of blondes, shouting 'I fucking hate blondes, they should all fucking die', she said. 'He'd wrap his belt round my throat, choke me and rape me'" (Fricker, 2011).

Johanna would later describe how he would use a claw hammer when physically assaulting her — the same weapon that he used to attack and subsequently murder his victims (Manzoor, 2009). These aggressive and sexually-motivated criminal activities, along with his constant, unwavering, targeting and selection of young women, all of which fall within a similar age range of his future victims, again demonstrates how particular serial murderers not only have a propensity to be drawn to similar forms of occupation, but also a shared a history of sexual deviancy and violence.

Stalking London's Roads

Levi Bellfield, a night club bouncer and, by day, a wheel-clamper, committed his murders over a large geographical area whilst supposedly carrying out work-related activities. Thirteen-year old Milly Dowler, Bellfield's confirmed first victim, was last seen on CCTV leaving the railway station in Walton-on-Thames, Surrey, on 21 March 2002 (Twomey, 2008). Bellfield's second known victim, 19-year old Marsha McDonnell, was assaulted and subsequently died from her injuries sustained from a blunt instrument near her home in Hampton in February 2003 (Barton, 2008). Bellfield's third and final victim, 22-year old French student Amelie Delagrange, Was attacked in Twickenham Green on 19 August 2004 (Twomey, 2008). Wansell (2011) notes that Bellfield did not commit any of his known murders whilst working as a nightclub bouncer, but instead exclusively during the hours in which he was supposedly working as a self-employed, wheel-clamper. Wansell continued, noting how:

> "Bellfield's appetite for driving around West London at night looking for female prey hadn't dimmed. As his wheel-clamping business expanded, his search seemed to grow in intensity" (Wansell, 2011, p. 137).

Whilst Bellfield's nightclub occupation may have provided proximity to young women similar to those whom he attacked and murdered, this particular form of employment did not generate the necessary conditions prescribed by routine activity theory in order for a successful crime to occur. This particular occupation would be considered as being a busy "mode of activity" due to it being a place of recreation and "entertainment" (Brantingham and Brantingham, 2008). So too it would have been a part of many individuals' routine activities—including, among other demographs, young, single women. Specifically, due to the large volume of people that would enter the nightclub, along with Bellfield's colleagues, the probability of there being suitable guardians that could offer some form of protection would have increased, and subsequently been a deterrent for Bellfield.

Building upon the original routine activity theory presented, Eck (1994) generated the "problem analysis triangle". This triangle, which added an outer-layer to the initial routine activity triangle, examines how the presence, or absence, of components makes a crime either difficult or "feasible" (Felson, 2008, p. 74). A "handler", who is an individual who can exert some form of control over them, is often described as being either their parents, siblings, or spouse (Eck, 1994). With regards to their occupation, this control, it could be argued, could extend to supervisors and superiors. Within the confines of his role as a nightclub bouncer, Bellfield would have been under the supervision of a manager who would have made his ability to engage in his offending behaviour much more difficult than when undertaking his role as a wheel-clamper. Away from such pressures prescribed by Eck (1994), Bellfield was able to freely travel across a large geographical space and actively engage in offending without the fear of either a "handler" or the presence of capable guardians.

Similar to Scottish serial murderer Robert Black (*Chapter Seven*), Bellfield also used his access to large geographical space in order to dispose of one of his victim's body. Specifically, due to Bellfield reportedly living very close, "just 50 yards from where Milly was last seen alive" (Davies, 2011), he drove a considerable distance in order to physically remove any connection between himself and Milly:

> "The judge also noted that the applicant was familiar with, and had walked his dogs in the wood 25 miles away from Milly Dowler's home, where her remains were sadly found six months later after her body had been deposited in the position in which it was found following her disappearance" (Court Transcript, Court of Appeal, February, 2012).

This would be the only murder where Bellfield used a vehicle as a means to transport his victim's body after they had been murdered. Applying journey-to-crime principles, in which it is argued that offenders' probability to offend decreases the further they travel away from their home, it is reasonable to conclude that the rationale behind this decision was due to the relative proximity between Milly's abduction site and Bellfield's home. However, unlike Robert Black, Bellfield was operating from his place of residence and had no legitimate reason associated with his occupation to drive further than necessary. Given this much more confined space of activity in comparison to delivery van driver Black, Bellfield was still bound to the confines of his awareness and activity space, which was why a location he repeatedly visited was ultimately selected. Despite these factors, it still took the police nine years to successfully link Bellfield to Milly's murder.

Benefits of Being the Boss

Whilst Bellfield's occupation as a nightclub bouncer placed him within close proximity to young women similar to those whom he attacked and subsequently murdered, it was his job as a wheel-clamper that offered him the time to successfully murder. Specifically, unlike his duties as a bouncer where he would have been under some form of managerial oversight, Bellfield owned and managed his wheel-clamping business (Bell, 2011). Bellfield, who would often "go wheel-clamping during the day at a vast range of sites across West London and beyond" (Wansell, 2011, p. 182), had the managerial freedom to go where he wanted and to engage in behaviour that, if he had been under the supervision of others, would have been considered suspicious and a cause for concern. For example, on one occasion when he was wheel-clamping, it was noted that Bellfield resorted to violence by using a bat and knuckle-dusters that were hidden in the car (Wansell, 2011). On another occasion Bellfield engaged in inappropriate verbal behaviour whilst supposedly engaging in work-related activities:

> "Bellfield was driving along Staines Road and had just turned into Hospital Bridge Road when he suddenly told him, 'I want to talk to that slut' and

promptly stopped the car. He would wind the window down and shout abuse and obscenities at them" (Wansell, 2011, p. 113–114).

It is evident that Bellfield lacked much in the way of the managerial oversight of "handlers". Due to this "occupational freedom" he was afforded significant amounts of time to engage in his search for suitable victims. He also had ample opportunity to spend time with his victims, as demonstrated during the murder of Milly Dowler (Gammell and Hughes, 2011). With regard to his ability to spend a considerable amount of time seeking out suitable victims, Wansell observes that:

> "He started using [his van] not only for wheel-clamping, but also for his by now habitual nightly drives around West London and his old stomping grounds of Twickenham Green and Strawberry Hill" (Wansell, 2011, p. 184).

On another occasion it was reported that an individual who worked as part of Bellfield's wheel clamping crew was a witness to an attempted murder, with Bellfield telling his employee to "jump in the driving seat" (Wansell, 2011, p. 154) before fleeing the scene of the crime. This ability to engage in offending behaviour without fear of repercussions at an occupational level can also be demonstrated in the manner in which he abducted and subsequently murdered Milly Dowler, for example. Evidence was put forward in the Court of Appeal regarding Milly's murder and her connection to Bellfield:

> "…His strange behaviour in relation to the removal of bed sheets from the bed which he shared with his then partner at the address at which he had lived at the time when Milly Dowler was abducted" (Court Transcript, 8 February, 2012).

Here it becomes apparent that Bellfield, after abducting Milly during the day, took her back to his home prior to attacking and, more than likely, murdering her. Not only did the use of his work-related vehicle provide him the means to transport her quickly from the abduction site to his residence, a lack of managerial oversight allowed him to be able to successfully disengage with his ordinary day-to-day activities, and offend without the fear of the outside intrusion of a work superior.

The use of a vehicle proved to be essential in providing Bellfield with the necessary time needed in order to carry out a successful attack on his victims. This is perhaps best demonstrated by his attack on French student Amelie Delagrange, whom he followed in his vehicle prior to murdering her. The events leading up to her death were reconstructed at his trial. Brian Altman QC stated that:

> "Bellfield was driving the van and spotted Amelie at some point along the route and determined to engage her. There was more than enough time for him to wait for her in his van by the green, wait for her to catch up and, when she walked across the green, intercept and attack her …return to the van and drive off" (Wansell, 2011, p. 197).

In other words Bellfield's vehicle provided him with the means and time to plan and co-ordinate an attack, whilst also ensuring that he was able to quickly leave the scene of the crime — generating physical space between himself and his victim.

Occupation and Offending Collide

So too Bellfield's offending was closely intertwined with his occupation. His wheel-clamping, in comparison to the rather static role of a night-club bouncer, greatly expanded his activity space and, as a result, his awareness space. Due to this occupational requirement, Bellfield's first known murder, that of Milly Dowler, set the template for his subsequent murders. Specifically, Bellfield, who was supposedly engaging in tasks pertaining to his wheel-clamping business, used an absence of managerial control as a means to engage in offending behaviour. For example, Milly was last seen at a bus stop that is situated close to where Bellfield lived at the time ("His Name is Evil: Levi Bellfield", *The Mirror*, 2012; see also Wansell, 2011). Whilst this would be the only known case in which Bellfield abducted and murdered his victim during the day, other characteristics of this were replicated in all his subsequent murders and attacks. During a Court of Appeal hearing, it was noted that:

"He said that the Crown argued that the applicant had been convicted of two offences of murder and one of attempted murder in 2003 and 2004, each of which involved an attack on a lone young woman who had alighted from public transport, but with the additional feature that each of the offences took place in an area of West London bordering on Surrey with which the applicant was familiar and within which the offences involving Milly Dowler were committed" (Court Transcript, Court of Appeal, 8 February 2012).

This "expansion" in Bellfield's activity space appeared to intensify his "appetite" for offending (Wansell, 2011, p. 182). Similar to Robert Black, Bellfield appeared to identify and capitalise on criminal opportunities that were conveyed to him by his immediate environment, which was significantly altered and shaped by his decision to start a wheel-clamping business in 2000 (McShane, 2001). Bellfield's second victim, Marsha McDonnell, was attacked after she got off her bus from Kingston-upon-Thames (Moore, 2008); Kate Sheedy, Bellfield's third victim, who survived the attack, was hit by Bellfield's van after she noticed his vehicle following the bus she was on (Wansell, 2011); and Bellfield's final victim, Amelie Delagrange, was attacked after "she missed her stop after taking a bus home from an evening out with friends in the town" ("Bus stop killer's chain of violence", *BBC News*, 2008). Again reminiscent of Black, all of Bellfield's known murders occurred whilst he was working as a wheel-clamper, suggesting that he associated his opportunities to offend with his employment. This notion is further strengthened by the fact that Bellfield learnt to take advantage of his occupation with the ability to distance himself from his crimes. Bellfield also had access to a vast array of vehicles (Wansell, 2011). Similar to Fred West (*Chapter Nine*), who learnt to apply his occupationally-oriented skills to remove evidence, Bellfield used one of the key facets of his occupation as a means to obfuscate authorities and hinder their ability to identify the owner of the vehicles they were seeking. For example, Wansell notes:

"One of them was the silver hatchback Y57 RJU that Bellfield had purchased the previous November to use in his new clamping business. But that hadn't proved easy to track back to him as, significantly, and for no apparent reason, Bellfield had sold the Corsa on 11 February 2002, just a week after Marsha's murder" (Wansell, 2011, p. 143).

This ability to quickly buy and sell vehicles was evidently perceived by Bellfield as a significant advantage afforded to him with regard to evading the authorities—and Bellfield also sold the vehicles he used in his other murders (Wansell, 2011). For Bellfield, his occupation not only shaped his activity and awareness space to overlap with a greater number of criminal opportunities that subsequently "informed" him where to look for, and take advantage of such opportunities, it also provided him with the necessary tools to successfully obfuscate matters for police.

CHAPTER ELEVEN

The Handyman

You stand convicted of the truly evil abduction and murder of a vulnerable young girl in 1991 and thereafter of attempting to defeat the ends of justice in various ways over an extended period ... Yet again you have shown yourself to be unfit to live in a decent society.

Judge Lord Emslie upon sentencing Peter Tobin to life imprisonment

---

Name: Peter Tobin
Born: 27 August 1946
Location: Renfrewshire, Scotland, Margate, Kent, and Havant, Hampshire
No. of victims: Three
Victims: Young women
Motive: Sexually motivated
Offending period prior to arrest: 15 years.

Peter Tobin: The Mobile Handyman

Tobin worked as a mobile odd job labourer. He was a handyman by occupation (Cramb, 2008). He again offers a completely different perspective on the "geographically transient" serial murderer. Armed with the skills necessary to be a handyman, he is known to have used false names during particular jobs (Cacciottolo, 2009). This conscious decision to hide his true identity gives insight into the level of premeditation he engaged in before committing his crimes. In some respects, Tobin has more in common with George Smith than with some of the more contemporary examples such as Peter Sutcliffe or Robert Black. This is primarily due to the nature of his travels. Smith was an English serial killer and bigamist. In 1915 he was convicted and subsequently hanged for the slayings of three women, the case becoming known as the "Brides in the Bath Murders". The events leading up to each murder were the same: Smith would enter a relationship with his victim and would shortly marry them before drowning them in a bathtub in an effort to make it seem as if they had suffered a fatal and unfortunate accident. In following this pattern of offending, Smith would inherit their wealth shortly before moving to a new location and repeating this cycle of manipulation and eventual murder.

Like Smith, Tobin, as a result of his occupation, would frequently move from house-to-house (Tran, 2010) leaving a victim behind. This constant moving from one part of the country to another also ensured that he crossed multiple police force boundaries. This important issue is often present with geographically transient serial murderers, and can create "linkage blindness" (Gaines and Miller, 2007), discussed in greater detail later in this chapter.

A Checkered Past

At least five recognisable forms of occupation can be identified for Tobin. Born in 1946 in Johnstone, Renfrewshire in Scotland, Tobin was, according to Wier (2011), sent to an approved school as a result of his parents being unable to control his "difficult" behaviour. He appeared to also get in trouble with the authorities in his youth, and spent time in young offender institutions and various prisons for offences including burglary and forgery ("Was Peter Tobin Bible John?" *The Scotsman*, 2008; see also Wier, 2011). Little is known about Tobin's occupational history prior to his murder of Angelika Kluk. This is most likely due to the fact that he was using a series of fake names and aliases throughout his life and, in particular, upon release from prison for sexually assaulting two girls ("Was Peter Tobin Bible John?" *The Scotsman*, 2008). Whilst it has been reported that he had a series of various occupation throughout his life (Parsons, 2010), his use of approximately 40 false names and aliases (Cacciottolo, 2010) required the police to make a televised public appeal for information about him, and this has made it difficult to create an in-depth and accurate picture of his working history (Mathieson, 2008).

Tobin's first known employment was as a cook for a boarding house in Glasgow in the late-1960s (Mathieson, 2008) Thereafter, whilst living in Brighton, he ran and operated a "small café in the late 80s" (Evans, 2010). This did not last for long, as Tobin took up employment as a caretaker for a sea front hotel, in which he has since been linked to the unsolved missing persons case of Louise Kay. Louise was 18 at the time of her disappearance and lived close to the hotel where Tobin worked (O'Hare, 2010). At the time of both the murders of Vicky Hamilton and Dinah McNicol, Tobin was reported as working as both a "lagger", which consisted of "travel[ing] the country fitting insulation panels in buildings" ("Timeline: Peter Tobin", *BBC News*, 2009), and as an odd-job labourer, which again required him to travel across the UK in search of work (Addley, 2009). With regards to his last known murder, Tobin worked as an odd-job labourer and handyman for St Patrick's Church, Anderston, in Glasgow ("Tobin guilty of Angelika's murder", *BBC News*, 2007). It was reported that Tobin used a false name and alias during this period in an effort to conceal his criminal history ("Peter Tobin: Timeline of his life of crime", *The Telegraph*, 2009).

In comparison to other British serial murderers included in this book, who held relatively few occupations prior to being arrested, Tobin's employment history is, despite the difficulties posed due to his use of false names, varied and extensive. All of his occupations were within work environments related to one particular personality-type according to Holland's model (*Chapter Four*). In particular, and in relation to the List of Occupations by RIASEC Interest Area (n.d.), Tobin's time working as a cook; his time as a café owner; caretaker; lagger; and finally odd-job labourer are all occupations that fall within the interest area of the Realistic personality-type.

A History of Sexual Violence

In examining Tobin's offending history, he appeared to start with instrumental crimes with the hope of gaining some form of material or financial gain before moving to more expressive and violent forms of offences. At the age of seven, Tobin was sent to a reform school due to being difficult to control (Addley, 2009). On leaving there he is known to have spent some time at a young offender institution ("Sex killer Tobin's violent past", *BBC News*, 2007), and was later charged with a series of robberies and burglaries ("Was Peter Tobin Bible John?" *The Scotsman*, 2008). Whilst it would be a number of years before Tobin was charged with any sex-related offences, his former partners informed the police after his arrest about his violent and aggressive behaviour towards them. Tobin's former partner, Cathy Wilson, for example, remembered:

> "Of course, that didn't stop him threatening me, imprisoning me, hitting me, abusing me and even promising that he would kill our son if I tried to leave but it did give me enough time to work out how to get away. Even so, I do sometimes think that I shouldn't really be alive today" (Stonehouse, 2011).

Mega (2009) interviewed two of Tobin's ex partners — Cathy Wilson and Margaret Mackintosh. They both revealed that he was not only physically violent towards them, but also forced them to perform "depraved" sexual acts. A 22-year-old Tobin, upon meeting 17-year-old Margaret Mackintosh, raped and beat her (Levy, 2009) — demonstrating similar behaviour that characterised his later offences. As demonstrated through his past behaviour towards these women, it is evident that Tobin had a history of violence and sexual aggression towards women, and that his occupation as an odd-job labourer provided him with close proximity to suitable targets and the managerial freedom to act upon his criminal tendencies expressed through his previous criminal actions.

In 1993, Tobin sexually assaulted two 14-year-old girls at his flat situated in Leigh Park, Havant. The girls asked Tobin if they could wait in his flat for his neighbour to return home, and it was during this time he made them drink cider and vodka at knifepoint, before proceeding to rape both girls and stabbing one of them. He then turned on the gas taps in his flat in an effort to ensure both girls died, and took his young son who was present during this time. He then moved to Coventry under a fake name in order to avoid being identified, but was ultimately apprehended in Brighton when his car was. Tobin ultimately served ten years in prison for this offence, and was released in 2004. This particular incident again further reinforces Tobin's history of sexually-oriented violence, and continues to build his crime template for future offences.

No analysis into Tobin's past would be complete without addressing the often-raised question as to whether he was in fact the infamous and never apprehended "Bible John" serial murderer. "Bible John", the nickname given to a suspected serial murderer, is thought to have attacked and killed three young women in Glasgow between 1968 and 1969 after meeting each of them at the Barrowland Ballroom. Nearly 50 years have passed since this killing spree, and the offender has never been identified, although some eminent criminologists, including Professor David Wilson, believe it is in fact Tobin who was responsible.

On 23 February 1968, 25-year-old Patricia Docker, as nurse, was found in a lane behind Carmichael Place, Glasgow. The victim's clothes and possessions, including her purse, had been removed. Upon further inspection by the police, it was determined that Patricia was raped, and was murdered by way of strangulation. It was believed by the police that Patricia had in fact met her attacker at the Barrowland Ballroom the previous night, where it was hosting an over-25s night.

Nearly six months passed before "Bible John" would strike again. On Monday, 18 August 1969, 32-year-old mother of three Jemima McDonald was found beaten, raped, and strangled to death in an old tenement building on MacKeith Street. Whilst the modus operandi of the perpetrator was similar to that of Patricia's, Jemima was found fully-clothed. Despite this difference, it was soon revealed that Jemima, similar to Patricia, had in fact visited the same ballroom the previous Friday.

Approximately three months passed before the third and final victim, 29-year-old Helen Puttock, was found murdered in Earl Street in Scotstoun. It was revealed that she too visited the Barrowland Ballroom on the night she was murdered. Helen, along with her sister, Jean, met two men, both called John, at the ballroom the night she was murdered. After spending the night with them at the ballroom, one of the men left to go home whilst the "other John" remained with Helen and her sister. Upon leaving the ballroom, they shared a taxi to Knightswood where Jean happened to live. When interviewed by the police, Jean informed them that the man often quoted passages from the Bible, resulting in the media nicknaming the suspect "Bible John". Jean also revealed that, upon arriving home, the taxi continued on with her sister and John still inside. Helen was later found in her back garden, having been raped and strangled — her handbag was also missing.

Despite the high-profile investigation for the unknown serial rapist and murderer, the case ultimately went cold due to a lack of evidence and leads. As the years passed, various suspects were linked to the "Bible John" murders but resulted in little other than the occasional newspaper headline. This changed, though, upon the trial and subsequent conviction of Peter Tobin for the murder of Angelika Kluk in 2007. David Wilson highlighted shortly after Tobin's conviction that he noticed parallels between Tobin's murders and those of Bible John, namely that Tobin was quite old for a recently-convicted serial murderer. As he noted, murder is usually a "young man's business" ("A life of crime: Professor David Wilson — trying to understand why serial killers kill", *The Scotsman*, 2010). Wilson also drew attention to the careful hiding of Angelika's body, along with his ability to quickly move a great distance from the murder site, as signs of experience in the commission of murder. Along with this information, as previously discussed, Tobin's former partners also revealed the serial murderer's propensity towards raping and physically assaulting them. Tobin had even met his first wife at the very ballroom where all the "Bible John" victims met their attacker; before leaving Glasgow in 1969 shortly after the last victim, Helen, was murdered.

Despite the striking parallels between Tobin's known murders and those of "Bible John", along with the fact that Tobin indeed frequented the same ballroom the victims visited prior to be murdered, there is still no definitive evidence that Tobin is responsible for these crimes. As it stands, the only person who can ever prove that he is responsible for these unsolved murders is Tobin himself, who is likely to take such secrets to his grave. Regardless of whether Tobin is in fact "Bible John", the fact that he used fake aliases, along with his continual movement across the country in a supposed effort to find work, raises important questions into the history of Tobin prior to his arrest for the murder of Angelika Kluk. What cannot be contested, though, is that Tobin clearly exhibited behaviour involving sexually-oriented violence towards both his former partners and his known victims prior to murdering them.

Hunting for Opportunities

Tobin appeared to have the ability to move from one part of the country after committing an offence on the pretence that he was following work-related opportunities. In particular, Tobin, who "lived in several places, including Glasgow, Brighton, East Sussex, Margate, Kent, and Havant, Hampshire" (Tran, 2010), did not raise any initial suspicion when moving from one residence to another, even after the family who moved into his former home "noticed a 'pungent' smell which would not go away" ("Peter Tobin 'buried teenage victim at suburban house'", *The Telegraph*, 2009). Tobin, after murdering Vicky Hamilton in Bathgate, quickly moved to Margate and transported her body to be buried in the garden of his new home. This was again masked under the assumption that the move was due to work opportunities, as was his nature to "flit from one temporary job to another" (Day et al, 2007). Whilst Tobin's profession provided him with a legitimate reason to constantly move from one location to another, the nature of his work, similar to that of Fred West (*Chapter Nine*), further provided him with "occupational camouflage" when disposing of his victims' bodies. For example, he was able to dig up areas of his garden in an effort to dispose of both Vicky's and Dinah's bodies. In this way his profession aided in reducing suspicion as he built a sandpit and patio over their respective bodies (Day et al, 2007; Chapman, 2009).

Tobin's third victim was Angelika Kluk. His profession again provided him with the necessary proximity and validity to attack and murder her. For example, as noted by Elias (2006), Tobin had in fact spent the day with Angelika painting a garage at St Patrick's Church, Glasgow, where he had been employed. Tobin's profession as a handyman, similar to that of Peter Sutcliffe and Robert Black, appeared to place him closely to his ideal victim-type — young women — without raising any initial fears or concerns for their safety. This reinforces the significance of how an occupation can provide such offenders with validity and access in relation to being close to their victims. This is further demonstrated by examining those serial murderers that lacked employment, in which the offending period was, on average, less than those of serial murderers that had some form of legitimate employment. For example, unemployed serial murderers such as Donald Neilson; Patrick Mackay; and, Colin Ireland were all apprehended within the space of a year. This is in stark contrast to Sutcliffe (five years); Black (five years); and Tobin, who committed his known offences over a 15-year period. With reference to routine activity theory, it is apparent that these unemployed serial murderers needed to actively and "artificially" create the circumstances for a successful crime to occur. In illustrating this point, it can be noted how Tobin was working alongside and conversing with Angelika prior to murdering her. This is in stark contrast to the case of Mackay, who had to physically break into his victims' homes to gain proximity and access. This reinforces the differences between those British serial murderers who lacked employment or whose occupations did not place them within the proximity of their ideal victims, in that Tobin's profession provided him with the necessary conditions prescribed by routine activity theory, without being perceived as an initial threat, or danger to his victim.

Similar to Scottish serial murderer Robert Black, Tobin used his occupation as an odd-job labourer in order to circumscribe the conditions set by the theory known as journey-to-crime. As already described in this book, this theory argues that crimes are more likely to take place closer to an offender's home and follow a distance-decay function, with the probability that a crime occurring lessens the further away an offender is from their home base or "anchor point". Further to this, there is a "buffer zone" between the offender's home and the space in which they commit their crimes — this space is often avoided by offenders in an effort to not draw attention to themselves and their home. With regard to Tobin, he was able to both murder Angelika within the location in which he worked, and also take his other known victims to his home or "anchor point". This was achieved by Tobin using his guise as a labourer in order to bury Angelika within the church where they both worked (Brocklehurst, 2013), and to bury both Vicky Hamilton and Dinah McNicol in his garden at his home in Margate (Wright and Kelly, 2010). Due to both the skills and requirements of his occupation, Tobin was able to select and abduct victims far from his home, or "anchor point", whilst also being able to commit crimes closer to home or his actual work site—with the knowledge that he was able to hide their bodies after murdering them.

Perks of the Job

Tobin worked for a variety of different individuals at numerous locations ("Is this Peter Tobin, the UK's worst ever serial killer?" *The Mirror*, 2010), and lacked any consistent form of managerial control and oversight. This lack is an important factor in thinking about the nature of two of Tobin's murders. Specifically, with reference to the abduction and murders of Vicky Hamilton and Dinah McNicol, both of their bodies were found buried in Tobin's garden at his home in Margate (Evans, 2009). After identifying them, pathologists were able to use the conditions of their remains as a means to re-construct the immediate events leading up to, and after their deaths:

> "She [Vicky Hamilton] was waiting for a bus in the town centre to take her home to her mother in Redding, Stirlingshire...Tobin preyed on her nervousness and lured her to his home...He drugged her with the sedative Amitriptyline, strangled her, carried out a serious sex attack and murdered her. Tobin then tried to cover his tracks by hiding Vicky's body and getting rid of some of her clothing and belongings. He cut her body in two, wrapped it in a curtain and bin bags, and stashed the knife in his loft. Tobin left the schoolgirl's purse near Edinburgh's main railway and bus stations to fool police into thinking she had run away from home" ("Peter Tobin convicted of third murder: Vicky Hamilton his first victim", *The Telegraph*, 2009).

Here we should note that Tobin was afforded considerable time both by way of his occupation and by his vehicle. This latter issue again demonstrates the unique time-saving advantage of being able to flee the scene of the abduction site quickly, and in providing the offender with the ability to find a suitable location to continue their offending behaviour. This ability to offend over an extended period of time is further enhanced by a lack of managerial control or oversight. Due to these factors, Tobin was able to spend a considerable amount of time assaulting Vicky prior to murdering her. He was also able to plan and execute the removal of evidence, including the burial of her body, in meticulous detail—all apparently without raising any suspicions as to his whereabouts or behaviour ("Vicky Hamilton murder: How police closed the net on Peter Tobin", *The Guardian*, 2008).

A Skill for Murder

For handyman Tobin, whose occupation took him all over across the UK, the knowledge that he gained through the nature of his employment was eventually incorporated into his offending behaviour. Tobin's occupation consisted of "a number of jobs, including painter and decorator, manual labourer and carpenter" (Bell, 2009). These various labour-oriented occupations afforded him a specific skill set that provided a means for him to bury his victims at his various homes. Tobin used these skills in each of his consecutive murders, with Detective Superintendent David Swindle of Strathclyde police noting that "he [Tobin] is determined to conceal the bodies of his victims, sometimes burying them very far down" (Townsend, 2009). It was not simply a matter of concealing the victims' bodies, Tobin actually applied occupational knowledge and the skills of his trade to ensure that they were difficult to find and recover:

> "Her body was discovered two years ago, bound and gagged, wrapped in 16 heavy-duty refuse bags and buried under concrete in the garden of Tobin's former home in Margate, Kent. A few metres away, cut in two and also wrapped in bin bags, was the corpse of Vicky Hamilton, 15, whom Tobin had abducted, raped and murdered in Bathgate, West Lothian, in February 1991" (Townsend, 2009).

Of particular interest is the case of Vicky Hamilton, as Tobin constructed a sand pit on top of the area of land in which she was buried, (Day et al, 2007). With both the murder of Vicky and Dinah, he was able to use his occupationally-oriented skills to successfully kill and conceal his victims' bodies. So effective was Tobin's ability to dig up, bury, and subsequently build over the areas of his garden where he disposed of his victims' remains, that he was able to avoid suspicion or concern from his partner at the time who was, along with their children, living in the same residence. Nicola Downing, Tobin's former partner, was reported at stating, "We lived in the house for 12-years and had a happy family home. What they have found is awful; it has turned our family upside down" (Day et al, 2007).

Whilst the murder of Angelika Kluk presents a change for Tobin with regard to attacking and murdering a young woman away from the confines of his own home, his skills as a labourer are still apparent. After murdering Angelika, he buried her body although this time beneath the floorboards of the church where he was working (Townsend, 2009). Again, whilst Angelika's murder presented a change in modus operandi for Tobin, his efficiency at labour-oriented tasks meant that it was not "until five days later that her battered body was discovered underneath the pews" (Elias, 2007). Again, this demonstrates how, with regard to Tobin, his respective occupations in fact provided him with a skill set that subsequently leaks through his every-day work-related activities and into the more sinister realm of serial murder.

A Convenient Lie

Tobin's ability to move from one part of the country after committing an offence on the pretence that he was following work-related opportunities afforded the Scottish serial murderer with an occupational "camouflage" of sorts. In particular, Tobin, who "lived in several towns and cities, including Glasgow, Brighton, East Sussex, Margate, Kent, and Havant, Hampshire" (Tran, 2010), did not raise any initial suspicion when moving from one residence to another, even after the family who moved into his former home "noticed a 'pungent' smell which would not go away" ("Peter Tobin 'buried teenage victim at suburban house'", *The Telegraph*,

2009). Tobin, after murdering Vicky Hamilton in Bathgate, quickly moved to Margate and transported her body to be buried in the garden of his new home. This was again masked under the assumption that the move was due to work opportunities, as was his nature to "flit from one temporary job to another" (Day et al, 2007). Whilst Tobin's profession provided him with a legitimate reason to constantly move from one location to another, the nature of his work further provided him with "occupational camouflage" when disposing of his victims' bodies. For example, he was able to dig up areas of his garden in an effort to dispose of both Vicky's and Dinah's remains. In this way his profession aided in reducing suspicion as he built a sandpit and patio over their respective bodies (Day et al, 2007; Chapman, 2009) as it did with relation to his third victim Angelika Kluk.

On the Job, On the Hunt

Tobin held a similar form of occupation to odd-job labourer Fred West, and also had a penchant for targeting victims within a similar age range. Both Tobin and West would have also had a comparable amount of occupational freedom due to the nature of their jobs—self-employed labourers who regularly changed clientele. Despite these similarities, though, Tobin tended to commit his offences whilst also supposedly carrying out his work-related duties. This would seem to have been the result of a lack of an offending accomplice or "partner", such as wife Rosemary for West. This may explain why Tobin attacked and murdered Angelika Kluk whilst also providing his labouring services to the church where they both worked (Brocklehurst, 2013). In relation to routine activity theory, Tobin, an already motivated offender who had murdered twice before, was put in close proximity to a suitable victim due to his occupation and, his victim lacked any form of protection. Tobin, unconstrained by the use of an accomplice, was able to take immediate advantage of this proximity whereas, for example, West may have hesitated whilst engaging in work-related duties due to the lack of his offending partner being present (as described in *Chapter Nine*).

Tobin also appeared to avoid sex workers, and to be drawn towards young, isolated women. With this in mind, he may have struggled to find a suitable target outside of his work related activities and especially at night. This is reinforced by the fact that all three of Tobin's victims were either abducted or murdered during the day (Cramb, 2008; see also Addley, 2007). Whilst the full details behind the abductions of Vicky and Dinah are unknown, it was revealed that both had traces of the drug Amitriptyline, which causes drowsiness (Taylor, 2010). The use of such a drug not only seemed to incapacitate them, but also suggests that Tobin planned to spend a considerable amount of time with them prior to murdering them. Indeed all three of his victims were sexually assaulted (Evans, 2009). This further reinforces the potential influence of holding a transient occupation with very little or no managerial control in that offenders such as delivery driver Robert Black and Tobin were able to not only abduct and kill their victims whilst carrying out work related duties, but also to spend a considerable amount of time with them prior to killing them. Here we can reference rational choice theory, which argues that individuals weigh up the cost to benefit ratio of engaging in criminal behaviour, in order to rationalise these findings. Tobin's occupation combined with factors such as access to a large geographical space, managerial freedom, and, in relation to the murder of Angelika Kluk, proximity to his preferred victim-type, may have created an increased benefit to risk ratio to commit such a crime whilst supposedly also engaged in work-related activities.

CHAPTER TWELVE

The Forklift Truck Driver

He had an ability to have a violent row one minute and then have a calm conversation with you straight afterwards, as if nothing had happened. The only way I can describe it is to say he was a real Jekyll and Hyde character. He definitely had a psycho side to him.

Elizabeth Roche, neighbour to Steve Wright

Name: Steven Gerald James Wright
Dubbed by the Media: Suffolk Strangler
Born: 24 April 1958
Location: Suffolk
No of victims: five confirmed
Victims: Sex workers
Motive: Sexually motivated
Offending period prior to arrest: 3 months

The "Suffolk Strangler"

Steve Wright brings us to one of the more contemporary British serial murderers who held some form of transient dependent occupation. Wright, while committing his crimes almost 30 years after Peter Sutcliffe ("the Yorkshire Ripper"), also targeted sex workers but was apprehended within the space of three months—a much shorter period than Sutcliffe's five year period of offending prior to being caught by the police. Why was Wright, a serial murderer who held a transient occupation and who targeted the same type of victim that Sutcliffe did get caught so much sooner than the Yorkshire Ripper? While it may be sensible to assume that Wright was perhaps less organized and forensically aware than Sutcliffe, he was in fact very aware of police procedures and worked hard to create distance between himself and his crimes. In fact, Wright was so forensically aware that he placed a number of his victims in water in an effort to remove any traces of forensic evidence—exhibiting signs of a well organized and intelligent serial murderer. There were ultimately two important factors that lead to his apprehension in the space of three months. First, Wright, whilst displaying signs of forensic awareness, appeared to grow in confidence very quickly and soon preferred to lay his victims in the woods surrounding Ipswich and display them in a crucifix position. While it has been argued that he positioned his victims in such a position in an effort to mask the true motivations behind his crimes and cause the police to pursue inaccurate leads, this change in modus operandi would ultimately result in the preservation of more forensic evidence. Second, the collecting and subsequent analysis of forensic evidence has significantly improved since the time of the Yorkshire Ripper, with the authorities having access to "new techniques allowing microscopic fibres to be identified" (Addley, et al, 2008) during the course of the Suffolk Strangler investigation. With access to such investigative tools and a serial murderer who grew in confidence over a very short period of time, Wright was ultimately apprehended through the finding of forensic evidence that linked one of his victims, sex worker and drug addict Tania Nicol, to his vehicle. Whilst these two factors were important in his quick apprehension, Wright also held a transient dependent occupation that differs in some interesting ways to the other serial murderers so far presented. With this in mind, this chapter attempts to determine just how much Wright's occupation impacted upon his offending, and whether, despite these difference in occupation, his profession still afforded him some instrumental advantages.

Occupational History

Steve Wright, similar to handyman Peter Tobin (*Chapter Eleven*), had an extensive and varied occupational history, which would see him regularly change employment and work environments. Described by friends as being quiet and socially awkward, Wright was also noted as being 'a bit unlucky when it came to finding and holding down a decent job' (O'Neill, 2008). Wright's childhood was characterised by instability due to his father's occupation as an RAF policeman. He left school at an early age and without any formal qualifications (McVeigh, 2008). He joined the merchant navy shortly afterwards, and worked as a chef (Allen and Rayner, 2008). He would remain in this profession for a number of years (Malkin, 2008) before leaving to become a steward on the *Queen Elizabeth II* ocean liner (QE2). This profession would take him all over the world, including such locations as New York, the Everglades, Los Angeles, Australia, New Zealand, Singapore, the Seychelles and South Africa ("The ex-wife's story: My violent life with the Suffolk strangler — and his flirtation on the QE2 with Suzy Lamplugh", *London Evening Standard*, 2008). His time serving on the QE2 was also marked by his propensity to visit local brothels in search of sex workers whilst on shore leave ('Suffolk Murders 2006', *BBC News*, 2008):

> "He went back to sea, working on the QE2 where, he admitted in court, he first acquired his taste for prostitutes, visiting massage parlours in various ports whenever he 'got the urge'" (Allen and Rayner, 2008).

Wright ultimately spent six years working as a steward on the QE2 prior to taking employment managing a pub. Whilst working on the QE2, he courted and subsequently married window dresser Diane Cassell as he was notified that to manage the pub he would have to be married ('The ex-wife's story: My violent life with the Suffolk strangler — and his flirtation on the QE2 with Suzy Lamplugh', *London Evening Standard*, 2008). The marriage, though, did not last long, with Diane leaving Wright within a year (Williams and Greenhill, 2008). As a result, his tenancy ran out and he subsequently ended up working at two different pubs: the *White Horse* in Kent; and the *Rose and Crown* in South-east

London. He also worked briefly as a barman at a hotel (McVeigh, 2008). He was eventually convicted of stealing £80 from the cash register at the hotel in which he worked at, which resulted in him signing up for "driving and labouring jobs with Gateway Recruitment Agency" (McVeigh, 2008). During this period Wright is known to have worked as both a lorry driver and, more importantly, a forklift truck driver — the profession that he held whilst he committed his known murders (O'Neill and Bird, 2006).

Again, similar to Tobin, Wright's occupational history may appear to be varied but, in relation to Holland's model (*Chapter Four*), all of these individual work environments fall under the interest area of one particular personality-type. In particular, Wright's profession as a chef for the Merchant Navy; a steward on the QE2; various bartender positions; lorry driver; and forklift truck driver are all noted by the List of Occupations by RIASEC Interest Area (n.d.) as work environments that are of "primary interest " to individuals with the Realistic personality type.

Setting the Template for Murder

As demonstrated by those British serial murderers so far presented who held some form of transient-oriented or dependent professions, all had histories of engaging in some form of sexually-oriented offending behaviour prior to gaining the professions they held whilst committing their murders. Wright, on the other hand, does not appear to be associated with any sexual or physical assaults prior to committing his known murders. Despite this, during his time working as a steward on cruises, he was known to be a frequent visitor to the red light districts of the various countries he visited ("Suffolk Murders 2006", *BBC News*, 2008). On one occasion, for example, he was filmed inside a bar in Thailand in the company of sex workers (Williams and Greenhill, 2008). Wright's propensity to seek out women for sex was not limited to his time working as a steward. A former sex worker, for example, stated that he was her first customer, eight years prior to him committing murder (Bulstrode, 2012). Similar to Duffy and Tobin, Wright also demonstrated aggressive behaviour towards his former partners. Whilst Pam Wright, his partner at the time of the murders, does not recall any violent behaviour towards her, Diane Cole, Wright's former partner, outlined in detail some of the aggressive and violent behaviour that he displayed whilst they were together:

> "[He] wrote 'slag' and 'whore' on her door, slashed her clothes to pieces and then attacked her with a knife when he thought she was with another man. Repeatedly banged her head against a wall—for folding bed sheets the wrong way. Battered her senseless, punching and kicking her when their four-year relationship came to an end" (Armstrong and McGurran, 2008).

Whilst Wright may only have been charged for more instrumental crimes, such as the stealing money from a cash register, it is apparent that he had a penchant to target red light districts and, as demonstrated by his former partner, showed violent behaviour towards women. Again, these past behaviours and actions towards women would appear to form the basis for Wright's crime template in relation to those murders that he committed whilst employed as a forklift truck driver.

Smaller Hunting Grounds

Fork-lift driver Steve Wright shares many similarities with Peter Sutcliffe—namely that, whilst their professions required them to use vehicles, they instead chose to commit their known offences outside of their typical working hours, and used their own vehicles. With regard to Wright, the use of a vehicle was vital in his ability to dispose of his victim's bodies. Specifically, the use of a vehicle was essential for Wright to travel to, and gain access, to "remote spots" (McVeigh, 2008)—where he would subsequently dispose of his victims' bodies. In comparison to Robert Black, Wright was not able to travel a considerable distance in order to generate "linkage blindness". Instead he used his vehicle as a means to reach isolated locations where there was minimal risk regarding the presence of witnesses or capable guardians, and also offered opportunities to remove potential forensic evidence. For example, with reference to the murders of Tania Nicol and Gemma Adams, both were placed in Belstead Brook, South-west of Ipswich (Addley and McVeigh, 2008). Placing their bodies in water assisted in the removal of potentially damning forensic evidence and made it difficult for the police to initially find and identify their bodies.

> "Tania was last seen on the evening of Monday October 30…Five and a half weeks passed between Nicol's disappearance and the discovery of her body, on December 8, trapped in debris in Belstead Brook" (Addley and McVeigh, 2008).

Again, whilst Wright did not travel particularly far from the abduction sites of his victims to their disposal locations, his knowledge of the area, along with the use of a vehicle, provided him the means to both physically and temporally remove himself from those murdered individuals. With regard to his remaining three victims, they were all found in secluded locations around the outskirts of Ipswich—but were not placed in water (O'Neil, 2008). Instead, it was reported that Wright placed two of his victims, Anneli Alderton and Annette Nicholls, in isolated areas and they "were found arranged with their arms outstretched in a crucifix pose" ("Suffolk Murders 2006", *BBC News*, 2008). Whilst the reason as to why Wright changed his methods in disposing of his victims' bodies is not known, what can be observed is that, due to his access to a larger geographical space, he was afforded more time in order to engage in behaviour pertaining to his offending—a theme that will be discussed in more detail later.

Setting the (Crime) Scene

Like Sutcliffe, Wright targeted sex workers whilst not engaged in work-related duties. After all, Wright's role as a forklift truck driver would have seen him employed within a confined space over an extended period of time. So too, it is interesting that he often alternated between the storage facilities in which he operated as a forklift truck operator (McVeigh, 2008). This was primarily a result of Wright "sign[ing] on for driving and labouring jobs with Gateway Recruitment Agency, first based in Levington, Suffolk, and then in Nacton" (McVeigh, 2008). Taking this into consideration, Wright would have been under the supervision of a variety of employers who required the skills of a forklift truck operator.

Such work would also result in him operating a vehicle within a relatively small and confined geographical area. Thus, whilst the nature of his occupation did not grant him flexibility and, as a result, time to offend, the use of his vehicle still afforded him the more immediate instrumental advantage of time.

All of this is perhaps best demonstrated in the manner in which a number of Wright's victims were found, and in the quantity of DNA that was discovered in his car and home. For example, in the case of victims Anneli Alderton and Annette Nicholls, both women were found in isolated woodland areas and posed in a crucifix position ("Suffolk Murders 2006", *BBC News*, 2008). Due to using a vehicle, necessary because of his constantly changing work location, Wright was able to ensure that he could spend more time with the victims' bodies after killing them. Whilst the reasoning for placing two of his victims in such a position has yet to be determined, what is apparent is Wright's ability to access isolated areas to dispose of his victims' bodies. Here we should note that, in one case, the disposal site was closely situated by the work agency he visited (McVeigh, 2008). Time afforded Wright the opportunity to not only physically remove himself from the victim, but to also leave them exactly how he wanted them to be found. Like Sutcliffe, Wright used this time to examine whether there was any obvious forensic evidence that may have linked him to the victim, with Wright "wash[ing] and vacuum[ing] his car afterwards to remove evidence" (Allen and Rayner, 2008). It has also been suggested that Wright spent a great deal of time with his victim prior to disposing of their bodies. At his trial, forensic scientist Peter Hau has suggested:

> "...there were 'extensive' samples of Steve Wright's DNA, unlikely to have come from 'casual contact', on the bodies of Paula Clennell, Anneli Alderton and Annette Nicholls. 'I would say it would be more likely to be a prolonged physical contact,' said Hau" (Siddique, 2008).

Similar to West and Tobin, Wright is known to have brought his victims back to his home, and, in some cases, engaged in sexual intercourse with them prior to murdering them (McVeigh, 2008). Again, the instrumental benefit of using a vehicle afforded these offenders the necessary time to fully engage in their offending behaviour without fear of being caught or interrupted.

From being able to travel to remote and far-reaching locations, to spending a considerable amount of time with his victims, Wright's occupation and, more importantly, use of a vehicle during the course of his offending provided him with significant "freedom behind the wheel".

Hidden Intentions

In comparison to delivery driver Robert Black and lorry driver Peter Sutcliffe, Wright had a much smaller activity and awareness space. This appears to be primarily due to Wright, whilst operating a fork-lift truck, working within an enclosed location as opposed to the relative freedom afforded to other transient serial murderers. This, it would appear, prevented Wright from taking advantage of the "occupational camouflage" to the same degree as the other serial murderers presented in this book. For example, he would have been unable to drive his fork-lift truck in the same manner as Black drove his van, who was able to successfully hunt for potential victims whilst giving the impression he was simply a van driver who was either on his way or returning from making deliveries. Further to this, even if Wright was indeed able to move his forklift from the enclosed spaces he worked within to the road, he would not have been able to have abducted his victims in the same way that Black was capable of doing. Another important factor to consider is that both serial murderers targeted very different victims, albeit while for similar sexually-oriented reasons, and this would have been another factor that would have impacted upon Wright's ability to fully take advantage of his "occupational camouflage". For Black, who targeted young girls, his ability to use the space afforded to him in the back of his delivery van would have been that much easier while for forklift truck driver Wright, both his victim preference and work vehicle would require this serial murderer to adopt different offending strategies and techniques. For example, despite these occupation restrictions, Wright's profession still provided him a form of "concealment" with regard to his partner at the time, who had no suspicions about what Wright was doing. Pam Wright remembered:

> "What is startling about the portrait she paints of him is his ability to switch seamlessly from a life of cosy domesticity to frenzied killing, and casually back again. 'On the nights the girls were murdered he would come home from work as normal, have a shower and change into his jogging bottoms, polo shirt and fluffy brown slippers,' says Pam…he'd slip on a pair of trainers without socks, put on his coat and drive me to work. 'After he dropped me off he didn't go home but, as I now know, went looking for prostitutes to have sex with and then kill'" (Gallagher, 2008).

Wright's former partner's account of his day-to-day behaviour, shaped by his employment, presents a sense of normality and familiarity that prevented those close to him from ever suspecting his behaviour during the period in which he murdered his victims. Pam Wright also noted that she would regularly phone Wright at 4.30 am whilst she was at work to ensure that he was awake for his job, again reducing any initial suspicion that she may have had during the time in which he committed his murders. So, whilst Wright was unable to effectively "hide in plain sight" in the same way, for example, as Black, his status in holding employment shaped how those close to him perceived him, and raised him "above suspicion". This instrumental advantage highlights how significant holding an occupation can be for an individual committing multiple acts of murder and, more importantly, how occupations that may appear similar on the surface in fact impact upon these serial murderer's offending behaviour in various ways. While Wright may not have had the same level of managerial freedom or geographical mobility afforded to other serial murderers who held transient dependent occupations, his job assisted in creating a sense of normality and, as demonstrated by his former partner, routine that prevented others from initially suspecting or discovering his night time activities.

CHAPTER THIRTEEN

The Transient Serial Murderer: A New Perspective

*If there is such a thing as an ideal profession for a serial
killer, it may well be as a long-haul truck driver.*

The Federal Bureau of Investigation

The preceding six chapters have acted as case studies of sorts, intricately each exploring a known British serial murderer, and their respective offences, who held a transient dependent occupation. An array of instrumental advantages afforded to these offenders emerged, along with other, more psychological factors that may assist in better understanding this unique form of serial murder. This chapter seeks to summarise the key themes that emerged across these case studies, before exploring the significance of this form of occupation to other professions, or lack thereof, held by British serial murderers. Such information will not only assist in better understanding transient serial murder, but also the phenomenon of this unique form of crime more generally — and, from a law enforcement perspective, may assist in the apprehension of such offenders.

Instrumental Advantages

As demonstrated in the preceding six chapters, it has been suggested that those serial murderers who held occupations that were transient in nature were afforded a number of instrumental advantages that assisted in their offending. In saying this, we refer to how their occupation and,

by extension their use of vehicles, assisted them in successfully committing numerous murders before eventually being apprehended by the
authorities. These instrumental, or practical, advantages afforded to these
particular British serial murderers come in a variety of forms, and some
are more readily apparent than others—though each is evidently important in the successful commission of serial murder. So, similar to how
Dr Harold Shipman and nurse Beverley Allitt had access to lethal doses
of morphine, which he would administer to his patients, this section
outlines how occupationally specific conditions for driving-oriented
professions provides ideal advantages for those committing serial murder.

Firstly, transient-oriented occupations provided these particular serial
murderers with the ability to access a considerably increased geographical space. While the range of this geographical space would often
differ between each serial murder case—from the relatively small space
covered by forklift-truck driver Steve Wright to the significantly larger
space covered by PDS delivery driver Robert Black—they each utilised
their ability to traverse a larger than normal distance when committing
murder. With their ability to do so, a number of advantages emerged that
assisted these offenders from being apprehended by the authorities. The
most significant factor was their ability to cross multiple police jurisdictions. From lorry driver Peter Sutcliffe who travelled between a number
of towns and cities including Manchester and Leeds, to PDS delivery
driver Robert Black who committed murders in England, Scotland, and
Northern Ireland, these individuals were able to commit their crimes in
various jurisdictions, which raises a host of investigative issues. Firstly,
these serial murderers' ability to cross jurisdictions or, in the case of
Robert Black, borders, creates "linkage blindness", which may assist in
explaining why it took a number of years before most of these offenders
were apprehended. "Linkage blindness" is a significant issue for law
enforcement, as investigators do not see, or are prevented from seeing,
beyond their own jurisdictional responsibilities. So, while there may
have been a murder that took place in a particular jurisdiction, they
may be searching for suspects within their area of responsibility, and not
realising that the offender may have simply been a visitor who in fact
resides many miles away from the location where they committed that

particular offence. So too, as demonstrated in the case of Robert Black, some serial murderers may in fact not only commit their offences in locations they simply visited, but they may also dispose of their victims' bodies in an entirely different area far removed from the abduction site and the home of the offender—creating further confusion for the authorities. This is further aggravated by the fact that most law enforcement officers' areas of responsibility stop at the boundary of their own jurisdiction. So, whilst there may be a suspect living in a different area that the authorities wish to interview or apprehend, they would need to get in contact, and liaise with, the relevant authorities that are responsible for that particular area. The very nature of local law enforcement in the UK, along with a police department's responsibility and receptiveness to the needs of those within their jurisdiction effectively quarantines the department from the other jurisdictions in the UK and, as such, serial murderers who are transient by way of their occupation pose a series of unique challenges to the authorities. "Linkage blindness" illustrates the chief limitations of law enforcement, and, more importantly, draws attention to the general structural weaknesses of such agencies and the difficulties transient-oriented serial murderers pose. Whilst in recent years there have been strides to create a multitude of national databases and resources such as the Police National Database (PND) and Police National Computer (PNC) to assist in investigations that may involve criminals that cross multiple jurisdictions, the exchange of investigative information among various police departments in this country is generally poor. With this in mind, "Linkage blindness" is the almost total absence of distribution or organizing of investigative data or evidence and the non-existence of sufficient networking by the law enforcement agencies that make up the UK's police service. As a consequence of this lack of communication and networking, linkages are rarely recognised among multiple murders that share similar crime patterns, modus operandi, and signatures, but are spread across a large geographic area that is comprised of more than one police jurisdiction. Such structural and organizational weaknesses evidently prevent or obstruct any potential early warning signs that a serial murderer is active and preying on multiple victims in various locations.

Echoing the work of Quinet discussed in *Chapter Three* of this book, not only were these particular serial murderers drawn to the road due to the nature of their jobs, but so were their victims. For the sex worker, a common victim of the serial murderer who held a transient dependent occupation, they are forced to the road in order to advertise their services to the vehicles that pass them by. This particular trait of the sex worker's profession is more present in countries in which prostitution is illegal and, as a result, individuals are forced to work in unprotected and supervised areas quite unlike those that are present in countries such as Holland, for example. In examining the UK, the laws around prostitution in England and Wales are far from straightforward. The act of prostitution is not in itself illegal — but a string of laws criminalise activities around it. Under the Sexual Offences Act 2003, it is an offence to cause or incite prostitution or control it for personal gain. It has been argued that this move towards the criminalisation of prostitution stems from Victorian society, which labelled sex workers as wicked, immoral and a public nuisance that needed to be removed from modern, civilised society. Whilst it has been argued that keeping prostitution illegal is done in the name of women and the upholding of model civil behaviour, it would appear through the course of this book that it only perpetuates violence against sex workers by driving the trade further underground rather than making women safer. In this need to remain hidden from the eyes of the law, sex workers are unfortunately compelled to the streets in order to make a living and, as a result, this exposes them to the likes of those individuals presented in this book who harbour sinister intentions towards them. Runaways and throwaways, as defined by Wilson (2009), are those victims that lack a stable place of residence. Similar to sex workers, individuals who fall within these groups are hidden from mainstream society and, due to a lack of stability in relation to where they are living, are also drawn to the road in search for better opportunities. Unfortunately, as argued by Opack (2000), roads act as literal and metaphorical paths away from "the abyss of the social, economic, and personal impoverishment of the 'throwaway' world" (p. 65). While these "paths" can indeed lead away from the "throwaway" world, they can also lead towards it. It is this "abyss" — a lack of economic support and social ties — that hides these individuals away from necessary protection and instead leaves them open for victimisation. This is perhaps best illustrated in the murders of Fred West who, along with his wife and partner in crime Rosemary, targeted young women who lacked a stable home. Not only would it be less likely that these victims would be missed once they have been murdered, but their lack of a home consequently meant they were more at risk of encountering a serial murderer hunting on Britain's roads.

In relation to the targeting of children only one serial murder, Robert Black, appeared to target this group. Despite this, analysing Black's offences provides an insight into how the role of a child has changed over recent decades, and how cultural and societal perceptions may assist in explaining why Black was an anomaly amongst these particular serial murderers. The historic relationship between children and the road can perhaps be best demonstrated in Black's abduction and murder of his first victim, Jennifer Cardy, a case which went unsolved until 2011. The investigation into her abduction and murder was left open for twenty-eight years and it was only in 2005 that the case was revisited. It is often assumed that the "golden age" of childhood, in which children were able to enjoy growing-up in a relatively stress free and safe environment came to an abrupt end with the "Moors Murders" committed by Ian Brady and Myra Hindley in the 1960s. Whilst the public outcry was indeed significant at the time, with many calling for the death penalty to be reinstated, it was in fact the murders of Robert Black and the widespread moral panic with regards to paedophiles in the 1980s that resulted in a cultural shift regarding the nature of childhood. As Professor David Wilson notes, 20 years after the crimes of Brady and Hindley, young children were still running errands for their parents and playing without supervision in the streets and parks nearby. But after Robert Black was arrested and brought to the public's awareness, along with the growing fear of "stranger danger", the very definition of what it meant to be a child was altered, resulting in more control and surveillance in an effort to protect them. Why is it that this victim group received such a powerful response from the public in comparison to the other victim-types previously discussed? Here we refer to the work of David Garland (2001) and the concept of the "ideal victim". Garland noted the following regarding this concept:

> "If victims were once forgotten, hidden casualties of criminal behaviour, they have now returned with a vengeance, brought back into full public view by politicians and media executives who routinely exploit the victim's experience for their own purposes. The sanctified persona of the suffering victim has become a valued commodity in the circuits of political and media exchange, and real individuals are now placed in front of the cameras and invited to play this role" (Garland, 2001, p. 143).

In continuing Garland's examination of the "ideal victim", such an individual needs to exhibit a number of characteristics in order to be seen as a "valued commodity". Such traits include: they are vulnerable and weak; they were carrying out a respectable activity when the crime occurred; they were where they could not possibly be blamed for being; and, the offender was "big and bad". When examining each of these unique traits, it is clear that the victims of Black's murders indeed fall under the "ideal victim" category — especially when you consider that Black himself, with his heavy-set build that could easily overpower his small victims, ticked the "big and bad" criteria. In comparison to those other victims discussed, this particular victim group were not drawn to the road due to necessity and neither were they marginalised from mainstream society. Instead, Black's crimes reflect the nature of childhood from a different time, a time when children were able to play outside without fear of being abducted as they walked along the roads or spent time in play areas or public parks. Unlike sex workers or runaways or throwaways, who are still at risk from serial murder to this day due to a lack of protection and visibility, the victims of Robert Black sparked a reaction from society which pulled children away from the road and, as a result, away from the predatory gaze of individuals like Black.

It is also important to note that each of the serial murdererers included in this book has been associated (if not, it should be stressed, finally or actually linked) with a number of unsolved murders throughout the country. For example, Peter Sutcliffe has been linked to a considerable number of unsolved murders of women and sex workers (Corcoran, 2013). So too, "Railway Rapists" John Duffy and David Mulcahy have also become suspects regarding over 180 unsolved cases which police examined at a "national" level (Tendler, 2001). The relatively recent conviction regarding the murder of Jennifer Cardy has already demonstrated how viable Robert Black has become regarding unsolved murders and disappearances of young girls. Since Black's initial conviction, he has indeed become a viable suspect in at least 40 unsolved cases of murders involving young girls (Tozer, 2011). Fred West was also a suspect for a number of unsolved murders, including the "Llandarcy double murders"—which have since been linked to another individual. However, West was viewed as a suspect because:

> "The Western Mail has said that West—the man behind the 'House of Horror' in Cromwell Street, Gloucester—is believed to have lodged at a house in Crythan Road in the Melin area of Neath while labouring" ("Fred West 'link' in murder puzzle", *BBC News*, 2001).

As we can see in the above statement, given West's history of transient dependent and labour-oriented professions, he became a viable suspect for other murders that occurred in different regions of the UK. Levi Bellfield's relatively recent conviction for the murder of Milly Dowler again demonstrates how his transient activities related to his occupation made him a viable suspect for unsolved murders post-conviction. Since his apprehension, Bellfield "has been connected to 20 attacks on women including a number of rapes" (Orr and Sturcke, 2008)—though to date he has yet to be officially charged with any of these offences. Peter Tobin is also a viable suspect for 15 unsolved murders (Townsend, 2009), and has, since his arrest, been associated with the "Bible John" murders that occurred in Glasgow in the late-1960s (Harrison and Wilson, 2010). Lastly, Steve Wright, who travelled extensively due to a variety of labour-oriented occupations, has also been linked with other unsolved murders—both in this country and abroad. Specifically, Wright is seen to be a suspect post-conviction for the murder of estate agent Suzy Lamplugh in 1986—20 years prior to him being arrested for his known murders (Edwards, 2008).

Despite those murders identified above which have been formally linked to one of the serial murderers under examination, there has been, to date, no conclusive evidence that any of these serial murderers were responsible for other murders. However, what is of interest is the fact that the very nature of their respective employments resulted in them being viable suspects in other murders post-conviction. For these British serial murderers, the fact that they only became viable suspects post-conviction demonstrates the instrumental significance of transient-oriented occupations with regards to serial murder.

So too, due to both a lack of managerial supervision and the immediate advantage of using a vehicle, they could spend a considerable period of time engaging in their offending behaviour. From Sutcliffe being able to take his time as he scouted potential targets whilst making deliveries, to his ability to quickly flee the scene of the crime with the aid of his own car — the use of a vehicle provided a multitude of time-saving advantages. The size and type of vehicle used also provided different time-saving benefits. For example, PDS delivery driver Black had access to a van, which provided him with ample space to not only abduct his victims but to also spend significant time sexually assaulting them prior to murdering them. Whilst other transient-oriented serial murderers may have lacked this space afforded to Black, the nature of their professions — rather than the size of their vehicles — afforded them other means to spend long periods of time engaging in offending behaviour. In particular, for odd-job labourers Fred West and Peter Tobin who, while transient dependent but odd-job labourers and handymen by trade, were able to exploit their lack of managerial control in order to spend a significant amount of time sexually assaulting their victims before carefully removing any evidence after murdering them. This relationship between a lack of managerial oversight and an increase in time available to offend can also be witnessed with wheel-clamper Levi Bellfield. Not only was his occupation transient dependent, he was also self-employed and lacked any form of legitimate managerial control and oversight. So, along with the already established time-saving advantages of using a vehicle afforded to him, his lack of managerial control provided him with the ideal means to travel through the streets of London and hunt for potential victims without the fear of superiors asking him of his whereabouts or questioning his behaviour. All those serial murderers included in this book were provided with some time-saving advantages by way of using a vehicle, but the varying nature of their respective employment and the extent, or lack of, managerial control and oversight was also a contributing factor for some of these serial murderers to engage in offending behaviour for extended periods of time without fear of being caught.

These particular forms of occupations also provided them with a varying degree of "occupational camouflage". For example, for lorry driver Peter Sutcliffe, PDS van driver Robert Black, and wheel-clamper Levi Bellfield, their various occupational duties and tasks would legitimately put them within general proximity of potential victims. Not only were these motivated offenders able to successfully hide in plain sight by being concealed within the confines of their vehicles, the legitimacy that their professions provided them with meant that many people, including the authorities, would not have initially thought they were a potential threat. This instrumental advantage is further compounded when we take into consideration that these serial murderers were able to also cross multiple police jurisdictions. With the ability to travel across extensive geographical distances, they would ensure that they did not hunt for victims in the same area over a short period of time, and instead visit locations in which awareness that a potential serial murderer may be active was much lower. Similar to other previously discussed practical advantages afforded to these serial murderers, this "occupational camouflage" would differ between offenders, and be implemented into their offending in a variety of ways. For example, it was utilised by the likes of Robert Black throughout all stages of offending. From searching for suitable victims as he made his way through various small towns after making his deliveries, to eventually disposing of their bodies as he made his way back to London, Black used the cover of his PDS delivery van, and the various duties associated with it, to successfully avoid raising suspicions of his criminal behaviour. As is often the case with serial murder cases, it was only when a witness saw Black abduct a young girl that the police were informed and he was eventually apprehended. Otherwise he may have continued to kidnap, rape and murder further victims whilst operating under the veil of a delivery driver. In comparison to Black, serial murdering "team" John Duffy and David Mulcahy used their respective occupations as labourers for the council and, in the case of Duffy, his time working as a carpenter for British Rail, to effectively search for and stake out suitable locations that they would later return to in order to ambush and attack isolated women at night. In this instance, their "occupational camouflage" was primarily useful as a means to find and select suitable offending locations, and less a factor in the actual instances of attacking their victims. With this in mind, these occupations provided these particular serial murderers with varying degrees of concealment that both allowed particular offenders to gain close proximity to their victims and, for others, the ability to seek out and plan future offences whilst all the while masking their true, sinister intentions.

Lastly, with regards to instrumental advantages, these occupations also provided these offenders with situational knowledge for selecting suitable stalking grounds and, as demonstrated in particular by Peter Tobin and Fred West, practical skills that, when applied to their offending behaviour, may have assisted in their ability to avoid capture. This particular instrumental advantage, which is intricately linked with the "occupational camouflage" previously discussed, is effectively a "seepage" of sorts, in which knowledge and skills gained in the course of these serial murderers' day-to-day employment activities and duties informs their offending behaviour. For example, Sutcliffe, Black, Duffy and Mulcahy, and Bellfield all used the geographical knowledge they gained through the course of their respective professions in order to select ideal locations in order to offend. So too, odd-job labourers Tobin and West used their knowledge of building and construction in order to successfully conceal their victims' bodies and any other incriminating evidence — all the while using their occupation in order to provide a valid reason for their extensive digging and building in their homes and gardens.

All the aforementioned instrumental advantages — from the ability to cross multiple police jurisdictions to effectively hiding in plain sight — subsequently made these serial murderers very efficient killers. When examining their length of offending prior to being apprehended by the authorities, it is clear that these instrumental advantages provided them with an effective means to avoid detection. In some cases, such as Fred West and Peter Tobin, they were actively engaging in the commission of murder for decades before finally being apprehended.

Psychological Factors

Outside of these instrumental advantages, the British serial murderers at the heart of this book also shared a number of other, more psychological, similarities in relation to both occupational choice and offending behaviour. These factors may—assist in shedding light on whether these serial murderers selected these occupations in order to offend, or whether their murders are more opportunistic and a result of the environmental context generated by their professions. Secondly, by examining when they committed their crimes, we can determine how subtle differences between these serial murderers' occupations and offending behaviour ultimately influenced how much their professions enabled and facilitated their criminal behaviour.

Through the theoretical application of Holland's RIASEC model (*Chapter Four*), in which it is argued that an individual's career choices and work environments are an expression of their personality, some interesting themes emerged. In particular, in examining the occupational history and job selection of these eight serial murderers, it was demonstrated that they each exhibited specific traits related to the Realistic personality-type. To reiterate, this particular personality-type, it is suggested, is most satisfied when employed in professions and work environments that require little in the way of creativity and social interaction, and instead involve significant amounts of time engaged in labour-oriented activities that are also rather solitary in nature. In essence, the Realistic personality-type prefers tools and machines than having to work with others, and enjoys the solitary nature that occupations—such as driving over long distances—provides. This was not only reinforced by the occupational histories of these offenders, but also in the responses of some of these serial murderers when such occupational characteristics were threatened. For example, for "Yorkshire Ripper" Peter Sutcliffe, when his freedom to be alone was interrupted due to a promotion, he would state that he was "deeply upset" (Bilton, 2003, p. 730) by having to work with others—no longer alone with his thoughts. Further to this, he would go on to convey how he was unable to "concentrate at work" due to working with an assistant who "didn't fully understand the mechanics of the job". Not only did Sutcliffe clearly exhibit qualities closely associated with the Realistic personality type, but the very use of the word "mechanic" provides some insight into the way in which he both perceived and associated with his profession. Whilst it is extremely difficult to determine whether these serial murderers consciously selected their professions in order to offend, the application of Holland's RIASEC model would suggest that these individuals were drawn to similar professions prior to them holding the occupations they did whilst committing their murders due to each serial murderer having a Realistic personality-type. Not only is this information potentially useful in understanding the chain of events that lead to particular individuals becoming serial murderers, it may also be a vital factor in both the profiling and ultimate apprehension of future transient serial offenders. This shared personality-type is an important psychological similarity between all of the serial murderers included in this book and, as such, provides an important aspect of the rationale as to why these individuals were drawn to both labour and transient-oriented occupations. Whilst these eight serial murderers appeared to share similar personality types, there were also other, more criminally-oriented, psychological similarities that further unifies this group of offenders beyond just sharing a similar profession—their motivation to kill.

Along with their shared Realistic personality-type, it was also established that each of these serial murderers committed previous offences that were sexually motivated. From Sutcliffe's earlier assaults on sex workers to Bellfield's violent and sadistic behaviour towards former partners, each serial murderer who held some form of transient occupation had a history of sexual deviancy. These previous cases of sexually-oriented behaviour would subsequently form the foundations for these individuals' crime templates, which would ultimately shape the type of crimes they would commit later in life and in driving-related employment. For instance, taking the early criminal behaviour of Robert Black into account, who repeatedly targeted young girls prior to becoming a PDS delivery driver, it is quite apparent as to how his earlier offences set the template for his later murders. Whilst there may have been some differences with regard to victim selection — with victim groups such as sex workers; young women; runaways and throwaways; and, young girls being at one time or another victims of this particular group of serial murderers — they were all chosen in order to satisfy the sexual fantasies and motivations of their attacker. As illustrated throughout this book, the sexual fantasies that propelled these eight serial murderers to offend would manifest in different ways — sometimes in subtle ways or more overt ways. In the cases of Robert Black, Peter Tobin, and "Railway Rapists" John Duffy and David Mulcahy, for example, they would sexually assault and rape their victims prior to murdering them — thus displaying more evident and explicit sexual motivations behind their offending. On the other hand, serial murderers such as Peter Sutcliffe and Levi Bellfield rarely sexually assaulted their victims, with both offenders often violently attacking their targets before fleeing the scene of the crime. Whilst it is here acknowledged that Sutcliffe indeed had intercourse with victim Helen Rytka prior to murdering her (Bilton, 2003), she was, like many of his victims, a sex worker by trade and proved to be an anomaly in his modus operandi. Instead Sutcliffe, similar to wheel-clamper Bellfield, demonstrated less overt sexual motivations that tend to fit Brooks et al's (1988) description of serial murder in that they "reflect[ed] sadistic sexual undertones" (cited in Castle and Hensley, 2002, p. 455). This element manifested in both Sutcliffe's and Bellfield's use of sheer brutality and infliction of pain upon their victims, with both men using hammers and, in the case of the former, knives and screwdrivers to attack their victims. Here it is argued that the combination of a shared personality-type subsequently placed them within occupations that correlated with it, whilst also generating close proximity to either their preferred victim or stalking grounds — each informed by their past criminal histories, which shaped their "crime templates". Taking these two factors into consideration, it could be argued that these serial murderers selected their occupations by their personality requirements as opposed to the single desire to commit murder. Instead, the very nature of these occupations provided these motivated offenders with opportunities to offend that may have not been present in other work environments.

It was also established that there were those serial murderers who engaged in their offending whilst also carrying out work-related activities, and those that appeared to only commit their murders once completing such obligations. On further analysis, there were a number of factors that may have influenced such decisions. These included the need for little or no managerial oversight in order to successfully disengage from the activities they were supposed to be undertaking whilst working. For example, it was much easier for the likes of long distance van driver Black and self-employed odd-job labourer West to offend whilst supposedly carrying out work-related duties due to a clear lack of managerial presence or — in the case of the latter — control. On the other hand, serial murderers such as fork-lift truck driver Wright and rail carpenter Duffy who was employed by the council, lacked this managerial freedom so they were unable to offend as freely as the aforementioned serial murderers. Another important factor to consider is the type of victim these particular serial murderers would target. For instance, for Sutcliffe and Wright who both targeted sex workers, this particular type of victim would likely be more present after dark due to both an awareness of an increased clientele due to the night-time economy, and a desire to remain hidden from the eyes of the law. With this in mind, both Sutcliffe's and Wright's preferred victim-type would be much more difficult to abduct and murder as they engaged in their day-time specific work-related activities. This is in stark contrast to Black's preferred victim-type, in which it was much more likely for him to encounter a lone child during the day-time — as he engaged in work-related activities — as opposed to at night.

Lastly, another important factor to consider in relation to whether or not these serial murderers could offend whilst engaging in work-related duties is if they offended alone or with an accomplice. In the case of serial murdering "team" Duffy and Mulcahy, whilst they worked in similar professions, they did not actually work together in the same work environment. With this in mind, it makes sense that they would instead use their time at work to perhaps search for potential victims or suitable hunting grounds, and wait for when until they were together before actually engaging in criminal behaviour. All of the above aforementioned points are important influences in whether or not these serial murderers could psychologically "engage" with offending behaviour when supposedly carrying out tasks related to their work.

The Significance of a Transient Dependent Occupation

Whilst there has been little academic attention towards the potential significance of occupational choice for serial murderers, it is evident that there are important facets of their offending that appear to be susceptible to the influence of these individuals' occupation, or lack of occupation. Most notably, particular forms of employment appear to provide offenders with the means to continue offending over an extensive period of time—namely that of healthcare, as demonstrated by Dr Harold Shipman, and those occupations that rely extensively on the use of vehicles. With reference to the questions raised in *Chapter Two* regarding whether particular forms of employment generate the necessary proximity to the victim types outlined by the "structural tradition", it is apparent that both these occupational groups generate both proximity and access to, in the case of healthcare, the elderly and women who work within the sex industry for transient-oriented professions. When British serial murderers lack this type of employment, or lack an occupation entirely, the ability to generate proximity and access to these victim-types becomes that much more difficult and, as a result, more likely to result in capture. This is best illustrated by unemployed Stephen Griffiths, Patrick Mackay, and Kenneth Erskine, who were all identified and apprehended in a short period of time, despite targeting similar victim-types as those serial murderers in healthcare and transient-oriented professions. Here it also important to acknowledge that there were those serial murderers who, whilst holding distinctly different forms of occupation, still used vehicles in their offending. Whilst Welsh serial murder Peter Moore and the serial murdering "team" Ian Brady and Myra Hindley used vehicles in aiding their offending, they differed in key aspects to those serial murderers that drove, or depended on driving, as part of their occupation. Specifically, Brady and Hindley targeted both young girls and boys within the general vicinity of where they lived in Greater Manchester ("Crimes that made Ian Brady and Myra Hindley notorious", *The Telegraph*, 2012). This was arguably due to the pair's occupations preventing them from travelling over an extensive geographical area in comparison, compared to for example PDS delivery driver Black — thus limiting their ability to generate "linkage blindness".

Moore also differs from those serial murderers who held transient-oriented professions in that he targeted gay men, or men whom he encountered whilst searching for suitable victims. Gay men, although considered a vulnerable group according to the "structural tradition", are not so explicitly drawn to the road as sex workers. Nor are they considered to be suitable or ideal victims when compared with isolated sex workers. These factors, along with the lack of proximity and access that was provided to those serial murderers who held transient-oriented occupations, may help to explain why those serial murderers who used a vehicle to offend but not in the course of their occupation were consequently apprehended, on average, sooner.

Serial murderers who held other forms of occupations including, for example: Reginald Christie (war-time constable); Dennis Nilsen (army and police); and John Haigh (entrepreneur), were not able to generate the same level of constant and necessary proximity to the victim groups outlined within the "structural tradition". Serial murderers falling into either one of these, or similar, occupations would have had to seek out their victims, and "artificially" generate the necessary conditions needed in order commit a successful murder. When we say successful, we refer to the presence of both a motivated offender and a suitable victim but a lack of a capable guardian or protection. For example, as demonstrated in *Chapter Six*, Robert Black would be in the process of returning to London in his PDS van after making his deliveries and, as such, his presence in the small rural towns he would often use to find a young girl would not be initially questioned. On the other hand, unemployed serial murderers or those in different occupations would have to remove themselves from their day-to-day activities and engage in movement that falls outside of their usual routines — arguably raising more suspicions and questions from others.

When examining both the victim-types and length of offending period in relation to the occupation, or lack thereof, those occupations that readily supply the offender with the situational context (Cornish and Clarke, 2008) to offend are, on average, more "successful" serial murderers. With the application of rational choice theory, in which immediate contextual factors influence how an individual weighs up the cost to benefit ratio of committing a crime, it is arguable that those serial murderers who worked within transient-oriented professions were influenced by their work environment with regard to their decision-making process to commit a crime. In particular, as Cornish and Clark (2008) note:

> "Event decisions…are frequently shorter processes, utilizing more circum-scribed information largely relating to immediate circumstances and situa-tions" (Cornish and Clarke, 2008, p. 2).

Here it is argued that occupations containing significant amounts of driving generate the "immediate circumstances and situations" neces-sary for a serial murderer to decide that the benefit of committing a crime outweighs the risk of being caught and apprehended. In applying this rational choice perspective, it could be argued that these particular occupations provide the ecological context with regards to the physical proximity generated between offender and victim, that the potential deci-sion to engage in offending behaviour is significantly increased. With regard to those serial murderers who held other occupations, the ecolog-ical context shaped by their routine activities would have not generated this same level of proximity to their victims. This, in turn, may have negatively influenced their decision to engage in their offending whilst undertaking work-related duties, and to instead seek out victims outside the confines of their occupation. Such decisions may indeed appear to be rational with regards to attempting to generate the "ideal" circumstances that outweighs the benefits of engaging in criminal behaviour compared to the risk of being apprehended. However, they are, in fact, losing the vital "occupational shielding" that was afforded to those serial murderers who worked within transient-oriented professions.

When we look at the length of the offending periods of those serial murderers included in this book, it is evident that their occupations assisted in their ability to not get caught for an extended period of time.

It is important to note here that, despite these generally long offending periods (Peter Sutcliffe: five years; Robert Black: five years; Peter Tobin: 15 years), this length of offending appears to be decreasing, with more contemporary serial murderers such as Levi Bellfield (two years) and Steve Wright (three months) being apprehended much quicker. The potential reasons behind this decreasing offending period is certainly worthy of deliberation, and will be discussed in the following chapter as we examine how the development of technology may be changing the occupations of contemporary and future serial murderers.

A Look to the Future: Hunting on the "Technological Highway"

If the Internet has become a very useful tool for people interested in serial killers, there's some indication that it may also prove to be a resource for serial killers themselves.

Harold Schechter (1997, Pocket Books) *The A to Z Encyclopedia of Serial Killers*

Is Serial Murder Adapting?

It was mentioned in the previous chapter that those more contemporary British serial murderers who held some form of transient-oriented occupation were apprehended at a much faster rate than their historic counterparts. This is perhaps best illustrated when we look at cases such as Fred West and Peter Tobin who committed their respective murders over the span of two decades, whilst more recent cases, such as fork-lift truck driver Steve Wright, was apprehended in the space of a few months. Whilst subtle differences in their offending behaviour and work environments may have a part to play in this disparity, we also need to acknowledge how police investigative techniques; forensic capabilities; and the advancement of surveillance technology may have also been an instrumental factor in this shortening of offending periods. With the development of police national databases, information can more readily be shared across multiple jurisdictions. With access to such a database, the risk of "linkage blindness" occurring when a serial murderer is geographically mobile is significantly reduced. So too, the police's ability to find and analyse forensic evidence has improved significantly since the time of Peter Sutcliffe, Robert Black and Fred West. In particular, forensics has made incredible strides over the last 30-years, providing law enforcement with an wide range of important tools that were unavailable during the time of, say, the "Yorkshire Ripper". The forensic sciences include the disciplines of pathology, toxicology, forensic DNA analysis, psychiatry, psychology, entomology, and computer and digital science. With access to such disciplines and techniques, police are now able to examine biological traces, such as fingerprint analysis, footwear, tyre impressions and tool-mark evidence, along with such things as drug analysis, ballistics and firearm examinations. This ability to cover a wide range of potential forensic evidence means that even the most highly organized serial murderer may unwittingly leave evidence that will ultimately lead to their downfall. This is perhaps best illustrated in the investigation into "Suffolk Strangler" Steve Wright who, despite displaying the hallmarks of an organized serial murderer by way of disposing his victims' bodies in water, was ultimately identified due to both DNA and fibre evidence that linked him or his victims. There was another, equally important factor that lead to Wright's arrest and conviction—CCTV footage. It was revealed during his trial that cameras within the red light district of Ipswich had captured Wright driving his Ford Mondeo prior to picking up Tania who disappeared later that same night. Wheel-clamper Levi Bellfield is a case of another contemporary serial murderer in which the use of CCTV recordings as evidence was crucial in securing a conviction. In fact, when examining the murder of French student Amelie Delagrange in which there were no witnesses, DNA evidence or any form of forensic evidence to work with, the authorities turned to the ever-present and watchful gaze of London's CCTV system. It was in this analysis that a breakthrough in the investigation was finally reached:

"Three months into the investigation of Delagrange's murder at Twickenham Green in August 2004, police on Operation Yeaddiss used CCTV footage to identify a white Ford van parked nearby at the time of the attack" (McVeigh, 2008).

It was this identification of the white Ford van that eventually led police to Levi Bellfield, and the CCTV footage played a vital part in securing his conviction. Whilst there have been many debates surrounding the use of surveillance technology—especially in relation to its potential threat to the right to privacy—there is little doubt that the rise of such crime prevention tools has been instrumental in identifying transient serial murderers much sooner than previously possible.

These advancements in investigative techniques, along with the rise of surveillance technology, has made it much more difficult for contemporary serial murderers who are geographically mobile to remain hidden from the eyes of the law. These difficulties faced by more modern serial murderers begs the question as to whether the occupations of active and future serial murderers will change in order to evade capture. Ever since the birth of the internet, organized crime has exploited its lack of borders and ability to remain anonymous in order to engage in criminal activities. With this in mind, will the serial murderers of tomorrow perhaps also make the move to the internet? Similar to how Sutcliffe drove around the right district of Bradford, and Bellfield followed buses in pursuit of suitable victims, serial murderers may be using the internet as means to target and select victims. As such, they reduce the likelihood of being caught and subsequently identified on CCTV, which proved both hazardous and, in the case of Bellfield, vital to their detection. Does this suggest that the occupations of serial murderers will now adapt in response to an ever-increasing "surveillance culture"? Have more contemporary and yet unidentified serial murderers abandoned the physical road, and now stalk the "technological highway"? In an attempt to provide an answer to this question, a number of cases in which murderers used the internet in order to commit their offences will be examined.

The "Craigslist Ripper"

In December of 2010 police in Long Island, situated within the state of New York, were tasked with the search for 24-year-old sex worker Shannan Gilbert—who had been reported missing back in May of that year. During this particular search police discovered the skeletal remains of a woman's body, which had been placed inside of a burlap sack. As it turned out, the body was not Shannan's but that of another 24-year-old sex worker—Melissa Barthlemy—who went missing in July 2009 after meeting a client she had met through Craigslist, an online based classified advertisements website. Within days, officers scouring Gilgo Beach in Long Island had found three more bodies, all of them in burlap bags and all belonging to missing sex workers.

With the information police had on the bodies so far discovered, detectives working on the case discovered an interesting link between the victims that extended beyond their profession. It was determined that three of the women were approximately five feet tall and had advertised their services online through the website Craigslist. This piece of information would ultimately earn the unidentified killer the local nickname of the "Craigslist Ripper". Despite the speed in which bodies were being discovered and identified, the investigation into who this killer could be failed to move forward.

In March 2011, the severed head, hands and forearms of a fifth woman were found within the same area as the other victims. She was identified as 20-year-old sex worker Jessica Taylor, who went missing in July 2003. Of note is that on 26 July 2003, her naked torso, chopped in pieces and missing its head and hands, was discovered 45 miles East of Gilgo Beach in Manorville, New York. Whilst the thought that the killer must have been using a vehicle to dispose of his victims' bodies must have already crossed detectives' minds, the fact that there was such a great distance between Jessica's various remains all but confirmed the use of transport.

Over the next few weeks police continued to search the Long Island area and discovered a further five bodies—none of which have been identified. Despite this lack of identification, it is strongly believed that many of these victims were also sex workers. It is also worth noting that one of these unidentified victims, an Asian man dressed in women's clothing and understood as having been a male sex worker, had been dead for approximately five years prior to being discovered. This subsequently led the authorities to believe that a number of different murderers had used this particular geographical location in order to dispose of their victims' bodies. Despite these initial thoughts, Suffolk County Police

Commissioner Richard Dormer returned to the initial theory that there was just one person responsible for the murders:

"It appears that one person, comfortable with the area, comfortable with Long Island is involved in these crimes … the body parts have been spread over an area of great distance. There's a connection that indicates that this person feels comfortable enough to drive with remains in his vehicle" ('Single serial killer responsible for Long Island beach murders, police say', *The Telegraph*, 2011).

While Commissioner Dormer draws attention to this unknown serial murderer using a vehicle in order to dispose of victims' bodies, the fact that this particular offender used the internet to search for victims would result in him or her not requiring to physically search for, and pick up, potential victims. With the aid of the internet, the "Craigslist ripper" reduced the amount of time he spent on the road and the watchful gaze of surveillance technology — technology that ultimately assisted in the apprehension of both Wright and Bellfield. Given the rather unique natrure of the case of the "Craigslist Ripper", there appears to be some disagreement with regard to the number of individuals responsible, with Dormer highlighting that:

"The theory now is that one person is responsible for these killings, one serial killer. That's what we're leaning towards, although there are other people in the police business, and even in the department, that have other theories" (Ibid).

This inability to come to a clear consensus in relation to the number of potential killers involved, along with the fact that some of victims had been murdered a number of years prior to being discovered, has resulted in very little progress in identifying the individual[s] responsible for these murders. These factors, along with the fact that this case is one of the first examples of a serial murderer using the internet in order to hunt for victims, poses unique obstacles for law enforcement that will need to be overcome if this person is to be caught.

As noted, what appears to be an important element in this particular case is the use of the Internet. Whilst the killer evidently uses a vehicle in order to dispose of their victims' bodies, the internet appears to be a vital tool in his or her "serial killing arsenal"—specifically in order to hide both identity and to find and select suitable targets. But the "Craigslist Ripper" is unfortunately not an isolated example of a murderer using the internet in order to hunt for victims.

"Help Wanted"

The murders committed by Richard Beasley provides another noteworthy example of "internet homicide". In 2013, Beasley, a 53-year-old from Summit County, Ohio, was convicted and given the death penalty for luring three men to their deaths using a Craigslist ad for a nonexistent job in 2011. Beasley was convicted of kidnapping and killing David Pauley, 51, of Norfolk, Virginia; Ralph Geiger, 56, of Akron, Ohio; and, Timothy Kern, 47, of Massillon, Ohio. He was also convicted of the attempted murder of Scott Davis, 49, a South Carolina man who answered the Craigslist ad and was shot in the arm while escaping after meeting Beasley and his 16-year-old accomplice, Brogan Rafferty. Below is the online advertisement that Beasley posted on Craigslist:

> "Wanted: Caretaker For Farm. Simply watch over a 688 acre patch of hilly farmland and feed a few cows, you get 300 a week and a nice 2 bedroom trailer, someone older and single preferred but will consider all, relocation a must, you must have a clean record and be trustworthy—this is a permanent position, the farm is used mainly as a hunting preserve, is overrun with game, has a stocked 3 acre pond, but some beef cattle will be kept, nearest neighbor is a mile away, the place is secluded and beautiful, it will be a real get away for the right person, job of a lifetime—if you are ready to relocate please contact asap, position will not stay open" (Rosin, 2013).

Beasley received over 100 responses to his carefully crafted advertisement that was designed to appeal to a certain demographic. Namely, Beasley was interested in drawing the attention of 'a middle-aged man who had never been married or was recently divorced, and who had no strong family connections' (Rosin, 2013). Whilst not readily apparent, Beasley, similar to the "Craigslist Ripper" and the eight British serial murderers discussed throughout this book, targeted those individuals who lacked in a stable home, and who were isolated due to a lack of family or friends. Out of these applicants, three men who happened to fit this rather specific criteria were kidnaped by Beasley and his young accomplice in order to steal from them prior to killing them and burying their bodies in the remote and rural backdrop in which the murders took place.

Here we need to ask what makes Craigslist such an attractive website for murderers and serial murderers? Firstly, it is important to note that it is generally free to use, and, secondly and arguably most importantly, it's mostly anonymous. In particular, in many segments of the website, the individual placing the online advertisement does not have to give a name or other important identifying details—an essential factor in a murderer's quest to remain beyond the sight of the law. Specifically, the Craigslist email "anonymizer" hides the user's email address so, if a murderer placed an online advert from a public computer, and changes their appearance in some manner, the authorities will have hard time tracking them down after they have murdered and dispatched their victim[s]. On top of this, the website does very little vetting of its advertisers and users, offering little in the way of protection for those individuals who may fall victim to predators attempting to lure them with enticing advertisements. One could reasonably argue that the main reason the site exists is so people can search for sex. A lot of the people who patronise the Craigslist personals want to maintain their anonymity. This of course creates the perfect stalking ground for murderers and aspiring serial murderers—who can search for potential victims under false pretences and a false identity.

What both the "Craigslist Ripper" and Richard Beasley have in common is that they both were able to hunt for and select victims without ever having to leave the confines of their home. This provides such offenders with a distinct advantage over the serial murderers discussed throughout this book, who needed to physically hunt for suitable victims and, as a result, increase the risks of being identified and apprehended in a modern society that places much emphasis on surveillance. Taking this into consideration, it may be that the "Golden Age" of the serial murderer who held transient-oriented professions has come to an end, and that the serial murderers of tomorrow may hold occupations that require the use of technology such as computers.

Final Thoughts

Most scholarly work pertaining to serial murder has neglected the potential significance of these offenders' occupations and work environments. Specifically, the "medical-psychological" tradition has, for the most part, observed the phenomenon of serial murder as existing in a vacuum—removed from the everyday lifestyles and habits that these offenders disengage from, and subsequently re-enter after committing an offence. From a structural standpoint there has been, though only in a limited way, attention given to the social standing of serial murderers depending on the historical epoch they existed within. This, though, has been largely contested and demonstrated to be an inaccurate depiction of serial murder—especially within a British context. The majority of scholarly work pertaining to the "structural tradition" shifted from that of the serial murderer to that of their victims. In doing so, it became apparent that particular groups have been repeatedly targeted by serial murderers within Britain. Whilst this research highlighted how societal conditions and, with reference to sex workers, particular occupations and lifestyles, make these individuals susceptible to serial murderers, the question as to how similar conditions influences the offenders' behaviour has been largely neglected. Taking this into consideration, and with acknowledgement that there have been serial murderers who held an occupation that consisted of various levels of driving, the central aim of this book was established.

As demonstrated through the course of this book, driving as a form of employment significantly impacted upon these individuals' offending behaviour. So too were there commonalities between these individuals' offending behaviour—namely that they were all sexually motivated and targeted predominately similar victim-types. It was also established that, in comparison to the other serial murderers who held different occupations or lacked employment entirely, these particular serial murderers were capable of engaging in their offending whilst also supposedly carrying out work-related duties. This demonstrated that particular occupations and work environments do in fact provide the necessary status and/or access to suitable victims without the need to physically "disengage" from their everyday activities. This ability not to physically remove themselves from their work-related activity space has afforded these serial murderers a number of key advantages that are not available to those individuals who work in professions that do not create the necessary access and opportunity to their victims, along with those that lack employment entirely. This has been illustrated by the fact that those serial murderers who held driving and transitory dependent work were, on average, identified and apprehended after longer periods of offending. So whilst these offenders do, in the manner of the "medical-psychological tradition", psychologically "disengage" from their everyday activities, their employment provides a means to not physically "disengage" and consequently makes them less susceptible to being identified and apprehend.

Robert Black, for example, was making, and continued to make, deliveries pre and post-abducting his victims, and Peter Sutcliffe continued to engage in his work-related activities whilst searching for suitable victims. These cases illustrate just how significant an offender's occupation may be as an aid to their offending. So, as demonstrated throughout the book, it would be advantageous to move beyond the confines of analysing the slither of time in which these individuals offend, and broaden the scope to include how their everyday activities and lifestyles, largely influenced by their occupation, or lack thereof, impacts not only their offending behaviour, but also the level of success they achieve in such murderous pursuits.

It is apparent that driving as a form of occupational choice is a "popular" form of employment for British serial murderers. In an effort to determine why this may be, a case study of eight British serial murderers demonstrated just how such an occupation can impact upon these offenders' criminal behaviour after gaining employment. These findings may prove to be of benefit to scholars of serial murder, and to those who attempt to apprehend such offenders.

Adams, L. (2011) 'Predator with a grotesque history of abuse', *The Herald* [online] 27th October. Available at: http://www.heraldscotland.com/news/crime-courts/predator-with-a-grotesque-history-of-abuse.15608109?page=2 [Accessed 25th June 2014]

Addley, E. (2007) 'Angelika Kluk Murder', *The Guardian* [online] 4th May. Available at: http://www.theguardian.com/uk/2007/may/04/ukcrime.estheraddley [Accessed 26th June 2014]

(2008) 'FAQ Prostitution', *The Guardian* [online] 22nd February. Available at: http://www.guardian.co.uk/uk/2008/feb/22/suffolkmurders.ukcrime5 [Accessed 28th February 2012]

(2009) 'How the police caught Peter Tobin', *The Guardian* [online] 16th December. Available at: http://www.theguardian.com/uk/2009/dec/16/peter-tobin-dinah-mcnicol-police [Accessed 25th June 2014]

Addley, E. and McVeigh, K. (2008) 'Motive still unknown as serial killer faces rest of life in prison', *The Guardian* [online] 22nd February. Available at: http://www.theguardian.com/uk/2008/feb/22/suffolkmurders.ukcrime [Accessed 20th June 2014]

Addley, E., McVeigh, K and Batty, D. (2008) 'Suffolk serial killer Steve Wright jailed for life', *Guardian,* [Online] 22nd February. Available at: http://www.guardian.co.uk/uk/2008/feb/22/wright.sentenced [Accessed 26th February 2012]

Adler, P. A and Adler, P. (1988) 'Observational techniques', in N.K. Denzin and Y.S. Lincoln (eds.), *Collecting and Interpreting Qualitative Materials*, London: Sage Publications, pp. 79–109

Adoni, H. and Mane, S. (1984) 'Media and the Social Construction of Reality: Toward an Integration of Theory and Research', *Communication Research*, Vol. 11, pp. 323–440

Ainsworth, P. (2001) *Offender Profiling and Crime Analysis*, London: Willan

Allen, N. and Rayner, G. (2008) 'Steve Wright: A real Jekyll and Hyde', *The Telegraph* [online] 21st February. Available at: http://www.telegraph.co.uk/news/uknews/1579403/Steve-Wright-A-real-Jekyll-andHyde.html [Accessed 21st June 2014]

Ameen, E. J. and Lee, D. L. (2012) 'Vocational training in juvenile detention: A call for action', *The Career Development Quarterly*, Vol. 60, pp. 98–108

Amis, M. (2000) *Experience*, London: Vintage

Andresen, M. A. (2010) 'The place of environmental criminology within criminological thought', In M. A. Andresen, P. J. Brantingham, and J. Kinney (eds.), *Classics in Environmental Criminology*: CRC Press

Ansevics, N. and Doweiko, H. (1991) 'Serial murderers: Early proposed development typology', *Psychotherapy in Private Practice*, Vol. 9, pp. 107–222

Argyle, M., Furnham, A. and Graham, J. A. (1981) *Social Situations*, London: Cambridge University Press

Armstrong, J. (2013) 'Serial killer Steven Grieveson who strangled three teenagers found guilty of murdering FOURTH victim', *The Mirror* [online] 24th October. Available at: http://www.mirror.co.uk/news/uk-news/serial-killer-steven-grievesonwho-2509973 [Accessed 7th May 2013]

Armstrong, J. and McGurran, A. (2008) 'Steve Wright beat and abused his ex-wife Diane Cole', *Mirror* [online] 22nd February. Available at: http://www.mirror.co.uk/news/uk-news/steve-wright-beat-and-abused-his-ex-wife-294719 [Accessed 26th June 2014]

Auerbach, C. F. and Silverstein, L. B. (2003) *Qualitative Data: An Introduction to Coding and Analysis*, New York: New York University Press

Baker, P. and Ellece, S. (2011) *Key Terms in Discourse Analysis*, London: Continuum

Bandura, A. (1977) 'Self-efficacy: Toward a Unifying Theory of Behavioural Change', *Psychological Review*, Vol. 84, No. 2, pp. 191–215

Barkan, S. E. and Bryjak, G. J. (2014) *Myths and Realities of Crime and Justice*, Burlington: Jones and Bartlett Learning

Barrick, M. R. and Mount, M. K. (1991) 'The Big Five personality dimensions and job performance: A meta-analysis', *Personnel Psychology*, Vol. 44, pp. 1–26

Barton, F. (2008) 'Bellfield: The killer with a hatred of blondes who boasted "I'm above the law"' *Mail online* [online] 26th February. Available at: http://www.dailymail.co.uk/news/article-518574/Bellfield-The-killer-hatred-blondesboasted-Im-law.html [Accessed 1st June 2014]

Barzelay, M. (1993) 'The Single Case Study as Intellectually Ambitious Inquiry', *Journal of Public Administration of Research and Theory*, Vol. 3, No. 3, pp. 305–318

Batty, D. (2005) 'Q andA: Harold Shipman', *The Guardian* [online] available at: http://www.guardian.co.uk/society/2005/aug/25/health.shipman [accessed 2nd August 2012]

Baxter, P. and Jack, S. (2008) 'Qualitative Case Study Methodology: Study Design and Implementation for Novice Researchers', *The Qualitative Report*, Vol.13 No. 4, pp. 554–559

Bazeley, P. and Jackson, K. (2013) *Qualitative Data Analysis with NVivo* (2nd ed.) London: Sage Publications

Beccaria, C. (1995) 'On crimes and punishments', In R. Bellamy (ed.) (R. Davies, Trans.), *On Crimes and Punishments and Other Writings*, Cambridge: Cambridge University Press (Original work published 1764)

Becker, H. S. (1970) 'Field work evidence', In H. Becker (ed.) *Sociological Work: Method and Substance*, New Brunswick: Transaction Books, pp. 39–62

Bell, G. (2009) 'Tobin worked in north-east abattoir, police reveal', *Aberdeen Press and Journal*, 24th December, p. 4

Bell, S. (2008) 'Race against time to catch a killer', *BBC News* [online] 25th February. Available at: http://news.bbc.co.uk/1/hi/uk/7221852.stm [Accessed 24th June 2014]

Bell, S. (2011) 'Milly Dowler killer Levi Bellfield "controlling and evil"', *BBC News*, 24th June. Available at: http://www.bbc.co.uk/news/uk-13902337 [Accessed 20th June 2014]

Bell, S. and Shaler, R. C. (2008) *Encyclopaedia of Forensic Science*, London: Facts on File

Benhabib, S. (1990) 'Hannah Arendt and the Redemptive Power of Narrative', *Social Research*, Vol. 57, No. 1, pp. 167–196

Bennell, C., Alison, L. J., Stein, K., Alison, E. and Canter, D. V. (2002) 'Sexual Offenses Against Children as the Abusive Exploitation of Conventional Adult-Child Relationships', *Journal of Social and Personal Relationships*, Vol. 18, pp. 155–171

Bennell, C., Bloomfield, S., Emeno, K., and Musolino, E. (2013) 'Classifying serial sexual murder/murderers: An attempt to validate Keppel and Walter's (1999) model', *Criminal Justice and Behavior*, Vol. 40, pp. 5–25

Bennett, J. and Gardner, G. (2005) *The Cromwell Street Murders: The Detective's Story*, Brimscombe Port: The History Press

Bennett, R. (1991) 'Routine Activities: A Cross-National Assessment of a Criminological Perspective', *Social Forces*, Vol. 70, pp. 147–63

Bennett, W. (1995) 'The Horrific Secrets of 25 Cromwell Street', *The Independent*, [Online] 7th October. Available at: http://www.independent.co.uk/news/

the-horrificsecrets-of-25-cromwell-street-1576291.html [Accessed 22nd February 2012]

Bennett, W. and MacDonald, M. (1995) 'Inside 25 Cromwell Street: The Genial Neighbour at No 25', *The Independent* [online] 2nd January. Available at: http://www.independent.co.uk/news/uk/inside-25-cromwell-street-the-genialneighbour-at-no-25-1566338.html [Accessed 19th May 2014]

Bentham J. (1789) *An Introduction to the Principles of Morals and Legislation*, London: Payne

Berelson, B. (1952) *Content Analysis in Communication Research*, New York: The Free Press

Berry-Dee, C. and Morris, S. (2009) *Born Killers*, New York: John Blake Publishing Ltd

Beveridge, W. I. B. (1951) *The Art of Scientific Investigation*, London: William Heinemann

Bilton, M. (2003) *Wicked Beyond Belief: The Hunt for the Yorkshire Ripper*, London: Harperpress

Birch, H. (1994) 'If Looks Could Kill', H. Birch (ed.) *Moving Targets: Women, Murder, and Representation,* Los Angeles: University of California Press, pp. 32–62

Black, J. L. (2006) *The Broadview Anthology of British Literature: The Victorian Era,* Plymouth: Broadview Press

Blanche, T. and Durrheim, K. (1999) *Research in Practice: Applied Methods for the Social Sciences*, Cape Town: University of Cape Town Press

Bohan, J. S. (1993) 'Regarding Gender: Essentialism, Constructionism, and Feminist Psychology', *Psychology of Women Quarterly*, Vol. 17, No. 1, pp. 5–21

Borland, B. (2013) 'Moira search sparks fears of Fred West's hidden Scots victims', *Express* [online] 13th January. Available at: http://www.express.co.uk/news/uk/370402/Moira-search-sparks-fears-of-Fred-Wests-hidden-Scots-victims [Accessed 25th June 2014]

Boseley, S. (2010) 'GPs send Reforms Plan back to Drawing Board', *The Guardian* [online] 27th May. Available at: https://www.theguardian.com/society/2010/may/27/bma-rejects-doctor-gp-revalidation [Accessed 27th February 2012]

Bourke, F. (2006) 'Probation Staff used Fred West to Build Patios: Exclusive Killer on Remand in Birmingham was Cowboy Builder', *Birmingham Post,* 15th January. Available at: http://www.thefreelibrary.com/PROBATION+STAFF+USED+FRED+WEST+TO+BUILD+PATIOS%3B+EXCLUSIVE+KILLER+ON...-a0149115617 [Accessed 23rd June 2014]

Bracchi, P. and Wright, S. (2011) 'Humming along to Take That, playing Monopoly with her child-killer friends and parading in glitzy tops… the very cushy prison life of Rose West', *Mail online* [online] 2nd September. Available at: http://www.dailymail.co.uk/news/article-2033143/Rosemary-West-Humming-TakeThat-playing-Monopoly-child-killer-friends-parading-glitzy-tops — cushy-prison-lifeRose.html [Accessed 2nd May 2014]

Branson, A. (2013). 'African American Serial Killers: Over-Represented Yet Under Acknowledged', *The Howard Journal of Criminal Justice*, Vol. 52, No. 1, pp. 1–18 Brantingham, P. J. and Brantingham, P.L. (1981) 'Notes on the Geometry of Crime', in P. J. Brantingham and P. L. Brantingham (eds.), *Environmental Criminology*, London: Sage Publications, pp. 27–54

Brantingham, P. L. and P. J. Brantingham (2008) 'Crime Pattern theory' in R. Wortley and L. Mazerolle (eds.), *Environmental Criminology and Crime Analysis*, Crime Science Series. Culompton: Willan Publishing

(1978) 'A Theoretical Model of Crime Site Selection', In M. Krohn and R.L. Akers (eds.), *Crime, Law, and Sanctions*, Beverly Hills: Sage Publications

(1993) 'Environment, Routine and Situation: Toward a Pattern Theory of Crime', *Advances in Criminological Theory*, Vol. 5, pp. 259–294

British Society of Criminology (2010), *Code of Ethics,* [online] available at http://www.britsoccrim.org/codeofethics.htm [last accessed 10th April 2012]

British Sociological Association. (2002), *Statement of Ethical Practice,* [online] available at: http://www.britsoc.co.uk/media/27107/StatementofEthicalPractice.pdf [Accessed 10th April 2012]

Britten, N. (2006) 'Drifter "Had Desire to be City's First Serial Killer"', *The Telegraph* [online] 17th January. Available at: http://www.telegraph.co.uk/news/uknews/1508012/Drifter-had-desire-to-be-citysfirst-serial-killer.html [Accessed 3rd March 2012]

Brocklehurst, S. (2013) 'CSI Scotland: How forensics caught Peter Tobin', *BBC News* [online] Available at: http://www.bbc.co.uk/news/uk-scotland-24430345 [Accessed 17th June 2014]

Brooks, P. R., Devine, M. J., Green, T. J., Hart, B. L. and Moore, M. D. (1988) *Multiagency Investigation Team Manual,* Washington: Police Executive Research Forum

Brunt, M. (2014) 'Rose West Urged To Break Silence Over 'Killing', *Sky News* [online] 21st February. Available at: http://news.sky.com/story/1214962/rose-westurged-to-break-silence-over-killing [Accessed 18th May 2014]

Bullen, M. (1998) 'Participation and critical thinking in online university distance education', *Journal of Distance Education*, Vol. 13, No. 2, pp. 1–32

Bulstrode, M. (2008) 'Steve Wright was my first "punter", says ex sex worker', *BBC News Suffolk* [online] 23rd May. Available at: http://www.bbc.co.uk/news/uk-england-suffolk-18163426 [Accessed 26th June 2014]

Burgess, C. D. (1980) *Field Research: A Sourcebook and Field Manual*, London: Allen and Unwin

Burn, G. (1984) *Somebody's Husband, Somebody's Son: The Story of the Yorkshire Ripper*, London: Faber and Faber Ltd.

Burnard P. (1991) 'A method of analysing interview transcripts in qualitative research.', *Nurse Education Today*, Vol. 11, pp. 461–466

Burr, V. (2003) *An Introduction to Social Constructionism* (2nd edn.), London: Routledge.

'Bus Stop Killer's Chain of Violence', (2008) *BBC News* [online] 25th February. Available at: http://news.bbc.co.uk/1/hi/uk/7230063.stm [Accessed 24th June 2014]

'Cardy family "do not hate" child killer Robert Black', (2011) *BBC News* [online] 8th December. Available at: http://www.bbc.co.uk/news/uk-northern-ireland-16086642 [Accessed 22nd June 2014]

'Child killer Robert Black's past "wrongly revealed", (2013) *BBC News* [online] 14th January. Available at: http://www.bbc.co.uk/news/uk-northern-ireland-21018816 [accessed 22nd June 2014]

'Child killer Robert Black's past revealed to Northern Ireland jury', (2011) *The Guardian* [online] 7th October. Available at: http://www.theguardian.com/uk/2011/oct/07/child-killer-robert-black-trial [Accessed 26th May 2012]

'Court cleared in Angelika Kluk murder trial' (2007) *Herald Scotland* [online] 14th April. Available at: http://www.heraldscotland.com/court-cleared-in-angelika-klukmurder-trial-1.856178 [Accessed 26th June 2014]

'Crimes that made Ian Brady and Myra Hindley notorious', (2012) *The Telegraph* [online] 17th August. Available at: http://www.telegraph.co.uk/news/uknews/crime/9481684/Crimes-that-made-Ian-Brady-and-Myra-Hindley-notorious.html [Accessed 20th May 2013]

Cacciottolo, M. (2009) 'Piecing together serial killer Peter Tobin's past', *BBC News* [online] 16th December. Available at: http://news.bbc.co.uk/1/hi/uk/8132283.stm [Accessed 24th June 2014]

Cameron, D. and Frazer, E. (1987) *The Lust to Kill: A Feminist Investigation of Sexual Murder.* Cambridge: Polity Press

Campbell, D. (2011) '"Angel of Death" Colin Norris could be Cleared of Insulin Murders', *The Guardian* [online] 4th October. Available at: http://www.guardian. co.uk/uk/2011/oct/04/angel-of-death-murder-case-new-evidence [Accessed 27th February 2012]

Campbell, D. T. (1975) 'Degrees of Freedom and the Case Study', *Comparative Political Studies*, Vol. 8, No. 1, pp. 178–191

Canter, D. (2004) *Mapping Murder,* London: Virgin Books
(2005) *Mapping Murder: Walking in Killers' Footsteps,* London: Virgin Books

Canter, D. and Larkin P. (1993) 'The Environmental Range of Serial Rapists', *Journal of Environmental Psychology*, Vol. 13: pp. 63–69

Canter, D. and Hammond, L. (2006) 'A Comparison of the Efficacy of Different Decay Functions in Geographical Profiling for a Sample of US Serial Killers', *Journal of Investigative Psychology and Offender Profiling*, Vol. 3, No.2, pp. 91–106

Canter, D. V., Bennell, C., Alison, L. J. and Reddy, S. (2003) 'Differentiating sex offenses: A Behaviourally Based Thematic Classification of Stranger Rapes', *Behavioural Sciences and the Law*, Vol. 21, pp. 157–174

Canter, D., Alison, L., Alison, E. and Wentink, N. (2004) 'The Organized/Disorganized Typology of Serial Murder: Myth or Model?', *Psychology, Public Policy*, and Law, Vol. 10, No. 3, pp. 293–320

Canter, D., Coffey, T., Huntley, M. and Missen, C. (2000) '"Predicting Serial Killers" Home Base Using a Decision Support System', *Journal of Quantitative Criminology*, Vol. 16, Vol. 4, pp. 457–478

Canter, D. and Youngs, D. (2009) *Investigative Psychology: Offender Profiling and the Analysis of Criminal Action*, Chichester: John Wiley and Sons Ltd

Carter, H. (2000) 'Harold Shipman, Guilty of 15 Murders. But did he Kill 150?', *The Guardian* [online] 1st February. Available at: http://www.guardian.co.uk/uk/2000/ feb/01/shipman.health4 [Accessed 27th February 2012]

Carter, H. and Ward, D. (2002) '"Britain's worst serial killer': 215 Dead but we still don't know why', *The Guardian* [online] 20th July. Available at: http://www.guardian. co.uk/uk/2002/jul/20/shipman.health5 [Accessed 27th February 2012]

Cassel, E. and Bernstein, D.A. (2007) *Criminal Behaviour* (2nd ed.), New York: Psychology Press

Castle, T. (2001) 'A case study analysis of serial killers with military experience: Applying learning theory to serial murder', *Unpublished master's thesis*: Morehead State University

Castle, T. and Hensley, C. (2002) 'Serial Killers With Military Experience: Applying Learning Theory to Serial Murder', *International Journal of Offender Therapy and Comparative Criminology*, Vol. 46, No. 4, pp. 453–465

Chapman, J. (2009) 'Murderer said grave was to be "sand pit"', *Express* [online] 25th June. Available at: http://www.express.co.uk/news/uk/109779/Murderer-said-gravewas-to-be-sand-pit [Accessed 24th June 2014]

Clark, E. (2009) 'Arson: a Burning Desire', *The Telegraph* [online] 15th October. Available at: http://www.telegraph.co.uk/news/uknews/crime/6325967/Arson-aburning-desire.html [Accessed 28th February 2012]

Clarke, R. V. G. and Felson, M. (1993) *Routine Activity and Rational Choice*, London: Transaction Publishers

Clough, S., Alleyne, R. and Laville, S. (2001) 'They were like two bodies with one brain, raping and killing for kicks', *The Telegraph* [online] 3rd February. Available at: http://www.telegraph.co.uk/news/uknews/1320832/They-were-like-two-bodies-withone-brain-raping-and-killing-for-kicks.html [Accessed 22nd February 2012]

Clubb, M. J., Erik, W. A., Geda L. C. and Traugott, W. M. (1985) 'Sharing research data in the social sciences', In Fienberg, S. E., Martin, M. E., and Straf, M. L. (eds.), *Sharing Research Data* Washington: National Academy Press

Cohen, L. and Felson, M. (1979) 'Social change and crime rate trends: A routine activity approach', *American Sociological Review*, Vol. 44, pp. 588–608

Cohen, S. (2002) *Folk Devils and Moral Panics: The Creation of the Mods and Rockers*, (3rd ed.) Abingdon: Routledge

Cohen, S. and Young, J. (1981) *The Manufacture of News: Deviance, Social Problems and the Mass Media* (2nd ed.), London: Constable

Corbin, J. M. and Strauss, A. L. (2008) *Basics of Qualitative Research: Techniques and Procedures for Developing Grounded Theory*, London: Sage Publications

Corcoran, K. (2013) 'Did the Yorkshire Ripper kill SEVENTEEN more women? Retired policeman "strongly believes" catalogue of unsolved murders have the hallmarks of Peter Sutcliffe', *Mail Online*, 24th November. Available at: http://www.dailymail.co.uk/news/article-2512616/

Did-Yorkshire-Ripper-killSEVENTEEN-women-Retired-policeman-strongly-believes-catalogue-unsolvedmurders-hallmarks-Peter-Sutcliffe.html [Accessed 19th June 2014]

Cornish, D.B. (1993) 'Theories of action in criminology: Learning theory and rational choice approaches', In R. V. Clarke and M. Felson (Eds.), *Routine Activity and Rational Choice*, New Brunswick: Transaction, pp. 351–382

Cornish, D. B. and Clarke, R.V. (1987) 'Understanding Crime Displacement', *Criminology*, Vol. 24, No.4, pp. 933–947

(2008) 'The rational choice perspective', In R. Wortley and L. Mazerolle (eds.) *Environmental Criminology and Crime Analysis*, Cullompton: Willan Publishing

Costa, P.T., McCrae, R. R . and Holland, J. L. (1984) 'Personality and vocational interests in an adult sample', *Journal of Applied Psychology*, Vol. 69, pp. 390–400

Coulthard, M. and Johnson, A. (2007) *An Introduction to Forensic Linguistics: Language in Evidence,* New York: Routledge

Courtenay, W. H. (2000) 'Constructions of masculinity and their influence on men's well-being: a theory of gender and health', *Social Science and Medicine*, Vol. 50, pp. 1385–1401

Crace, J. (2004) 'Two Brains' *The Guardian* [online] 2nd November. Available at: http://www.theguardian.com/uk/2004/nov/02/ukcrime.highereducationprofile [Accessed 25th June 2014]

Craig, W. M., Pepler, D. and Atlas, R. (2000) 'Observations of bullying in the playground and in the classroom' [Special Issue: Bullies and Victims], *School Psychology International*, Vol. 21, pp. 22–36

Cramb, A. (2008) 'Handyman Peter Tobin guilty of murdering schoolgirl Vicky Hamilton', *Telegraph* [online] 12th March. Available at: http://www.telegraph.co.uk/news/uknews/scotland/3543265/Handyman-Peter-Tobinguilty-of-murdering-schoolgirl-Vicky-Hamilton.html?mobile=basic [Accessed 26th June 2015]

Critcher, C., Petley, J., Hughes, J. and Rohloff, A. (2013) *Moral Panics in the Contemporary World*, London: Bloomsbury Academic

Cross, R. (1981) *The Yorkshire Ripper*, London: Granada Publishing Ltd.

Crowley, C., Harré , R., and Tagg, C. (2002) 'Qualitative research and computing: Methodological issues and practices in using NVivo and NUD*IST', *International Journal of Social Research Methodology*, Vol. 5, No. 3, pp. 193–197

D'Cruze, S. Walklate, S. Pegg, S. (2006) *Murder: Social and Historical Approaches to Understanding Murder and Murderers*, Cullompton: Willan

Dagnell, A. (2012) '"I never told the police that Fred West raped me when I had the chance. He murdered all those other poor girls because of me"–The Wests Nanny: Pain and Guilt of the One who Got Away', *Sunday Mirror* [online] 29th April. Available at: http://www.thefreelibrary.com/'+I+never+told+the+police+that+Fred+West+raped+m e+when+I+had+the...-a0287985088 [Accessed 25th June 2014]

Davey, E. (2009) 'Snaring the Stockwell Strangler', *BBC News* [online] 14th July. Available at: http://news.bbc.co.uk/1/hi/england/london/8149921.stm [Accessed 28th February 2012]

David, H. A. and Nagaraja, H. N. (1970) *Order Statistics* (3rd ed.) London: Wiley.

Davies, C. (2011) 'Milly Dowler murder: Levi Bellfield convicted', *The Guardian* [online] 23rd June. Available at: http://www.theguardian.com/uk/2011/jun/23/milly-dowler-murderer-levi-bellfield [Accessed 6th June 2014]

Davis, C. A. (2005) *Couples Who Kill: Profiles of Deviant Duos*, London: Allison and Busby

Day, E., Poole, O. and Jenkins, L. (2007) 'Are there more Houses of Horror to be found?', *The Guardian* [online] 18th November. Available at: http://www.theguardian.com/uk/2007/nov/18/ukcrime.elizabethday [Accessed 23rd June 2014]

De Fruyt, F. and Mervielde, I. (1997) 'The Five-Factor model of personality and Holland's RIASEC interest types', *Personality and Individual Differences*, Vol. 1, 87–103

Deaux, K. (1984) 'From individual differences to social categories. Analysis of a decade's research on gender', *American Psychologist*, Vol. 39, pp. 105–116 Deng, C., Armstrong, P. I. and Rounds, J. (2007) 'The fit of Holland's RIASEC model to US occupations', *Journal of Vocational Behaviour*, Vol. 71, pp. 1–22

Denzin, N. K. (1970) the *Research Act in Sociology*, Chicago: Aldine

Diamond, Jared (1996) 'The Roots of Radicalism', *The New York Review of Books*, 14 November, pp. 4–6

'Did the Yorkshire Ripper murder five women in the Midlands?' (2014) *Birmingham Mail* [online] 16th March. Available at: http://www.birminghammail.co.uk/news/midlands-news/yorkshire-ripper-midlands-murders-probe-6837058 [Accessed 22nd June 2014]

Dimolianis, S. (2011) *Jack the Ripper and Black Magic: Victorian Conspiracy Theories, Secret Societies and the Supernatural Mystique of the Whitechapel Murders*, Jefferson: McFarland and Company Inc.

Ditmore, M. H. (2006) *Encyclopedia of Prostitution and Sex Work*, Vol. 2, Westport: Greenwood Press

Dixon, C. (2011) *The Crossbow Cannibal: The Definitive Story of Stephen Griffiths–the Self-Made Serial Killer*, London: John Blake Publishing Ltd

Donnelly, M. (2005) *Sixties Britain: Culture, Society and Politics,* Harlow: Pearson Education Ltd.

Doris, J., M. (2010) 'Foreword', in: S. Waller (ed.) 2010. *Serial Killers: Being and Killing Philosophy for Everyone,* West Sussex: Blackwell Publishing Ltd, pp. Viii–Xi

Douglas, J. E., Burgess, A. W., Burgess, A. G. and Ressler, R. K. (1992). *Crime Classification Manual: A Standard System for Investigating and Classifying Violent Crimes*, San Francisco: Jossey-Bass

Downe-Wamboldt, B. (1992) 'Content analysis: Method, applications, and issues', *Health Care for Women International,* Vol. 13, pp. 313–321

Durham, A. M., Elrod, H. P. and Kinkade, P. T. (1995) 'Images of crime and justice: Murder and the "true crime" genre' *Journal of Criminal Justice*, Vol. 23, No. 2, pp. 143–152

Eagly, A. H. (1983) 'Gender and social influence: A social psychological analysis' *American Psychologist*, Vol. 38, pp. 971–981

Eck, J. E. (1994) 'Drug Markets and Drug Places: A Case-Control Study of the Spatial Structure of Illicit Drug Dealing', *Unpublished Ph.D. dissertation*, University of Maryland: College Park

Edwards, R. (2008) 'Serial killer Steve Wright will die behind bars for killing five prostitutes, a judge has ruled', *The Telegraph*, 22nd February, p. 7

(2009) 'Convicted sex killer Peter Tobin "murdered A-level student and buried body in garden", court hears', *The Telegraph* [online] 24th June. Available at: http://www.telegraph.co.uk/news/uknews/law-and-order/5613946/Convicted-sexkiller-Peter-Tobin-murdered-A-level-student-and-buried-body-in-garden-courthears.html [Accessed 5th May 2013]

Edwards, R. (2010) 'Milly Dowler murder: parents to learn if Levi Bellfield will face trial', *The Telegraph* [online] 30th March. Available at: http://www.telegraph.co.uk/news/uknews/crime/7536046/Milly-Dowler-murderparents-to-learn-if-Levi-Bellfield-will-face-trial.html [Accessed 24th June 2014]

Egger, S. A. (1990) 'Serial Murder: A Synthesis of Literature and Research,' in S. A. Egger, Ed. *Serial Murder: An Elusive Phenomenon*. New York: Praeger Publishers, pp. 3–34

(1998) *The Killers Among Us: An Examination of Serial Murder and Its Investigation* (2nd ed.) Upper Saddle River: Prentice Hall

Eisenhardt, K. M. (1989) 'Building theories from case study research', *Academy of Management Review*, Vol. 14, pp. 532–550

Elder-Vass, D. (2012) *The Reality of Social Construction*, Cambridge: Cambridge University Press

Elias, R. (2006) 'Angelika Died Horrific and Very Violent Death' *Daily Record* [online] 2nd October. Available at: http://www.dailyrecord.co.uk/news/uk-world-news/angelika-died-horrific-and-very-violent-936355 [Accessed 24th June 2014]

(2007) 'Tobin was a travelling salesman, selling death' *Scotland on Sunday*, 6th May, p. 10

Elo, S. and Kyngas, H. (2008) 'The Qualitative Content Analysis Process' *Journal of Advanced Nursing*, Vol. 61, No. 1, pp. 107–115

Emsley, J. (2008) *Molecules of Murder: Criminal Molecules and Classic Cases*, Cambridge: The Royal Society of Chemistry 'Emotional scenes as Levi Bellfield is convicted of Milly's murder' (2011) *The Independent* [online] 24th June. Available at: http://www.independent.co.uk/news/uk/crime/emotional-scenes-as-levi-bellfield-isconvicted-of-millys-murder-2302026.html [accessed 24th June 2014]

Evans, M. (2009) 'Peter Tobin "buried teenage victim at suburban house"' *The Telegraph* [online] 14th December. Available at: http://www.telegraph.co.uk/news/uknews/crime/6810632/Peter-Tobin-buriedteenage-victim-at-suburban-house.html [Accessed 16th June 2014]

(2010) 'Police excavate former homes of serial killer Peter Tobin' *The Telegraph* [online] 13th July. Available at: http://www.telegraph.co.uk/news/uknews/crime/7885543/Police-excavate-formerhomes-of-serial-killer-Peter-Tobin.html [Accessed 24th June 2014]

Evans, S. and Gainey, P. (1998) *Jack the Ripper: First American Serial Killer*, London: Kodansha America

Farh, J. L., Leong, F. T. L. and Law, K. S. (1998) 'Cross-cultural validity of Holland's model in Hong Kong', *Journal of Vocational Behaviour*, Vol. 52, pp. 425–440

Farrell, G., Clark, K., Ellingworth, D. and Pease. K. (2005) '"Of Targets and Super targets" a Routine Activity Theory of High Crime rates', *Internet Journal of Criminology*

Feist, J. and Feist, G.J. (2006) *Theories of Personality*, New York: Mc Graw Hill

Felson, M. (2000) 'The routine activity approach as a general social theory', In S. S.Simpson (ed.) *Of Crime and Criminality: The Use of Theory in Everyday Life*, Thousand Oaks: Sage Publications

(2008) 'Routine activity theory', In: R. Wortley and L. Mazerolle (eds.) *Environmental Criminology and Crime Analysis*. Cullompton: Willan Publishing, pp. 70–77

Ferguson, C. J, White, D. E., Cherry, S., Lorenz, M. and Bhimani, Z. (2003) 'Defining and classifying serial murder in the context of perpetrator motivation', *Journal of Criminal Justice*, Vol. 31, pp. 287–29

Ferreira, J. A. A. and Hood, A. B. (1995) 'The Development and Validation of a Holland-Type Portuguese Vocational Interest Inventory', *Journal of Vocational Behaviour*, Vol. 46, No. 2, pp. 119–130

'Five murders in six weeks but no one knows why; Strangler was shy, ordinary man who didn't fit profile of a killer', (2008) *The Evening Standard*, 21st February, p. 6

Falk, G. (1990) *Murder: An Analysis of Its Forms, Conditions, and Causes,* North Carolina, McFarland and Company

Flyvbjerg, B. (2006) 'Five Misunderstandings About Case-Study Research', *Qualitative Inquiry*, Vol. 12, No. 2, pp. 219–245

'Fred West "link" in murder puzzle', (2001) *BBC News* [online] 10th February. Available at: http://news.bbc.co.uk/1/hi/wales/1163511.stm [Accessed 19th June 2014]

Freidson, E. (1970) *Profession of Medicine: A Study of the Sociology of Applied Knowledge*, New York: Harper and Row

Freud, S. (2003) *Beyond the Pleasure Principle*, London: Penguin

Fricker, M. (2011) 'Levi Bellfield was "6ft of pure evil"' *The Mirror* [online] 24th June. Available at: http://www.mirror.co.uk/news/uk-news/levi-bellfield-was-6ft-of-pure-evil-137037 [Accessed 25th June 2014]

Furnham, A. (1994) *Personality at Work*, London: Routledge

(2001) 'Self-estimates of intelligence: Culture and gender differences in self and other estimates of both general and multiple intelligences', *Personality and Individual Differences*, Vol. 31, pp. 1381–1405

Gaines, L. and Miller, R. (2007) *Criminal Justice in Action* (4th ed.) Belmont: Thomson Higher Education

Gallagher, I. (2008) 'My life with the Suffolk Strangler, by the partner he drove to work before murdering prostitutes', *Mail Online* [online] 25th February. Available at: http://www.dailymail.co.uk/femail/article-517797/

EXCLUSIVE-My-life-SuffolkStrangler-partner-drove-work-murdering-prostitutes.
html [Accessed 24th June 2014]

Gammell, C. and Hughes, M. (2011) 'Levi Bellfield trial: a blink of the eye and Milly
Dowler was gone', *The Telegraph* [online] 11th May. Available at: http://www.
telegraph.co.uk/news/uknews/crime/8506314/Levi-Bellfield-trial-a-blinkof-the-eye-
and-Milly-Dowler-was-gone.html?fb [Accessed 20th June 2014]

'Gay Serial Killer is given Three Life Sentences' (1996) *The Independent* [online] 29th
February. Available at: http://www.independent.co.uk/news/gay-serial-killer-is-
giventhree-life-sentences-1321584.html [Accessed 28th February 2012]

Geertz, C. (1973) 'Thick Description: Toward an Interpretive Theory of Culture' in *The
Interpretation of Cultures: Selected Essays*, New York: Basic Books, pp. 3–30

(1995) *After the Fact: Two Countries, Four Decades, One Anthropologist*, Cambridge:
Harvard University Press

George, A. L and Bennett, G. A. (2004) *Case Studies and Theory Development in the
Social Sciences*, Cambridge: Belfer Centre for Science and International Affairs

Gergen, K. (1985). 'The Social Constructionist Movement in Modern Psychology',
American Psychologist, Vol. 40, No. 3, pp. 266–275

Giannangelo, S.J. (1996). *The Psychopathology of Serial Murder: A Theory in Violence*.
Westport: Praeger

Gibson, D. C. (2006) *Serial Murder and Media Circuses,* Westport: Praeger Publishers

Giddens, A. (1982) *Profiles and Critiques in Social Theory*, Berkeley: University of
California Press

Glaser, B. A., Calhoun, G. B. and Bates, J. M. (2003) 'Self-reported career interests
among court referred adolescent males: A pilot study', *Journal of Addictions and
Offender Counselling*, Vol. 23, No. 2, pp. 73–82

Godwin, G. M. (1998) 'Inner themes — outer behaviours: A multivariate facet model
of U.S. serial murderers' crime scene actions'. *Unpublished doctoral dissertation*,
University of Liverpool

Godwin, G. M. and Canter, D. V. (1997) 'Encounter and death: the spatial behaviour
of us serial killers', *Policing: an International Journal of Police Strategy and
Management*, vol. 20, pp. 24–38

Goodman, J. (1986) *The Moors Murders: The Trial of Myra Hindley and Ian Brady*,
London: David and Charles

Graneheim U. H. and Lundman B. (2004) 'Qualitative content analysis in nursing research: concepts, procedures and measures to achieve trustworthiness' *Nurse Education Today*, Vol. 24, pp. 105–112

Gravetter, F. and Forzano, L. (2011) *Research Methods for the Behavioural Sciences*, London: Engage Learning

Greig, C. (2012) *Serial Killers: Horrifying True-Life Cases of Pure Evil*, London: Arcturus Publishing Ltd.

Groff, E. R. and McEwen, T. (2005) 'Disaggregating the journey to homicide' in

F. Wang (ed.), *Geographic Information Systems and Crime Analysis*, Hershey: Idea Group Inc., pp. 60–83

Grossman, D. (1996) *On Killing: The Psychological Cost of Learning to Kill in War and Society*, New York: Back Bay Books

Groth, A. N., Burgess, A. W. and Holmstrom, l. l. (1977), 'Rape: Power, Anger and Sexuality', *American Journal of Psychiatry*, Vol.134, pp. 1239–1243

Grover, C. and Soothill, K. (1997) 'British Serial Killing: Towards a Structural Explanation', *British Society of Criminology*, Vol. 2, July, pp. 1–17

Guest, G., Bunce, A. and Johnson, L. (2006) 'How many interviews are enough? An experiment with data saturation and variability', *Field Methods*, Vol. 18 No. 1, pp. 5982

Guillemin, M. and Gillam, L. (2004) 'Ethics, Reflexivity, and "Ethically Important Moments" in Research', *Qualitative Inquiry*, Vol. 10, No. 2, pp. 261–280

Haggett, P., Cliff, A. D. and Frey. A. (1977) *Locational Analysis in Human Geography*, Edward Arnold: London

Hamilton, T. (2011) 'The Monster Butler: Fake toff serial killer Archibald Thomson Hall murdered for riches', *Daily Record* [online] 30th March. Available at: http://www.dailyrecord.co.uk/news/uk-world-news/the-monster-butler-fake-toff-serial-1098917 [Accessed 20th July 2013]

Hammersley, M. and Atkinson, P. (1995) *Ethnography: Principles in Practice* (2nd ed), London: Routledge

Hammond, L. and Youngs, D. (2011) 'Decay Functions and Offender Spatial Processes' *Journal of Investigative Psychology and Offender Profiling*, Vol. 8, No. 1, pp. 90–102

Harbort, S. and Mokros, A. (2001) 'Serial murderers in Germany from 1945 to 1995: A descriptive study', *Homicide Studies*, Vol. 5, Vol. 4, pp. 311–334

Harris, S. and Wright, P. (2001) 'Scot who helped jail Railway Rapist; Evidence proved vital in serial killer case', *The Sunday Herald* [online] 11th February. Available at: http://www.highbeam.com/doc/1P2-19040369.html [Accessed 2nd June 2014]

Harrison, P. and Wilson, D. (2010) *The Lost British Serial Killer*, London: Sphere

Harrison, W. A. (1998) 'The occupations of drink drivers: Using occupational information to identify targetable characteristics of offenders', *Accident Analysis and Prevention*, Vol. 30, No. 1, pp. 119–132

Hartman, T. (1987) *The Colour Code*, New York: Taylor Don Hartman

Haverkamp, B. E., Collins, R. C., and Hansen, J. (1994) 'Structure of interests of Asian-American college students', *Journal of Counselling Psychology*, Vol. 41, No. 2, pp. 256–264

Hazelwood, R. and Douglas, J. (1980) 'The lust murderer', *FBI law enforcement Bulletin*, Vol. 49: pp. 1–5

Hedrick, T. E. (1985) 'Justifications for and obstacles to data sharing', in S. Fienberg, M. Martin and M. Straf (eds.), *Sharing Research Data*, Washington: National Academy of Sciences

Henderson, P. (1995) 'Making of a Monster', *Courier Mail*, 3rd January p. 2

Hepburn, C. and Hinch, R. (1997) 'Researching Serial Murder: Methodological and Definitional Problems', *Electronic Journal of Sociology*, Vol. 3, December [Online] Available at: http://www.sociology.org/content/vol003.002/hinch.html [Accessed 28th May 2012]

Hergenhahn, B. R. and Olson, M. H. (2007) *Introduction to Theories of Personality*, (7th edn.), Englewood Cliffs: Prentice-Hall

Heylighen, F. (1993) 'Selection Criteria for the Evolution of Knowledge', *13th International Congress on Cybernetics*, pp. 524–528

Heylighen, F. (1993) *Epistemology Introduction* [online] Available at: http://pespmc1.vub.ac.be/EPISTEMI.html [accessed 27th May 2012]

Hickey G. and Kipping E. (1996) 'A multi-stage approach to the coding of data from open-ended questions', *Nurse Researcher*, Vol. 4, pp. 81–91

Hickey, E. (1991) *Serial Murderers and Their Victims*, Belmont: Wadsworth
(1997) *Serial Murderers and Their Victims* (2nd edn.). Belmont: Wadsworth
(2006) *Serial Murderers and their Victims* (4th ed.), London: Thomson Higher Education

Hilliard, M., Harkin, G. and Young, D. (2011) 'Paedophile faces questions in missing teen's cold case' *Independent* [online] 28th October. Available at: http://www.

independent.ie/irish-news/courts/paedophile-faces-questions-in-missingteens-cold-case-26786394.html [Accessed 24th June 2014]

'His Name is Evil: Levi Bellfield' (2012) *The Mirror* [online] 15th May. Available at: http://www.mirror.co.uk/news/uk-news/his-name-is-evil-levi-bellfield-832593 [Accessed 23rd June 2014]

Hislop, R. D. (1999) *Construction Site Safety: A Guide for Managing Contractors*, Boca Raton: CRC Press

Hodgson, P. (2011) *Jack the Ripper: Through the Mists of Time*, Dartford Kent: Pneuma Publishing

Holland, J. L. (1973) *Making Vocational Choices: A Theory of Careers*, Englewood Cliffs: Prentice-Hall

   (1997) *Making Vocational Choices* (3rd edn.). Odessa: Psychological Assessment Resources, Inc.

Holmes, R. and DeBurger, J. (1988) *Serial Murder*. Newbury Park: Sage Publications

Holmes, R. M. and Holmes, S. T. (2009) *Serial Murder* (3rd edn.) London: Sage Publications

   (1994) *Murder in America*. Thousand Oaks: Sage Publications

Holmes, S. and Holmes, R. (2002) *Sex Crimes: Patterns and Behaviour* (2nd edn.), Thousand Oaks: Sage Publications

Holstein, J. A. and Gubrium, J. F. (1997) *The New Language of Qualitative Method*, Oxford: Oxford University Press

Homan, R. (1992) 'The ethics of open methods' *British Journal of Sociology*, Vol. 43, pp. 321–332

Honeycombe, G. (1982) *The Murders of the Black Museum, 1870–1970*, London: Hutchinson Press

Hopkins, N. (2000) 'Childhood bond "led to rape and murder"' *The Guardian* [online] 4th October. Available at: http://www.theguardian.com/uk/2000/oct/04/nickhopkins [Accessed 24th June 2014]

House of Commons (2008) *A Surveillance Society?, Fifth Report of Session 2007–08*, Vol. 2, London: TSO

Hsieh, H. F. and Shannon, S. E. (2005) 'Three approaches to qualitative content analysis', *Qualitative Health Research*, Vol. 15, No. 9, pp. 1277–1288

Huisman, O. and Forer, P. (1998) 'Towards a geometric framework for modelling space-time opportunities and interaction potential', *Paper presented at the International*

Geographical Union, Commission on Modelling Geographical Systems Meeting, 28–29 August, Lisbon: Portugal

'Is this Peter Tobin, the UK's worst ever serial killer?' (2010) *The Mirror* [online] 16th July. Available at: http://www.mirror.co.uk/news/uk-news/peter-tobin--uks-worst-235864 [Accessed 20th June 2014]

Jenkins, P. (1988) 'Serial Murder in England, 1940–1985,' *Journal of Criminal Justice*, Vol. 16, pp. 1–15

(1994) *Using Murder: The Social Construction of Serial Homicide*, New York: Aldine de Gruyter

Jewkes, Y. (2004) *Media and Crime*, London: Sage Publications

Johnson, R. B., and Onwuegbuzie, A. J. (2004) 'Mixed methods research: A research paradigm whose time has come', *Educational Researcher*, Vol. 33, No. 7, pp. 14–26

Jones, M. R. (2007) *Palmetto Predators: Monsters Among Us*, Charleston: History Press

Jones, N. J., Bennell, C. and Emeno, K. (2012) 'A multivariate model of serial homicide', Unpublished manuscript

Jouve, N., W. (1986) *"The Street Cleaner" The Yorkshire Ripper Case on Trial*, London: M. Boyers

Kalman, C. (1994) 'Increasing the Accessibility of Data', *British Medical Journal* Vol. 309, pp. 740–746

Kant, I. (2002) *Groundwork of the Metaphysics of Morals*, trans. Allen Wood, New Haven: Yale University Press

Kelly, L. and Radford, J. (1987) 'The Problem of Men: Feminist Perspectives on Sexual Violence', in P. Scraton, P. Gordon, eds. *Causes for Concern. British Criminal Justice on Trial?* Harmondsworth: Penguin

Kennedy, M. M. (1979) 'Generalizing from Single Case Studies', *Evaluation Quarterly*, Vol. 3, No. 4, pp. 661–678

Kent, J. (2003) 'Using Functional Distance Measures When Calibrating Journey to Crime Distance Decay Algorithms', *MSc Thesis*, Louisiana State University

Kent, J., Leitner, M. and Curtis, A. (2006) 'Evaluating the usefulness of functional distance measures when calibrating journey-to-crime distance decay functions', *Computers, Environment and Urban Systems*, Vol. 30, pp. 181–200

Keppel, R. D. and Birnes, W. J. (2003) *The Psychology of Serial Killer Investigations: The Grisly Business Unit*, London: Academic Press

Keppel, R. D. and Walter, R. (1999) 'Profiling killers: A revised classification model for understanding sexual murder', *International Journal of Offender Therapy and Comparative Criminology*, Vol. 43, pp. 417–437

Kerr, G. (2011) *World Serial Killers*, New York: Canary Press

Khan, S. B., Alvi, S. A., Shaukat, N., Hussain, M. A., and Baig, T. (1990) 'A study of the validity of Holland's theory in a non-western culture' *Journal of Vocational Behaviour*, Vol. 36, pp. 132–146

King, N. (1994) 'The qualitative research interview', In Qualitative methods in C. Cassell and G. Symon (eds.), *Oganizational Research: A practical guide*, London: Sage Publications, pp. 14–36

Kirby, T. (1993) 'Serial killer Locked up for Life: "To Take One Human Life is an Outrage, to Take Five is Carnage,"' says Judge', *The Independent* [online] 21st December. Available at: http://www.independent.co.uk/news/ serial-killer-locked-up-for-life-to-take-one-human-life-is-an-outrage-to-take-five-is-carnage-says-1468716.html [Accessed 28th February 2012]

Kirk, J. and Miller, M. L. (1986) *Reliability and Validity in Qualitative research*, Beverly Hills: Sage Publications

Kondracki, N. L., and Wellman, N. S. (2002) 'Content analysis: Review of methods and their applications in nutrition education', *Journal of Nutrition Education and Behaviour*, Vol. 34, pp. 224–230

Kracauer, S. (1952) 'The challenge of qualitative content analysis', *Public Opinion Quarterly*, Vol. 16, pp. 631–642

Krafft-Ebing, R. (1896) *Psychopathia Sexualis: With Especial Reference to Contrary Sexual Instinct: A Medico-legal Study*, Philadelphia: F.A. Davis

Krippendorff, K. (1980) *Content Analysis: An Introduction to its Methodology*, Beverly Hills: Sage Publications

Krueckeberg, D. A. and Silvers, A. L. (1974) *Urban Planning Analysis: Methods and Models*, New York: John Wiley and Sons

Lane, B. and Gregg, W. (1995) *The Encyclopedia of Serial Killers,* New York: Berkley

Lauri S. and Kyngas, H. (2005) *Developing Nursing Theories,* Werner Söderström, Dark Oy: Vantaa

Law, M. (2005) 'Reduce, Reuse, Recycle: Issues in the Secondary Use of Research Data', *IASSIST Quarterly*, Vol. 29, pp. 5–11

Leafe, D. (2010) 'Solved: How the Brides in the Bath Died at the Hands of their Ruthless Womanising Husband', *The Mail Online* [online] 22nd April. Available at: http://www.dailymail.co.uk/femail/article-1267913/Solved-How-brides-bath-diedhands-ruthless-womaniser.html [Accessed 28th February 2012]

Lee, K. and Ashton, M. C. (2012) *H Factor of Personality: Why Some People Are Manipulative, Self-Entitled, Materialistic and Exploitive and Why it Matters for Everyone*, Ontario: Wilfred Laurier University Press

Lester, D. (1995) *Serial Killers: The Insatiable Passion.* Philadelphia: Charles Press

'Levi Bellfield defence was a charade driven by hatred, victim's family claims' (2011) The Guardian [online] 27th June. Available at: http://www.theguardian.com/uk/2011/jun/27/levi-bellfield-defence-milly-dowler [Accessed 2nd February 2013]

Levin, A. (2001) 'They dragged me off the street, into a never-ending nightmare; Victim of sadistic pair who went hunting for women tells of the attack that nearly destroyed her life RAILWAY RAPISTS', *Daily Mail*, 3rd February, p. 8

Levin, F. and Fox, J. A. (1985) *Mass Murder: America's Growing Menace,* Plenum Press: London

Levin, J. and Fox, J. A. (2012) *Extreme Killing: Understanding Serial and Mass Murder,* London: Sage Publications

Levy, A. (2009) 'Serial killer Peter Tobin convicted of killing teenager Dinah McNicol… but how many more did he kill?' *Mail Online* [online] 18th December. Available at: http://www.dailymail.co.uk/news/article-1236349/Peter-Tobinconvicted-murder-guilty-killing-teenager-Dinah-McNicol.html [Accessed 25th June 2014]

Leyton, E. (1986) *Hunting Humans: The Rise of the Modern Multiple Murder,* London: Washington Mews Books

Liebert, J. (1985), 'Contributions to psychiatric consultation in the investigation of serial murder', *International Journal of Offender Therapy and Comparative Criminology*, Vol. 29, pp. 187–200

Lincoln, Y. S. and Guba, E. G. (1985) *Naturalistic Inquiry*, Beverly Hills, CA: Sage Publications

'List of Occupations by RIASEC Interest Area' (n.d.) [online] Available at: http://www.career-lifeskills.com/pdf/jst-576530-occupations.pdf [Accessed 24th June 2014]

Lock, A. and Strong, T. (2010) *Social Constructionism: Sources and Stirrings in Theory and Practice*, Cambridge: Cambridge University Press

Low, K. S. and Rounds, J. (2006) 'Interest change and continuity from early adolescence to middle adulthood', *International Journal for Educational and Vocational Guidance*, Vol. 7, No. 1, pp. 23–36

Lundrigan, S. and Canter, D. (2001) 'A Multivariate Analysis of Serial Murderers' Disposal Site Location choice', *Journal of Environmental Psychology*, Vol. 21, No. 4, pp. 423–432

(2008) 'A Multivariate analysis of Serial Murderers' Disposal Site Location Choice', in D. Canter and D. Youngs (eds). *Applications of Geographical Offender Profiling*, Aldershot: Ashgate Publishing Limited, pp. 25–41

MacIntyre, A. (1984) *After Virtue: A Study in Moral Theory* (2nd edn.), Notre Dame: University of Notre Dame Press

Malkin, B. (2008) 'Steve Wright Guilty of Ipswich Prostitutes Murders', *The Telegraph* [online] 21st February. Available at: http://www.telegraph.co.uk/news/uknews/1579404/Steve-Wright-guilty-ofIpswich-prostitutes-murders.html [Accessed 25th June 2014]

Manzoor, S. (2009) 'The murderer in our midst', *The Guardian* [online] 30th January. Available at: http://www.theguardian.com/lifeandstyle/2009/jan/30/family-levi-bellfield [Accessed 25th June 2014]

Martens, W. H. J. and Palermo, B. (2005) 'Loneliness and associated violent antisocial behaviour: Analysis of the case reports of Jeffrey Dahmer and Dennis Nilsen', *International Journal of Offender Therapy and Comparative Criminology*, Vol. 49, No.3, pp. 298–307

'Masculinity' (2007) *International Encyclopaedia of Men and Masculinities*, Abingdon: Routledge

Masters, B. (1995) *Killing for Company: the Case of Dennis Nilsen*, London: Arrow Books

(1997) *'She Must Have Known': The Trial of Rosemary West*, London: Doubleday

(2007) *The Shrine of Jeffrey Dahmer*, London: Hodder General Publishing Division

Mathieson, J. (2008) 'Links found in Angelika Kluk case helped cops nail Peter Tobin for Vicky Hamilton murder', *Daily Record* [online] 3rd December. Available at: http://www.dailyrecord.co.uk/news/scottish-news/links-found-in-angelika-kluk-case-1000203 [Accessed 24th June 2014]

Matthews, B. and Ross, L. (2010) *Research Methods: A Practical Guide for the Social Sciences*, London: Longman

Matza, D. (1964) *Delinquency and Drift*, New York: John Wiley and Sons, Inc.

Maxwell, J. A. (1992) 'Understanding and validity in qualitative research', *Harvard Educational Review*, Vol. 62, pp. 279–300

(2010) 'Using Numbers in Qualitative Research', *Qualitative Inquiry*, Vol. 16, No. 6, pp. 475–482

Mayring, P. (2000) *The Qualitative Content Analysis* (7th edn. 1st edition 1983) Weinheim: Deutscher Studien Verlag

Mayring, P. (2004) 'Qualitative Content Analysis', in U. Flick, E. V. Kardoff and I. Steinke (eds.) *A Companion to Qualitative Research*, London: Sage Publications, pp. 266–270

Mcaleese, D. (2011) 'Fuel receipts "link driver to Jennifer Cardy's murder"', *Belfast Telegraph*, 23 September [online] Available at: http://www.belfasttelegraph.co.uk/news/local-national/northern-ireland/fuel-receiptslink-driver-to-jennifer-cardys-murder-28661138.html [last accessed 12/10/13]

McCaffery, S. (2011) 'No mercy plea made for serial child killer Robert Black', *Belfast Telegraph* [online] 8th December. Available at: http://www.belfasttelegraph.co.uk/news/local-national/northern-ireland/no-mercyplea-made-for-serial-child-killer-robert-black-16088445.html [Accessed 21st February 2013]

McCain G. C. (1988) 'Content analysis: a method for studying clinical nursing problems', *Applied Nursing Research*, Vol. 1, No. 3, pp. 146–150

McClellan, J. (2008) 'Delivery Drivers and Long-Haul Truckers: Travelling Serial Murderers', *Journal of Applied Security Research,* Vol. 3, No. 2, pp. 171–190

McDonald, H. (2011) ' Child killer Robert Black sentenced to 25 years for murder of Jennifer Cardy', *The Guardian* [online] 8th December. Available at: http://www.theguardian.com/uk/2011/dec/08/robert-black-sentenced-25-years [Accessed 28th February 2012]

McEwen, A. (2013) 'Caroline Hogg murder: City scarred 30 years on' *The Scotsman* [online] 8th July. Available at: http://www.scotsman.com/news/scotland/topstories/caroline-hogg-murder-city-scarred-30-years-on-1-2992923 [Accessed 23rd June 2014]

McKay, D. A and Toker, D. M. (2012) 'The HEXACO and five-factor models of personality in relation to RIASEC vocational interests', *Journal of Vocational Behaviour,* Vol. 81, pp. 138–149

McLaren, A. (1995) *A Prescription for Murder: The Victorian Serial Killings of Dr. Thomas Neill,* London: The University of Chicago Press

McShane, J. (2001) 'Milly Dowler's murderer Levi Bellfield was a sadistic serial killer and stalker', *The Express* [online] 4th September. Available at: http://www.express.co.uk/expressyourself/269117/Milly-Dowler-s-murderer-LeviBellfield-was-a-sadistic-serial-killer-and-stalker [Accessed 23rd June 2014]

    (2011) *Predator — The true Story of Levi Bellfield, The Man Who Murdered Milly Dowler, Marsha McDonnell and Amelie Delagrange*, London: John Blake

McVeigh, K. (2008) 'Accused Admits sex with Victims', *The Guardian* [online] 8th February. Available at: http://www.theguardian.com/uk/2008/feb/08/ukcrime. uknews4 [Accessed 19th June 2014]

Mead, M. (1964) 'Cultural factors in the cause of pathological homicide', *Bulletin of the Menninger Clinic*, Vol. 28, pp. 11–22

Mega, M. (2009) 'Exclusive: Wives of serial killer Peter Tobin reveal torment at legacy of pain' *Daily Record* [online] 20th December. Available at: http://www.dailyrecord. co.uk/news/scottish-news/exclusive-wives-of-serial-killer-peter-1045432 [Accessed 25th June 2014]

Mega, M. and Montague, B. (2007) 'Bloody Past of the Margate Monster', *The Sunday Times*, 18th November, pp. 12–15

Mellor, L. (2012) *Cold North Killers: Canadian Serial Murder*, High Town: Gazelle Books Services Limited

Merriam, S. B. (1995) 'What can you tell me from N of 1? Issues of Validity and Reliability in Qualitative research', *PAACE Journal of Lifelong Learning*, Vol. 4, pp. 51–60

Merton, R. (1938) 'Social structure and anomie', *American Sociological Review*, Vol. 3, pp. 672–682

Miethe, T. D., Stafford, M. C. and Scott Long, J. (1987) 'Social Differentiation in Criminal Victimization: A Test of Routine Activities/Lifestyle Theories', *American Sociological Review*, Vol. 52, pp. 184–94

Miranda, C. (2007) 'Body finds Raises Serial Killer Fears', *Herald Sun*, 15th November, p. 43

Misselbrook, D. (2010) 'The General Practitioner and Abuse in Primary Care', in F. Subotsky, S. Bewley, and M. Crowe (eds.) *Abuse of the Doctor-Patient Relationship*, London: R C Psych Publications, pp. 78–91

Mitchell, R. G. Jr. and Charmaz, K. (1996) 'Telling Tales, Writing Stories: Postmodernist Visions and Realist Images in Ethnographic Writing', *Journal of Contemporary Ethnography*, Vol. 25, No. 1, pp. 144–166

Mitchell, W. E. (1996) 'The Aetiology of Serial Murder: Towards an Integrated Model', *University of Cambridge Paper London*, Trinity Hall Nightingale Scholar in Mental Health Law

Moore, M. (2008) 'Levi Bellfield guilty of murdering two women', *The Telegraph* [online] 25th February. Available at: http://www.telegraph.co.uk/news/uknews/1579748/ Levi-Bellfield-guilty-ofmurdering-two-women.html [Accessed 23rd June 2014]

Morris, B. (2014) '20 years after horror, brother begs West to reveal fate of teenage girl', *Herald Scotland* [online] 23rd February. Available at: http://www.heraldscotland.com/news/13147240.20_years_after_horror__brother_begs_West_to_reveal_fate_of_teenage_girl/ [Accessed 20th June 2014]

Morris, S. (2001) 'Love of "hunting" united rapists', *The Guardian* [online] 3rd February. Available at: http://www.theguardian.com/uk/2001/feb/03/stevenmorris [Accessed 25th June 2014]

Morrison, M. and Moir, J. (1998) 'The role of computer software in the analysis of qualitative data: efficient clerk, research assistant or Trojan horse?', *Journal of Advanced Nursing*, Vol. 28, No. 1, pp. 106–116

Mott, N. (1999) 'Serial murder: Patterns in unsolved cases', *Homicide Studies*, Vol. 3, pp. 241–255

'Murderer made serial killer boast' (2006) *BBC News* [online] 24th February. Available at: http://news.bbc.co.uk/1/hi/england/nottinghamshire/4747374.stm [Accessed 23rd May 2013]

Murphy, E. and Dingwall, R. (2001) 'The Ethics of Ethnography' in P. Atkinson, A. Coffey, S. Delamont, J. Lofland and L. Lofland (eds.), *Handbook of Ethnography*, London: Sage Publications, pp. 339–352

Murray, W. (2009) *Serial Killers*, New York: Canary Press

Myers, W. C., Reccoppa, L., Burton. K. and McElroy, R. (1993) 'Malignant Sex and Aggression: An Overview of Serial Sexual Homicide', *Journal of the American Academy of Psychiatry and Law*, Vol. 21, No. 4, pp. 435–451

'My Ride with a Serial Killer', (2009) *The Guardian* [online] 27th February. Available at: http://www.theguardian.com/lifeandstyle/2009/feb/27/4 [Accessed 4th May 2014]

Newton, M. (2006) *The Encyclopaedia of Serial Killers,* New York: InfoBase Publishing

Nicol, A. (2011) *The Monster Butler*, London: Black and White Publishing

Nicole, A. and Proulx, J. (2007) 'Sexual murderers and sexual aggressors: Developmental paths and criminal history', in J. Proulx, E. Beauregard, M. Cusson, and A. Nicole (eds.), *Sexual Murderers: A Comparative Analysis and New Perspectives,* Chichester: Wiley, pp. 29–50

Noaks, L. and Wincup, E. (2004), *Criminological Research: Understanding Qualitative Methods,* London: Sage Publications

Nunkoosing, K. (2005) 'The Problems with Interviews', *Qualitative Health Research*, Vol. 15, No. 5, pp. 698–706

Oates, J. (2012) *John Christie of Rillington Place: Biography of a Serial Killer*, Barnsley: Pen and Sword Books Ltd.

'Obituary of Professor Stuart Kind Forensic scientist whos "geographical profiling" helped to catch the Yorkshire Ripper' (2003) *The Daily Telegraph*, 30th April, pg. 25–26

O'Hare, P. (2010) 'Search of former homes of serial killer Peter Tobin could last a month, police reveal' *Daily Record* [online] 14th July. Available at: http://www.dailyrecord.co.uk/news/scottish-news/search-of-former-homes-of-serial-killer-1064299 [Accessed 25th June 2015]

O'Neill, S. (2008) 'He was rude and aggressive, but no one's idea of a killer' *The Times* [online] 22nd February. Available at: http://www.thetimes.co.uk/tto/news/uk/crime/article1873941.ece [25th June 2014]

   (2008) 'A loner whose quietness is now taken for secretiveness', *The Times*, 22nd February, pp. 6–7

O'Neill, S. and Bird, S. (2006) 'Police review old cases as hunt for serial killer widens' *The Times*, 21st December, p. 6

Opack, P. (2000) *Throwaway People: Danger in Paradise*, New York: Savage Press Orb, A., Eisenhauer, L. and Wynaden, D. (2000) 'Ethics in Qualitative Research', *Journal of Nursing Scholarship*, Vol. 33, No. 1, pp. 93–96

Orr, J. and Sturcke, J. (2008) 'Killer Bellfield suspected in Milly Dowler murder', *The Guardian* [online] 25th February. Available at: http://www.theguardian.com/uk/2008/feb/25/ukcrime [Accessed 19th June 2014]

O'Sullivan D and Haklay M, (2000) 'Agent-based models and individualism: Is the world agent-based?' *Environment and Planning*, Vol. 32, No.8, pp. 1409–1425

Oswald, F. L. and Ferstl, K. L. (1999) 'Linking a Structure of Vocational Interests to Gottfredson's (1986) Occupational Aptitude Patterns Map', *Journal of Vocational Behaviour*, Vol. 54, pp. 214–231

Oswald, L. (2001) 'Caught in the Clutches of Evil', *The News of the World*, 4th February, p. 4

Ouimet, M. and Proulx, J. (1994) 'Spatial and temporal behaviour of paedophiles: Their clinical usefulness as to the relapse prevention model', *Paper presented at the 46th Annual Conference of the American Society of Criminology*: Miami

Parkin, K. (2011) 'The Key to the Universe: Springsteen, Masculinity, and the Car', in D. G. Izzo (ed.) *Bruce Springsteen and the American Soul*, London: McFarland and Company, Inc.

Parsons, B. (2010) 'Homes searched in Peter Tobin murder inquiry' *The Argus* [online] 12th July. Available at: http://www.theargus.co.uk/news/videonews/102577/read/ [Accessed 24th June 2014]

Patterson, J. (2012) 'Why The Black Panther can hold its head up high', *The Guardian* [online] 6th June. Available at: https://www.theguardian.com/film/filmblog/2012/jun/06/the-black-panther-donald-neilson [Accessed 7th April 2013]

Patton M. Q. (1990) *Qualitative Evaluation and Research Methods*, Newbury Park: Sage Publications

Patton, Q. M. (1987) *How to Use Qualitative Methods in Evaluation*, London: Sage Publications

Pearson, P. (1997) *When She was Bad: Violent Women and the Myth of Innocence*, Toronto: Random House

Peattie, L. (2001) 'Theorizing Planning: Some Comments on Flyvbjerg's Rationality and Power', *International Planning Studies*, Vol. 6, No. 3, pp. 257–262

Penrose, J. (2009) 'Britain's 35 Serial killers who will Never be Released from Jail', *Mirror News* [online] 15th February. Available at: http://www.mirror.co.uk/news/uk-news/britains-35-serial-killers-who-377101 [Accessed 28th February 2012]

Perper, J. A. Cina, S. J. (2010) *When Doctors Kill: Who, Why, and How*, New York: Springer Media

Persaud, R. (1995) 'Locked in a Cell The Only One he could Kill was Himself: An Expert's View on the Motive', *Daily Mail*, 3rd January, p. 11–12

'Peter Tobin 'buried teenage victim at suburban house', (2009) *The Telegraph* [online] 14th December. Available at: http://www.telegraph.co.uk/news/6810632/Peter-Tobinburied-teenage-victim-at-suburban-house.html [Accessed 25th June 2014]

'Peter Tobin convicted of murdering Dinah McNicol', (2009) *The Telegraph* [online] 16th December. Available at: http://www.telegraph.co.uk/news/uknews/crime/6826316/Peter-Tobin-convicted-ofmurdering-Dinah-McNicol.html [Accessed 24th June 2014]

'Peter Tobin convicted of third murder: Vicky Hamilton his first victim', (2009) *The Telegraph* [online] 17th December. Available at: http://www.telegraph.co.uk/news/uknews/crime/6826469/Peter-Tobin-convicted-ofthird-murder-Vicky-Hamilton-his-first-victim.html [Accessed 20th June 2014]

'Peter Tobin: timeline of his life of crime' (2009) *The Telegraph* [online] 17th December. Available at: http://www.telegraph.co.uk/news/uknews/crime/6826530/Peter-Tobin-timeline-ofhis-life-of-crime.html?mobile=basic [Accessed 25th June 2014]

Philips, E. and Pugh, D. S. (2005) *How to Get a PhD: A Handbook for Students and Their Supervisors*, London: Open University Press

Phillips, P. D. (1980) 'Characteristics and Typology of the Journey to Crime', in

Georges-Abeyie, D. E. and Harries, K. D. (eds.), *Crime: A Spatial Perspective*, New York: Colombia University Press

Pokel, C. (2000) *A Critical Analysis of Research Related to the Criminal Mind of Serial Killers,* Research paper, The Graduate College University of Wisconsin-Stout: Wisconsin

Polit D. F. and Beck C. T. (2004) *Nursing Research. Principles and Methods*, Lippincott Williams and Wilkins: Philadelphia

Polit, D. F. and Hungler, B.P. (1999) *Nursing Research: Principles and Methods* (6th edn.), Philadelphia: Lippincott

Post, C. B. (2013) 'Ruling gives Notts serial killer "chance of eventual release", *Nottingham Post* [online] 10th July. Available at: http://www.nottinghampost.com/Ruling-gives-Notts-serial-killer-chanceeventual/story-19501560-detail/story.html [accessed 6th September 2013]

Potter, G. W. and Kappeler, V. E. (2006) *Constructing Crime: Perspectives on Making News and Social Problems* (2nd edn.), Prospect Heights: Waveland Press

Prediger, D. J. (1982) 'Dimensions Underlying Holland's Hexagon: Missing Link between Interests and Occupations?' *Journal of Vocational Behaviour*, Vol. 21, pp. 259–287

(2000) 'Holland's hexagon is alive and well — though somewhat out of shape: Response to Tinsley', *Journal of Vocational Behaviour*, Vol. 56, pp. 197–204

Prediger, D. J. and Vansickle, T. R. (1992) 'Locating Occupations on Holland's Hexagon: Beyond RIASEC', *Journal of Vocational Behaviour*, Vol. 40, pp. 111–128

Prentky, R. A., Burgess A. W. and Rokous, F. (1989) 'The presumptive role of fantasy in serial sexual homicide', *American Journal of Psychiatry*, Vol. 146, No. 7, pp. 887–891

Presser, L. (2009) 'The Narratives of Offenders' *Theoretical Criminology*, Vol. 13, No. 2, pp. 177–200

Pritchard, T. (2001) 'Inside the hunt for a serial rapist' *The Guardian* [online] 4th February. Available at: http://www.theguardian.com/uk/2001/feb/04/theobserver.uknews1 [Accessed 25th June 2014]

Putwain, D. and Sammons, A. (2002) *Psychology and Crime*, Hove: Routledge

Pyrek, K. M. (2011) *Healthcare Crime: Investigating Abuse, Fraud, and Homicide by Caregivers*, New York: CRC Press

Quinet, K. (2011) 'Prostitutes as Victims of Serial Homicide: Trends and Case Characteristics, 1970–2009', *Homicide Studies*, Vol. 15, No.1, pp. 74–100

Quinn, S. (1994) 'Handyman's House of Horror', *Courier Mail*, 12th March, p. 3

R v Black (2011) Armagh County Court: NICA 51

    (2011) Court of Appeal: NICC 40

    (2013) Court of Appeal, NICA 35

Ragin, C. C. (1992) '"Casing" and the process of social inquiry', in C. C Ragin and H. S. Becker (eds.) *What is a Case? Exploring the Foundations of Social Inquiry*, Cambridge: Cambridge University Press, pp. 217–226

Railey, M. G. and Peterson, G. W. (2000) 'The assessment of dysfunctional career thoughts and interest structure among female inmates and probationers', *Journal of Career Assessment*, Vol. 8, pp. 119–129

Raine, A. (2013) *The Anatomy of Violence: The Biological Roots of Crime*, London: Vintage

Ramsland, K. (2007) *Inside the Minds of Healthcare Serial Killers: Why They Kill*, New York: Praeger Publishers Inc.

Ramsland, K. M. (2007) *Inside the Mind of Healthcare Serial Killers*, Westport: Praeger Publishers

    (2006) *Inside the Minds of Serial Killers: Why They Kill*, Westport: Praeger Publishers Ltd.

    (2005) *The Human Predator: A Historical Chronicle of Serial Murder and Forensic Investigation*, London: Berkley Books

Rayner, G. (2011) 'Robert Black could have killed fifth girl', *The Telegraph* [online] 27th October. Available at: http://www.telegraph.co.uk/news/uknews/crime/8853137/Robert-Black-could-havekilled-fifth-girl.html [Accessed 20th June 2014]

Regina v Levi Bellfield (2012), Court of Appeal: No. 2011/04102/B5

Regina v West (1996) Court of Appeal: *Times Law Reports*

Regina v West (2006) Court of Appeal: Times Newspaper ltd.

Reid, M. (1995) 'Child killer Robert Black to be Charged Over Two More Murders from Decades Ago', *The Times Online,* [Online] 11th April. Available at: http://www.timesonline.co.uk/tol/news/uk/crime/article3724207.ece [Accessed 23rd February 2012]

Ressler, R. K. and Shachtman, T. (1997) *I Have Lived in the Monster: A Report from the Abyss*, New York: St. Martin's Press

    (1992) *Whoever Fights Monsters*, New York: St. Martin's Press

Ressler, R. K., Burgess, A. W. and Douglas, J. E. (1988*) Sexual Homicide: Patterns and Motives*, Lexington: Lexington Books

Ressler, R. K., Burgess, A. W., Douglas, J. E., Hartman, C. R. and D'Agostino, R. B. (1986) 'Sexual killers and their victims: Identifying patterns through crime scene analysis', *Journal of Interpersonal Violence*, Vol. 1, pp. 288–308

Reynald, D. M. (2011) *Guarding Against Crime: Measuring Guardianship within Routine Activity Theory*, Farnham: Ashgate Publishing

Richards, L. and Richards, T. (1994) 'From filing cabinet to computer', In A. Bryman, and R. G. Burgess (Eds.) *Analysing Qualitative Data*, London: Routledge, pp. 146–172

Roach, J. (2012) 'Long Interval Detections and Under the Radar Offenders', *Journal of Homicide and Major Incident Investigations*, Vol. 8, No. 1, pp. 1–19

'Robert Black Guilty of Fourth Child Murder' (2011) *The Telegraph*, 27th October, p. 9

'Robert Black jailed for murder of Ulster schoolgirl Jennifer Cardy' (2011) *Belfast Telegraph* [online] 8th December. Available at: http://www.belfasttelegraph.co.uk/news/local-national/northern-ireland/robert-blackjailed-for-murder-of-ulster-schoolgirl-jennifer-cardy-28689874.html [Accessed 2nd June 2014]

'Robert Black trial: Defendant had "tape and rags"' (2011) *BBC News* [online] 18th October. Available at: http://www.bbc.co.uk/news/uk-northern-ireland-15353002 [Accessed 3rd March 2013]

'Robert Black: profile of a serial killer' (2011) *The Herald* [online] available at: http://www.heraldscotland.com/news/crime-courts/robert-black-profile-of-a-serialkiller-1.1131626 [Accessed 25th June 2014]

Robinson, B. (2011) 'All Change in the Victorian Age', *BBC History* [Online] 17th February. Available at: http://www.bbc.co.uk/history/british/victorians/speed_01.shtml [Accessed 20th February 2012]

Rosch, E. (1978) 'Principles of Categorization', in E. Rosch and B. B. Lloyd (eds.), *Cognition and Categorization*, Killsdale: Lawrence Erlbaum, pp. 27–48

Rossmo, D. K. (2000) *Geographic profiling*. Boca Raton: CRC Press

Roth, P. A. (1989) 'How Narratives Explain', *Social Research*, Vol. 56, No. 2, pp. 449–478

Rounds, J.and Day, S. X. (1999) 'Describing, evaluating, and creating vocational interest structures' In M. L. Savickas and A. R. Spokane (eds.), *Vocational interests: Meaning, measurement, and counselling use*, Palo Alto, CA: Davies-Black, pp. 103–133

Rouse, J. (1990) 'The Narrative Reconstruction of Science', *Qualitative Inquiry*, Vol. 33, No. 2, pp. 179–196

Rowan, J. and Reason, P. (1981) *Human Inquiry: a Sourcebook of New Paradigm Research*, Chichester: Wiley

Rowley, J. (2002) 'Using case studies in research', *Management Research News*, Vol. 25 No. 1, pp. 16–27

Ryan, J. M., Tracey, T. J. G., and Rounds, J. (1996) 'Generalizability of Holland's structure of vocational interests across ethnicity, gender, and socioeconomic status', *Journal of Counselling Psychology*, Vol. 43, pp. 330–337

'Sadistic Couple's House of Horror; Murder by Numbers: How Dennis Nilsen Shared his Bed with Corpses plus the Story of UK's most Notorious Address' (2013) *Daily Star*, 17th November, pp. 4–5

Sagar, R. (1999) *Hell and Fire: The Extraordinary Story of Bruce Lee*, London: Highgate Publications

Sampson, R. J. and Wooldredge, J. D. (1987) 'Linking the Micro- and the Macro-level Dimensions of Lifestyle-Routines Activity and Opportunity Models of Predatory Victimisation', *Journal of Quantitative Criminology*, Vol. 3, pp. 371–393

Sanchez, R. (2011) 'Single serial killer responsible for Long Island beach murders, police say', *The Telegraph* [online] 1st December. Available at: http://www.telegraph.co.uk/news/worldnews/northamerica/usa/8929219/Single-serialkiller-responsible-for-Long-Island-beach-murders-police-say.html [accessed 23rd April 2014]

Sandelowski M. (1993) 'Theory unmasked: The uses and guises of theory in qualitative research', *Research in Nursing and Health*, Vol. 16, pp. 213–218

Schinka, J. A., Dye, D. A. and Curtiss, G. (1997) 'Correspondence between five-factor and RIASEC models of personality', *Journal of Personality Assessment*, Vol. 68, No. 2, pp. 355–368

Schlesinger, L. and Miller, L. (2003) *Learning to Kill: Contract, Serial, and Terroristic Homicide*, Springfield: Charles C. Thomas

Schlesinger, L.B. (2004). *Sexual Murder: Catathymic and Compulsive Homicides*. Boca Raton: CRC Press

Seale, C. (1999) 'Quality in Qualitative Research', *Qualitative Inquiry*, Vol. 5, pp. 465–478

Seale, C., and Silverman, D. (1997) 'Ensuring rigour in qualitative research' *European Journal of Public Health*, Vol. 7, No. 4, pp. 379–384

Searle, J. R. (1995) *The Construction of Social Reality*, London: Penguin Books

Seltzer, M. (1998) *Serial Killers: Death and Life In America's Wound Culture*, London: Routledge

'Serial child killer Robert Black fails to overturn Jennifer Cardy murder conviction',
(2013) *Belfast Telegraph* [online] 27th June. Available at: http://www.
belfasttelegraph.co.uk/news/local-national/northern-ireland/serial-childkiller-
robert-black-fails-to-overturn-jennifer-cardy-murder-conviction-29377626.html
[Accessed 25th June 2014]

'Serial killer Robert Black guilty of fourth child murder' (2011) *The Telegraph*
[online] 27th October. Available at: http://www.telegraph.co.uk/news/uknews/
crime/8852776/Serial-killer-Robert-Blackguilty-of-fourth-child-murder.
html?mobile=basic [Accessed 5th May 2013]

'Sex killer Tobin's violent past' (2007) *BBC News* [online] 4th May. Available at: http://
news.bbc.co.uk/1/hi/scotland/glasgow_and_west/6611765.stm [Accessed 25th June
2014]

'Sex Killers Link to 20 more Attacks Police Quizzing Convicted Pair', (2001)
Birmingham Evening Mail, 2nd June, p. 7 http://www.telegraph.co.uk/news/
uknews/crime/7770898/Stephen-Griffithsdescribed-himself-as-evil-on-MySpace.
html [Accessed 1st March 2012]

Shackleton, V. and Fletcher, C. (1984) *Individual Differences: Theories and Applications*,
London: Methuen and Co.

Shaw, A., Arnold, H. and Fisher, L. (2001) 'The Thrill Killers: 15 Crimes of Desolating
Wickedness; Real Life Monsters from Hell–Life in Jail for Rampage of Rape and
Murder', *The Mirror* [online] 3rd February. Available at: http://www.thefreelibrary.
com/THE+THRILLER+KILLERS%3A+15+CRIMES+OF+DESOLATING+WIC
KEDNESS%3B+REAL-LIFE...-a069885252 [Accessed 26th June 2014]

Sheller, M. (2004) 'Automotive Emotions Feeling the Car', *Theory Culture and Society*,
Vol. 21, No. 4, pp. 221–242

Shenton, A. K. (2004) 'Strategies for ensuring trustworthiness in qualitative research
projects', *Education for Information*, Vol. 22, pp. 63–75

Shrewsbury, C. B. (2008) *Career Profiles of Black Adult Male Substance Abuse Felons Using
Holland's Theory "RIASEC"*, Ann Arbor: ProQuest

Siddique, H. (2008) 'Forklift driver 'had prolonged physical contact' with Ipswich murder
victims', *The Guardian* [online] 31st January. Available: http://www.theguardian.
com/uk/2008/jan/31/ukcrime.haroonsiddique1 [Accessed 21st June 2014]

Silva, J. A., Ferrari, M. M. and Leong, G. B. (2002) 'The Case of Jeffrey Dahmer: Sexual
Serial Homicide from a Neuropsychiatric Developmental Perspective', *Journal of
Forensic Science*, Vol. 47, No, 6, pp. 1347–59

Silverman, D. (2001) *Interpreting Qualitative Data: Methods for Analysing Talk, Text, and Interaction* (2nd edn.) London: Sage Publications

Simpson, K. (1980) *Forty Years of Murder*, London: Grafton Books

Simpson, P. L. (2000) *Psycho Paths: Tracking the Serial Killer Through Contemporary American Film*, Carbondale: Southern Illinois University Press

Singh, A. (2011) 'Playing Fred West gave me Nightmares, Admits Wire Star', *The Telegraph* [online] 29th August. Available at: http://www.telegraph.co.uk/culture/tvandradio/8729718/Playing-Fred-West-gave-menightmares-admits-Wire-star.html [Accessed 28th February 2012]

Smith, T. S. (1976) 'Inverse distance variations for the flow of crime in urban areas', *Social Forces*, Vol. 54, No. 4, pp. 802–815

Snook, B., Cullen, R. M., Mokros, A. and Harbort, S. (2005) 'Serial murderer's spatial decisions: factors that influence crime location choice', *Journal of Investigative Psychology and Offender Profiling*, Vol. 2, pp. 147–162

Snook, B., Taylor, P. J. and Bennell, C. (2004) 'Geographic Profiling: the Fast, Frugal, and Accurate Way', *Applied Cognitive Psychology*, Vol. 18, No. 1, pp. 105–121

Soothill, K. and Wilson, D. (2005) 'Theorising the puzzle that is Harold Shipman', *Journal of Forensic Psychiatry and Psychology*, Vol. 16, No. 4, pp. 685–698

Sounes, H. (1995) *Fred and Rose: The Full Story of Fred and Rose West and the Gloucester House of Horrors*, London: Warner Books

Spokane, A. R. and Cruza-Guet, M. C. (2005) 'Holland's theory of vocational personalities in work environments', In S. D. Brown and R. W. Lent (eds.), *Career Development and Counselling: Putting Theory and Research to Work*, New York: Wiley

Standard occupational classification (2010) *Office for National Statistics* [online] available at: http://www.ons.gov.uk/ons/guide-method/classifications/currentstandard-classifications/soc2010/index.html [Accessed 9th October 2014]

Stevens, S. S. (1957) 'On the psychophysical law', *Psychological Review*, Vol.64, No. 3, pp. 153–181

Stewart, D. W. and Kamins, M. A. (1993) *Secondary Research: Information Sources and Methods*, London: Sage Publications

Stokes, P. (2010) 'Crossbow cannibal serial killer: Stephen Griffiths admits murdering three prostitutes' *The Telegraph*, [online] 21st December. Available at: http://www.telegraph.co.uk/news/uknews/crime/7770898/Stephen-Griffithsdescribed-himself-as-evil-on-MySpace.html [Accessed 1st March 2012]

Stokes, P. and Britten, N. (2008) 'Colin Norris, "Angel of Death" Nurse, Jailed for Life', *The Telegraph* [online] 4th March. Available at: http://www.telegraph.co.uk/news/uknews/1580651/Colin-Norris-Angel-of-Deathnurse-jailed-for-life.html [Accessed 28th February 2012]

Stommel, M and Wills, C. (2004) *Clinical research. Concepts and Principles for Aadvanced Practice Nurses*, Philadelphia: Lippincott: Williams and Wilkins

Stonehouse, C. (2011) 'I married a serial killer' *Express* [online] 29th September. Available at: http://www.express.co.uk/expressyourself/274285/I-married-a-serialkiller [Accessed 25th June 2015]

Stopher, P. R. and Meyburg, A. H. (1975) *Urban Transportation Modelling and Planning*, Lexington: Lexington Books

'Suffolk Murders 2006', (2008) *BBC News* [online] 21st February. Available at: http://www.bbc.co.uk/suffolk/content/articles/2008/02/21/steve_wright_guilty_profile_feature.shtml [Accessed 19th June 2014]

Surette, R. (2007) *Media, Crime, and Criminal Justice: Images, Realities, and Policies* (3rd ed.), Belmont: Thomson Wadsworth

Taylor, D. (2010) 'Peter Tobin prescribed same drug he used to help kill victims—but he swaps it for goodies inside jail', The Guardian [online] 21st December. Available at: http://www.dailyrecord.co.uk/news/scottish-news/peter-tobin-prescribed-same-drug-1070512 [Accessed 26th June 2014]

Taylor, P. (2012) 'Greater Manchester Serial Killers: Harold Shipman, Doctor Death', *Manchester Evening News*, 25th April, [online] Available at: http://www.manchestereveningnews.co.uk/news/local-news/greater-manchester-serial-killers-harold-687278 [last accessed 20th April 2013]

Tendler, S. (2001) 'Killer rapist suspected of more attacks', *The Times* [online], 3rd February. Available at: https://www.nexis.com/results/docview/docview.do?docLinkInd=trucandrisb=21_T212 63892107andformat=GNBFIandsort=BOOL EANandstartDocNo=1andresultsUrlKey=29_T 21263892111andcisb=22_T212638921 10andtreeMax=trueandtreeWidth=0andcsi=10939andd ocNo=1 [Accessed 19th June 2014]

'The ex-wife's story: My violent life with the Suffolk strangler: and his flirtation on the QE2 with Suzy Lamplugh', *London Evening Standard* [online] 22nd February. Available at: http://www.standard.co.uk/news/the-exwifes-story-my-violent-life-withthe-suffolk-strangler-and-his-flirtation-on-the-qe2-with-suzy-lamplugh-7301393.html [Accessed 25th June 2014]

'The secret world of Harold Shipman' (2001) *BBC News* [online] 5th January. Available at: http://news.bbc.co.uk/1/hi/uk/1102270.stm [Accessed 28 May 2013]

'The "wicked soul mates"' (2001) *BBC News* [online] 2nd February. Available at: http://news.bbc.co.uk/1/hi/uk/1150239.stm [Accessed 25th June 2014]

'Timeline: Peter Tobin' (2009) *BBC News* [online] 16th December. Available at: http://news.bbc.co.uk/1/hi/uk/8128188.stm [Accessed 25th June 2014]

Tinsley, H. E. A. (2000) 'The congruence myth: An analysis of the efficacy of the person-environment fit models', *Journal of Vocational Behaviour*, Vol. 56, No. 2, pp147–179

'Tobin guilty of Angelika's murder' (2007) *BBC News* [online] 4th May. Available at: http://news.bbc.co.uk/1/hi/scotland/glasgow_and_west/6623821.stm [Accessed 25th June 2014]

Tokar, D.M. and Swanson, J.L. (1995) 'Evaluation of the correspondence between Holland's vocational personality typology and the five factor model of personality', *Journal of Vocational Behaviour*, Vol. 46, pp. 89–108

Townsend, M. (2009) 'Serial killer Peter Tobin likely to take his secrets to the grave', *The Guardian* [online] 20th December. Available at: http://www.theguardian.com/uk/2009/dec/20/police-tobin-missing-women-search [Accessed 20th June 2014]

Tozer, J. (2011) 'Robert Black is Convicted of Murder of Fourth School Girl and Linked to 13 Other Unsolved Deaths', *Daily Mail* [online], 28th October. Available at: http://www.dailymail.co.uk/news/article-2054133/Robert-Black-convictedmurder-fourth-schoolgirl-Jennifer-Cardy.html [Accessed 19th June 2014]

Tracey, T. J. G. and Rounds, J. (1996) 'The spherical representation of vocational interests', *Journal of Vocational Behaviour*, Vol. 48, pp. 3–41.

Tracey, T. J. G. and Ward, C. C. (1998) 'The Structure of Children's Interests and Competence Perceptions', *Journal of Counselling Psychology*, Vol. 45, pp. 290–303

Tracey, T. J. G., Lent, R. W., Brown, S. D., Soresi, S. and Nota, L. (2006) 'Adherence to RIASEC structure in relation to career exploration and parenting style: Longitudinal and ideothetic considerations', *Journal of Vocational Behaviour*, Vol. 69, pp. 248–261

Tracey, T. J. G., Robbins, S. B. and Hofsess, C. D. (2005) 'Stability and change in adolescence: A longitudinal analysis of interests from grades 8 through 12', *Journal of Vocational Behaviour*, Vol. 66, pp. 1–25

Tran, M. (2010) 'Peter Tobin's former homes searched in hunt for more victims' *The Guardian* [online] 12th July. Available at: http://www.theguardian.com/uk/2010/jul/12/peter-tobin-serial-killer-brighton-search [Accessed 24th June 2014]

(2010) 'Peter Tobin's former homes searched in hunt for more victims', *The Guardian* [online] 12th July. Available at: http://www.theguardian.com/uk/2010/jul/12/peter-tobin-serial-killer-brighton-search [Accessed 1st March 2012]

Trasler (1993) 'Conscience, opportunity, Rational choice, and Crime' in R. V. G. Clarke and M Felson (eds.), *Routine Activity and Rational Choice*, New Brunswick: Transaction Publishers

Travers, M. (2001) *Qualitative Research Through Case Studies*, London: Sage Publications

Trestrail, J. H. (2007) *Criminal poisoning* (2nd ed.) New Jersey: Human Press Inc.

Turco, R. (2001) 'Child Serial Murder-Psychodynamics: Closely Watched Shadows', *Journal of The American Academy of Psychoanalysis*, Vol. 29, No. 2, pp. 331–338

Turvey, B., E., Petherick, W. (2009) *Forensic Victimology: Examining Violent Crime Victims in Investigative and Legal contexts,* London: Elsevier

Twomey, J. (2008) 'Cowardice of hammer killer condemned to die in prison' *The Express* [online] 27th February, p. 9

Vronsky, P. (2004) *Serial Killers: The Method and Madness of Monsters*, New York: Berkley Publishing Corporation

Vronsky P., Parker, R. J., Ramsland, K., Newton, M., Perrini, S. and Banaski, K. (2014) *Serial Killers True Crime Anthology: Volume 2*, United States of America: RJ Parker Publishing

Walby, S. (1990) *Theorizing Patriarchy*, Oxford: Blackwell

Wansell, G. (2011) *The Bus Stop Killer: Milly Dowler, Her Murder and the Full Story of the Sadistic Serial Killer Levi Bellfield*, London: Penguin

'Was Peter Tobin Bible John?' (2008) *The Scotsman* [online] 6th December. Available at: http://www.scotsman.com/news/was-peter-tobin-bible-john-1-1302021 [Accessed 24th June 2014]

Watson, J. B. (1925) *Behaviorism*, New York: People's Institute

Weber, R.P. (1990) *Basic Content Analysis*, Newbury Park: Sage Publications

Wehmeier, P. M., Barth, N. and Remschmidt, H. (2003) 'Induced delusional disorder: A review of the concept and an unusual case of *folie a famille*', *Psychopathology*, Vol. 36, pp. 37–45

Welch, M., Price, E.A. and Yankey, N. (2002) 'Moral Panic over Youth Violence: Wilding and the manufacture of Menace in the Media', *Youth and Society*, Vol. 34, No. 1, pp. 3–30

Welsh, E. (2002) 'Dealing with Data: Using NVivo in the Qualitative Data Analysis Process', *Qualitative Social Research*, Vol. 3. No. 2 [online] Available at: http://www. qualitative-research.net/index.php/fqs/article/view/865/1880 [last accessed 18/10/13]

White, H. (1990) *The Content of the Form: Narrative Discourse and Historical Representation*, Baltimore: Johns Hopkins University Press

White, J and Cooper, R. (2011) 'Serial child killer Robert Black sentenced to 25 years in prison for fourth schoolgirl Murder' *Mail Online* [online] 8th December. Available at: http://www.dailymail.co.uk/news/article-2071585/Robert-Black-Serial-killersentenced-25-years-prison-Jennifer-Cardy-murder.html [Accessed 24th June 2014]

Wier, N. (2011) *British Serial Killers*, Bloomington: Author House

Williams, D. and Greenhill, S. (2008) 'My violent life as Suffolk Strangler's wife – and how I fear he killed Suzy Lamplugh too' *Mail Online* [online] 22nd February. Available at: http://www.dailymail.co.uk/news/article-517219/My-violent-lifeSuffolk-Stranglers-wife—I-fear-killed-Suzy-Lamplugh-too.html [Accessed 25th June 2014]

Wilson, C. (2005) 'The brutal father who made him a monster' *Mail Online* [online] 21st February. Available at: http://www.dailymail.co.uk/news/article-334925/Thebrutal-father-monster.html [Accessed 24th June 2014]

Wilson, C. and Seaman, D. (2007) *The Serial Killers: A Study in the Psychology of Violence*, London: Virgin Books

Wilson, D. (2007) *Serial Killers: Hunting Britons and Their Victims 1960–2006*, Sherfield-on-Loddon: Waterside Press

(2009) *A History of British Serial Killing*, London: Sphere

(2011) *Looking for Laura: Public Criminology and Hot News*, Sherfield-on-Loddon: Waterside Press

(2013) *Mary Ann Cotton: Britain's First Female Serial Killer*, Sherfield-on-Loddon, Waterside Press

Wilson, D., and Jones, T. (2008) 'In My Own World': A Case Study of a Paedophile's Thinking and Doing and His Use of the Internet', *The Howard Journal of Criminal Justice*, Vol. 47, No. 2, pp. 107–120

Wilson, D., Tolputt, H., Howe, N. and Kemp, D. (2010) 'When Serial Killers go Unseen: the Case of Trevor Joseph Hardy', *Crime, Media, Culture*, Vol. 6, pp. 153167

Winter, J. C. F. (2013) 'Using the Student's t-test with extremely small sample sizes', *Practical Assessment, Research and Evaluation* [online] Vol. 18, No. 10. Available at: http://pareonline.net/getvn.asp?v=18andn=10 [Accessed 27th June 2014]

Woodrow, J. C. (2011) *Rose West: The Making of a Monster*, London: Hodder Paperbacks

Woods, S. A. and West, M. A. (2010) *The Psychology of Work and Organizations*, Andover: Cengage Learning

Wortley, R. and Mazerolle, L. (2008) *Environmental Criminology and Crime Analysis*, London: Willan

Wright, J. and Hensley, C. (2003) 'From Animal Cruelty to Serial Murder: Applying the Graduation Hypothesis', *International Journal of Offender Therapy and Comparative Criminology*, Vol. 47, No. 1, pp. 71–88

Wright, S. and Kelly, T. (2010) 'Peter Tobin police to search basements of serial killer's former properties', *Mail online* [online] 13th July. Available at: http://www. dailymail.co.uk/news/article-1294006/Peter-Tobin-police-search-victimsgarden-serial-killers-homes.html [Accessed 19th June 2014]

Wunsch, D. and Hohl, K. (2009) 'Evidencing a "Good Practice Model" of Police Communication: The Impact of Local Policing Newsletters on Public Confidence', *Policing: A Journal of Policy and Practice*, Vol. 3, No. 4, pp. 331–339

Wyre, R. and Tate, T. (1995) *The Murder of Childhood*, London: Penguin Books Ltd.

Yardley, E., Wilson, D. and Lynes, A. (2014) 'A Taxonomy of Male British Family Annihilators, 1980–2012', *Howard Journal of Criminal Justice*, Vol. 53, No. 2, pp. 117–140

Yardley, E. and Wilson, E. (2014) 'In Search of the "Angels of Death": Conceptualising the Contemporary Nurse Healthcare Serial Killer', *Journal of Investigative Psychology* [Early View]

Yin, R. K. (1994) *Case Study Research: Design and Methods* (2nd edn.), Newbury Park: Sage Publications

(1998) 'The abridged version of case study research: Design and method', in L. Bickman, and D. J. Rog (eds.), *Handbook of Applied Social Research Methods*, Thousand Oaks: Sage Publications, pp. 229–259

Young, J. (1999) *The Exclusive Society: Social Exclusion, Crime and Difference in Late Modernity*, London: Sage Publications

Yu, G. and Raine, A. (2010) 'Successful and Unsuccessful Psychopaths: A Neurobiological Model', *Behavioural Sciences and the Law*, Vol. 28, pp. 194–210

Index

Serial Killers and the Phenomenon of Serial Murder:
A Student Textbook
David Wilson, Elizabeth Yardley and Adam Lynes
Foreword Steve Hall

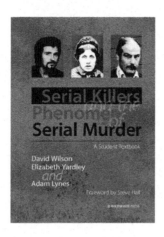

A superbly targeted resource for those learning about serial killings. *Serial Killers and the Phenomenon of Serial Murder* examines and analyses some of the best known (as well as lesser) cases from English criminal history, ancient and modern. It looks at the lifestyles, backgrounds and activities of those who become serial killers and identifies clear categories of individuals into which most serial killers fall. Led by Professor David Wilson the authors are all experts and teachers concerning the ever-intriguing subject of serial killing: why, when and how it happens and whether it can be predicted. Taking some of the leading cases from English law and abroad they demonstrate the patterns that emerge in the lives and backgrounds of those who kill a number of times over a period. The book is designed for those studying the topic at advanced level, whether as an academic discipline on one of the many courses now run by universities and colleges or as a private quest for understanding. It contains notes on key terms and explanations of topics such as co-activation, Munchausen syndrome, cooling-off period, psychopathy checklist, social construction, case linkage, family annihilation, activity space, rational choice theory, medicalisation and rendezvous discipline. As the first textbook of its kind it is an invaluable resource for teachers and students of serious crime.

Paperback & ebook | ISBN 978-1-909976-21-4 | 2015 | 224 pages

Lightning Source UK Ltd.
Milton Keynes UK
UKOW05f0047290317

297775UK00003B/78/P